Dedication

This book and the effort, passion and principles herein are dedicated to my sons, David, Ryan, and Jim Linderman with whom I share a path towards integrity, compassion and persistence, and to whom I am appreciative for the lessons of the same that they have taught me through their life examples. This book is also dedicated to our next generation, Max, Sophie, Emery and Owen; may you share this similar path.

I also dedicate this book to my friend and husband, John, who patiently and without hesitation shared his greater wisdom and computer skills with me in my moments of crisis, set up our garage to organize and facilitate display of the immense number of documents received from Ron Steen Jr. and kept encouraging me to keep going on this important project. And I thank Ron Steen Jr. for trusting me with his father's collection of saved and important documents. I also dedicate this book to Sheryl Ann Rhodes, a close friend and at one time my office manager who left work one Friday afternoon, and was shot and killed that evening. That experience caused me to connect with other vicitms of tragedy and the loss they experienced. Such a tragedy takes only seconds of time, but for us, who are left, lasts forever.

I extend special and sincere thanks to the Gulfport Senior Center Friday morning Writers' Group, who made me love writing all over again, mentored, helped and supported me to find the right words to express what I wanted to say. I thank my friend Roseann Blass for her early writing encouragement and I offer special appreciation to Jocelyn Pihlaja for her editing of my manuscript, assisting me in telling my story clearly and reminding me of the magic of the English language.

ABOUT THE AUTHOR

In 1992 I began a second career by completing an APA Approved program in Clinical Psychology at the Minnesota School of Professional Psychology in Minneapolis, Minnesota. As part of this program I completed separate assessment and diagnostic practicums, at the Federal Medical Center U.S. Bureau of Prisons, in Rochester, Minnesota and at a Community Mental Health Center in Owatonna, Minnesota. I would also complete a 12 month, APA Approved clinical internship at Florida State Hospital in Chattahoochee, the oldest and largest hospital for the criminal insane in Florida. My doctoral research project, "A Descriptive Study of Minnesota State and Federal Judges' Evaluations of Psychiatrists' and Psychologists' Forensic Performance," Linderman, 1991, volume 3, involved ratings by judges of doctoral level clinical psychologists, versus psychiatrists, in 25 forensic areas. Results indicated psychologists were perceived as significantly different from psychiatrists in 7 of 25 forensic areas. Completed surveys numbered 157 or 62% of the 251 judges contacted. Of these 157 surveys, judges indicated having from 1-41 years of experience on the bench and using psychologists more frequently than psychiatrists (means of 3.10 and 2.87 respectively).

In 1993, following additional supervision and assessment I was granted registration in the National Register of Health Service Psychologists, and in 1993 following additional supervision and assessment I was granted Diplolamate status in the American Board of Professional Psychology (ABPP) in Clinical Psychology.

As a forensic psychologist, I traveled all over Minnesota from southern Minnesota, bordering Iowa, to northern counties bordering Canada, from the western border next to the Dakotas to eastern Minnesota next to Wisconsin. I was engaged in many complex, serious and demanding cases.

Meeting Ron Steen, and being part of his case over three years' time, was the incentive I needed to start writing. After his death and my receiving several boxes of his personal records from his son, Ron Jr., records that spanned fifty years of Ron's life, I began organizing his story, writing it in sections which was a daunting task. The lessons of his story could educate others, perhaps assisting them to understand the complexities of treatment for mental illness and shed some light on situations and occurrences that can take place within psychiatric care and confinement that are due for change.

Sources of information for this book consisted of legal and personal documents of Ronald L. Steen related to events leading up to the 1986 shooting of his partner, followed by his admission to the Minnesota State Hospital system and subsequent experiences at sister institutions including Willmar State Hospital, Arrowhead House in Duluth, and the Mentally Ill and Dangerous Transition Building, and Shantz Hall in St. Peter, Minnesota. References reviewed and summarized were clinical and legal sources of information as well as the deposition taken of him following the January 15, 1986 shooting incident, jury selection, and January 1986 Indeterminate Civil Commitment as Mentally Ill and Dangerous Judicial Appeal Panel File No. AP089003 dated July 31, 2009, and following his 2009 provisional release. Also included was information from Ron's personal documents, interviews and conversations we had over time. Psychiatric records spanned 1986-2009: legal records were those shared with me through May of 2018.

Also noted is information related to his living briefly at Reflections, in Austin, Minnesota. Incorporated are personal letters to various attorneys related to his Transmatic grain dryer business, advertising related to such, newspaper information from the Echo Press in Alexandria, Minnesota, during and following his 1986 trial.

Other sources of information included Mr. Steen's personal correspondence and records, along with numerous interviews with family, friends, medical staff and synopses of reports related to and regarding Ron as included in his vast collection of personal papers, letters, and copied medical files.

Also invaluable to the writing of this book was the steady, stream of appreciated information and support by and from Ronald Steen Jr. who stayed in contact with me over several years' time.

Rose Linderman

Chapters

Prologue...1

2009: The Beginning of the End..6

1970 and Onward: The Unfolding of Events............................21

1986 The Turning Point in Time 39

The Grand Jury 52

The Jury Decision 82

The Trial Verdict...85

State Security Hospitals: Who is Most Secure?.......................93

Placements in Willmar and Duluth 112

2004 Back to Square One: St. Peter 130

Driving Thoughts..147

2006 150

Collateral Information from the Family..................................170

The Rest of the Story...187

The Other Experts' Reports..208

My Report..225

Surprise!..245

The Issue re: Dangerousness 250

Continued "Treatment" Failures...265

Special Review Board Hearings: Special or Unusual?............270

The Three Appellate Judges 284

The Last Step 290

The End is not The End 307

Treasure Trove...321

How Change Doesn't Happen...338

The Weakest Link of the Chain 352

Epilogue...360

Photographs...365

Prologue

Alexandria, Minnesota is an idyllic lake region in Douglas County, long known for generations of family lake cottages, fishing lore, fast boats and summer memories. It is a scenic haven of both humble and grand lake-front homes. One could imagine this area similar to that which inspired the Percy Faith, 'Theme from a Summer Place," especially after you explored and discovered magical coves in the woods adjoining lake beaches and heard the call of the loons. One large Lake Miltona home had an oversized garage that appeared ordinary enough on the outside—but inside, it teemed with treasures collected over more than 30 years, *notably* a 1977 Lincoln Mark V, the same car known to be a favorite of Elvis Presley.

On August 16, 1977, the day Elvis died, an Alexandria grain dryer businessman, Ronald Lee Steen, drove to a nearby Lincoln dealership, bought the car with cash, and drove it home. It was a soft teal green color, or as he described it to his son, "It's the color of money." For three decades the car would remain enshrined inside the garage, protected from the damage that might be inflicted if it moved through the world. The Lincoln was never driven; decades later it still had had the original price sticker on the window and 19 miles on the odometer; the exact distance from the local dealership to its new home. The Lincoln joined a collection of 32 vehicles, antique trucks, Harleys, and a few airplanes, the latter which Ron laughingly admitted he never learned to fly. For Ron, these treasures were more about the having than the using, when it came to his "toys." It was as though he just wanted to protect what he loved best.,

No one seeing this healthy, happy man enjoying his hobbies could have ever guessed what his future held for him. No one walking through Ron's personal museum, listening to him explain both provenance and passion of each vehicle, could have imagined this affable man being found Not Guilty by Reason of Insanity in 1986 for shooting his girlfriend, then designated Not Guilty by Reason of Insanity, and, finally indeterminately civilly committed as Mentally Ill and Dangerous to the Minnesota State Hospital system for the next 23 years.

I met Ron in the summer of 2006 when, as a forensic psychologist, I was asked to evaluate him to assess whether he continued to meet the statutory criteria for civil commitment or was able and safe to be released to the community. My recommendation was that he met the statutory criteria for release; he was not actively mentally ill and could manage in the community with assisted resources. Ron was in his 60's when I met him. He was tall, with black thinning hair, and somewhat overweight. I had read records that spanned his lifetime, both the good and tragic events, settings and environments of challenge, joy and sorrow. When we met in person, I experienced him as a social individual, amidst fellow patients he enjoyed and trusted, he proved intelligent and somewhat of a perfectionist and a stickler for detail. Throughout our time together, I would also experience his sense of humor, even in a state hospital setting, and his capacity to be personable despite his situation. The majority of people I interview are criminals and psychopaths. Ron did not fit into either group.

If Ron had been tried in a criminal court, he could have been imprisoned roughly 17 years. His defense attorney told him his stay in the hospital would be short. Not so. He instead found himself isolated if not forgotten in what seemed like an endless abyss with no way out. Folded into his sentence were less than top-rated health, dental, and psychiatric care, topped off by three meals a day of institutional food and a hopeless future.

Worst of all, Ron's comments related to his prior successes, and certain folks being out to get him, while truthful, when said in a state hospital setting sounded delusional. His threats to sue the staff for what he saw as injustices came across as paranoid and threatening. Added to this mix was the hospital's mandated compliance with treatment programming, despite these groups being unsupported by research that they actually improve symptoms of mental illness, let alone reduce future risk of harm. Further complicating Ron's chances for release were other unclear treatment goals, staff who engaged in less than honorable patient care, capricious definitions of programming and inconsistent medical file entries. Multiple treatment teams, each claiming to have the patient's best interests in mind, cemented in place what seemed like an endless, hollow experience. By the end of Ron's 23 years of jumping thorough illogical, nonsensical hoops, onlookers could only ask: whose purposes did the institution serve?

This story of Ron Steen challenges many people's understanding of mental health services and treatment, to the point that they see psychiatric care having its own delusions of grandeur. Others hearing about Ron's story wonder how it is that people get caught within certain systems for decades of time, seemingly unnoticed. His story is one of ongoing injustice and good intentions thwarted by bureaucracy.

In the fall of 2009, more than two decades after the nightmare began, Ron was provisionally discharged from state confines. Thanks to a 20-year habit of grinding his teeth day and night, his teeth were nearly level with his gums. He would die in his sleep after finally moving closer to family in July of 2010. His funeral was on his 70th birthday. Ron's story is that of the fragile relationship between perception and reality. It is also a story of treachery spawned in the face of over two decades of opportunity in areas of morality, professional ethics, financially, and related to his personal rights.

This is my story about Ron's story.

2009: The Beginning of the End

I entered my office Monday morning in the summer of 2009 with no expectation of anything spectacular occurring that week, let alone that day. I was looking forward to my noon Rotary meeting where I always enjoyed the varied programs, the people, the food, the whole experience. Where else could I sit at a table with three older gentlemen who had served in the military at Normandy beach?

Mid-morning the phone rang, and my secretary, called out, "That was Mr. Magnus' office. They are faxing a court order for Ron's release!" Her words broke the silence of the morning routine like a clap of thunder. I closed out the file document that I had opened on my computer, grabbed another file I needed to pass on to my secretary, and asked if we had any additional information related to the fax. "That's it, she said smiling. It was Mr. Magnus' secretary and she sounded excited. The fax should be coming any minute. Can you believe this might be over? That poor man. No one should be treated that badly for that long."

This was a case we had been working on for three years. It was one of those cases you ended up thinking about on random occasions, waiting for stop lights to change, rainstorms to end, appointments to start and food orders to arrive at a restaurant. Certainly, it had always been a challenging case, memorable for a lot of reasons, at this point related to a man's freedom being in the balance. I walked quickly to the room where our fax machine was located, set down my cup of coffee, and pulled a chair close to the printer to be ready for the first glimpse of the release paperwork, and waited. Impatiently, I waited. I was both excited and apprehensive. This case had included more than the usual ups and downs, dashed hopes, moments of complete frustration and the forced acceptance of bureaucratic set-backs that made conclusion, let alone resolution, a daydream. More than once, excitement and hopefulness had been followed by huge disappointment and frustration.

I am a private practice forensic psychologist and have worked in this capacity since 1992. The people I evaluate are involved in a variety of court proceedings where the issue of their behavior and mental health is a factor in decisions made by the court. In all my cases, while I am asked by attorneys to interview their clients, the bottom line is, that my client is the court. The guidelines that shape what I offer as the basis of my opinions and are anchored in state, and sometimes federal court statutes. The people I interview are involved in civil or criminal situations where their mental health, and in many cases, acts of violence are involved. Most of the people I get involved with are in some type of legal situation, either a civil or criminal situation. Their situations are serious and stressful. I try to put them at ease the best I can, and during my interview I explain the reasons for the questions I am asking. I also need to be on my guard for deception, if not outright lying. My goal is to treat everyone respectfully.

The first time I met Ron Steen in person I remembered being impressed by his calm and relaxed demeanor and his polite social skills. He stood about 6 feet tall which meant we could look eye to eye, and he had neatly combed, black, hair and although he did not have a moustache, he could have been a double in appearance and demeanor for Oliver Hardy. He was intelligent, witty, and personable. Interviewing him was easy and productive; he had good reasoning skills and was articulate. This was not how he had been described in many of his records that I reviewed ahead of meeting him in person.

I was also impressed that Ron was relaxed and friendly, assertive in offering additional information as well as asking for clarification when he had questions. He was obviously intelligent, discerning, and willing to share relevant examples of information from a stack of documents and paperwork he brought with him to the interview. He had a good sense of humor and despite his situation he was upbeat and sociable. Mostly he was eager to talk about his case, his story, his dilemma, and his life of gains and a lot of losses. As he talked about his situation I was struck with his personal strengths and wondered how it was that he had become so entangled in this system.

The incoming facsimile was going to specify the terms and details of what is termed a provisional discharge, a discharge with attached conditions or provisions. Ronald Lee Steen had been civilly committed as Mentally Ill and Dangerous in 1986 after being diagnosed with schizoaffective disorder, a major affective disorder, that originally included intermittent psychotic features, the psychosis having been in remission for a number of years. His medical records over time continued to debate whether his diagnosis was better defined as that of a bipolar disorder. I wondered how it was that so many entry's in his records by trained caregivers, professionals in the mental health systems for years, noted varying diagnostic considerations as though they were unable to agree with each other.

By the mid-1990s he had earned his right to walk freely on the state hospital grounds. In 2006, the hospital cleared him of his designation as 'dangerous,' but he was still seen as mentally ill related to his anchoring diagnosis of a mood disorder. State hospital records noted Special Review Boards had denied Ron's petition for discharge in 2006. The same board made up of different professionals in law and psychiatric services denied a second petition in 2008. An earlier petition in 2002 was also denied, even after Ron had lived for three years in a community-based group home where he drove his own car to his doctor's appointments and to visit family in other parts of the state.

The reasons for these denials included repeated statements of his "long history of delusional beliefs and paranoia," as well as an unwavering lack of support for discharge by his treatment teams over time, related to his uneven attendance at his treatment groups. His current treatment teams had not, and still did not, support either a full or provisional discharge. Their reasoning was Ron's open "refusal to re-involve himself in treatment programs that in his opinion failed to be helpful to him." Ignored was the fact that he had completed similar programs in the first decade of hospitalization. When I met Ron in 2006, he openly talked about the newer programs as not personally helpful to him after he attended them a few times to see what they included.

When Ron's case was advanced to the three judges on the Supreme Court of Appeals Panel (SCAP) in 2009, they not only reversed the Special Review Boards' plan to keep Ron confined, but they also called into question the hospital's position that he complete treatment programs that had become the sole barrier to his discharge. To my way of thinking, this was a boldly hopeful sign demonstrating these judges had been listening to what the defense for Ron's case had been saying; he was a man caught within a system in which there were few to no options. How could a state funded system of supposedly learned caregivers, disallow release unless patients completed programming unsupported by research as treating anything specific? Who was benefitting most from the insistence that all patients participate regularly in treatment groups aimed at filling hours than providing genuinely helpful content?

As I listened to and watched these proceedings, I was impressed that the three women judges' combined opinions included expressed limited patience for hospital rules that favored the institution and not the individual patient. This observation was heartening, as it shored the feeling Ron and I

11

shared about his case; it was ridiculous to require fully functional adults to live within a system of protocols that were irrelevant to his mental health.

The State of Minnesota, Office of Appellate Courts Judicial Appeal Panel Findings of Fact, Conclusions of Law and Order dated July 30, 2009 summed up the Findings of Fact and Conclusions of these Findings, noting evidence that "Respondent's Motion for Dismissal of Appellant's Petition for a Full Discharge from his civil commitment is hereby GRANTED.

The Order of the Commissioner of Human Services dated January 8, 2008, denying Appellant's Petition for Provisional Discharge is REVERSED." The final order added: "Appellant shall be provisionally discharged from his civil commitment. Appellant's treatment team shall work with him in the next thirty (30) days to ensure that the necessary supportive plan services are in place for discharge to the community."

Further noted was the dilemma that had plagued Ron for decades: "Appellant's treatment team does not support either a full or provisional discharge because they do not believe his discharge plan has sufficient specificity and they have not assisted him in preparation of his plan. The catch for Mr. Steen is that on unit where he had been briefly placed, staff will not assist with discharge planning because patients on that unit are not eligible for discharge services."

I so enjoyed this judicial candor, including their acknowledging Ron's situation as a catch-22. How can a patient be designated for discharge and then transferred to a ward from which NO ONE is directly released? The judges' decision that day was cause for joy, not only for Ron, but also for me. I had been losing faith in the system in which I worked.

The last two pages of the Order included one of the three appellate judges' concurring opinions, related to particular problems noted in this case. Carefully worded was a number of statements, one being, "It is unclear who exactly made the decision to place Mr. Steen in a particular mental health security unit form which no one was ever released...compared with his long history of failing to demonstrate evidence of aggression or danger toward himself or others."

Other noted statements included: Ron's "psychotropic medication was discontinued by his treatment psychiatrist in late 2006 because he was exhibiting no signs of psychotic symptomology and had for some time been psychiatrically stable." Also noted: "The head of the Security Hospital acknowledged that the programming on Mr. Steen's unit, was geared to lower functioning individuals. No one testified that activities and groups including "Happy Hour," "Harmonizing," "Frisbee Golf," and "Movie Classics" would have any therapeutic value for Mr. Steen. He is simply required to attend and complete them with the proper attitude because that is the unit where he is placed. Because he does not attend, he is identified as having negative attitudes."

This security unit from which no one, was ever directly released was none other than the notorious Unit 800, a ward specifically reserved for the most dangerous and psychotic patients within the confines of the entire hospital. Unit 800 patients were severely mentally retarded or mentally ill, or both, unpredictably violent, requiring frequent, if not ongoing physical restraint along with chemical restraint in the form of tranquilizing drugs to prevent them from hurting themselves, the staff or other patients. As noted by the court, the real catch was that the behavior of patients in this unit was not in any way similar to Ron's behavior/symptoms prior to his being placed in this unit! Clearly, he had been wrongly placed in the unit and then continually penalized for not fitting in.

What actually took place, according to the wording in Ron's medical records, was Ron's psychiatrist pre-ordering Ron's transfer to Unit 800 in anticipation of Ron's resistance to re-starting his Risperdal, a neuroleptic that evened out his recently noted agitation. However, when the psychiatrist informed Ron he wanted him to resume taking the Risperdal, Ron simply agreed. There was no arguing; there was no scene. To make this situation more rational, when Ron was documented as being informed, he was going to be transferred to Unit 800, his only comment as recorded in his medical record was, "I want my attorney informed of the transfer." The point here is that he knew, what Unit 800 involved and wanted someone to know where he was in case something happened to him.

While Ron's medical record dated April 27, 2007 included the statement, "Mr. Steen was transferred to Unit 800 due to his psychiatric decompensation," yet, bewilderingly, there were no corresponding documented behaviors in his medical record supporting this claimed "decomposition." Documented behaviors prior to and at the time of the transfer did not include any recorded symptoms of overt psychosis or acts of aggression whatsoever. Thus, in just one of many ethical injustices, it would appear that the existence of this information had been contrived to support the transfer.

The wrongful treatment of Ron only got worse. Upon Ron's admission to unit 800, there were entries made related to Ron reporting what could be seen as psychotic comments related to his expressing beliefs that his food and medication had been "poisoning" him. However, when I personally visited him in Unit 800, he reported to me the staff were trying to make him look crazy by claiming his having made such comments, which he said were untrue.

His history over 23 years had never included comments related to anyone poisoning him, nor had he been charted as reporting bizarre methods of receiving medication or bothered by unusual "fumes." Ultimately, no one would make anything of the discrepancy between his actual presentation and that noted in the chart at the time of transfer to Unit 800, any more than they did the substitution of mandatory program attendance, as the exclusive path for release, replacing the actual statutory criteria for release. For the duration of his time in Unit 800 Ron was treated with suspicion and condescension even though his words and behaviors were actually perfectly sane.

The justices' final order for Ron's release also noted another area that was an injustice not only to Ron, but also other patients. The judges' Order noted, "Mr. Steen, was "not the only patient the Court was aware of who had been subjected to endlessly changing and unclear release criteria that needed to be completed as a sign of making progress. Week after week and month after month the Court listens to cases involving psychiatric patients who report little or no value from the groups, they were required to attend...patients who describe meaningless rules to be followed simply because they were rules and the never-ending and continually changing criteria for what was labeled progress, and the lack of individuality in treatment." As such, Ron's case was one example of a much more pervasive problem in the system.

My clearest memory of the three judge panel is their huddling together on the raised stage following my testimony in the first of two parts of Ron's hearing for release. Their robes morphed into a single black intimidating mass, their arms extended around the shoulders of the person next to them to keep their conferring with each other as hushed as possible. When the huddle broke, they turned to those of us in the court room audience, and the chief judge announced that based on the testimony offered, Ronald Steen's case was "moving up." Later, to everyone's great relief, after the second phase of these proceedings, Ron's release was ordered for August 30, of 2009.

17

After the judges announced Ron's case was "moving up," I gloated for the entire two hour drive home. Drive time between where I lived and the various settings in which I conducted evaluations was necessary for my own mental health. Driving time for me was a way to review cases, think about conversations and interviews, plan my next step and chart my course related to a particular case. The miles between my home and prison settings, jails, court houses, state hospitals, VA centers, metro hospitals, group homes, chemical dependency treatment centers and points in between provided essential hours of processing and reflection allowing me to sift through the nuances of the cases I was handling.

Ron's case was no exception. There were many disappointing endings over two years' time that none of us who were supporting Ron's release knew how to act when we actually started winning. The reality of my profession is that most legal proceedings are not this exciting, nor do the wins feel so profound and sweet. But this latest win was especially sweet. Of course, there were also unknowns. Sometimes it is good not to know too much about what is actually about to happen next.

The next hurdle would be finding him an assisted living facility and a community with mental health services to meet his needs. Ron was no longer considered actively mentally ill, let alone dangerous; he had been a wealthy businessman and had assets to pay for housing and care (he had even sent his social security check of $1320 every month for years and years to his conservator for safe keeping). His defense attorney had a list of over a dozen available placements that he had visited along with his having been interviewed by each, with verbal notice of their being willing to accept him in the near future as one of their residents. Initially, we all assumed his next step would be easy.

Unfortunately, this was not the case. The problems began when Ron' original attorney, whom I refer to unfondly as Mr. Black, and the conservator of Ron's estate reportedly joined efforts and systematically called all possible placement options to inform them of Ron's history in 1986 and advise the placements he might not be an appropriate person for their community. One by one the housing options disappeared. Then, when a suitable living arrangement was finally accessed, related to my vouching for Ron's behavior and my understanding of his having financial assets, and this facility agreed to accept him as a resident, the financial reimbursement for Ron's needed services (housing, medical visits, hearing aids, dental care) would be sent late, short of the necessary amount, or not at all.

My impressions of these motives, if I was asked to guess about them were two-fold: not supporting his new found placement because their plan was to keep him confined at St. Peter forever, and/or creating stress for him, hoping he would get angry, create a scene and be returned to St. Peter as unacceptable. The most despicable possible motive for this behavior, which turned out to be not too far from the reality of the situation, was that paying for his expenses would lessen the size of his enormous nest egg.

Amazingly, Ron enjoyed his first home away from the hospital, despite the obstacles. By the spring of the following year he would transfer to an assisted living facility close to where his only son, Ron Jr. lived. I attributed his amazing resilience to his intelligence and his determination to make the most of his freedom after nearly three decades in a state system. I never knew Ron before 2006. Ron Jr. shared with me that in his prime his father was. "a mover and a shaker," on the go, living big and absorbed in wheeling and dealing, buying and selling and expanding his grain dryer business into an empire. He had lived in both worlds; the good life of excess and a life void of stimulation in a state hospital. His finally getting out of a confined setting may have been good enough; moving near to Ron, Jr. was better than he imagined. Nothing else was important enough to cause him distress compared with years of confinement. In some ways his current quieter existence was similar to how his life began in a small Minnesota rural community so many years ago.

Sometimes less is more. Ron's roots, after all, were from humble beginnings.

1970 and Onward: The Unfolding of Events

Ron Steen was the only child born to Leland and Dorothy Steen in Morris, Minnesota on July1, 1940. The few times he shared information about his family, Ron spoke of his parents with respect and love. He described them as "plain folks who worked hard for what they had, who embraced and lived a humble existence in a small and modest home." I would later learn that Ron's parents' emotional and verbal reticence with regards to the eventual 1986 shooting incident added to the paucity of an already isolated world.

Ron was part of the Morris High School Class of 1958; when his 50th class reunion was held he hoped he would get out of St. Peter State Hospital in time to attend it. Sadly, his student page of the Morris High School class reunion that took place in 2008 listed his state hospital address. In his records was a note from a high school friend who was organizing the event and wrote that she hoped he would be able to come to the reunion. Class photos included Ron in his "Elvis look alike days," and commented on his love of music, hunting, fishing and boating, nice cars and motorcycles. He was hailed as a talented pool shark who could beat just about anyone who dared to play with him.

Ron moved from Morris, on Minnesota's western border with South Dakota to Alexandria Minnesota, the central lake region of the state. In the 1960's he began selling Northland **DRYMOR** grain dryers. His folksy manner and energetic interest into the grain dryer business was a match. His first job in Alexandria was selling grain dryers. He was a quick learner and an astute salesman. It was not surprising that he soon became a nationally recognized salesman of the American Super B and Farm Fans Electronic Grain Dryers, a job he held for 13 years.

By the early 1970's Ron initiated the beginnings of what would bloom into a flourishing multimillion dollar grain dryer business of his own, known as Transmatic Big-R Save $ More Grain Dryer Capital Corporation. His company included a leasing option, something new and innovative at the time, that benefitted his growing list of customers. Eventually, he would move his parents to Alexandria join him, his father doing odd jobs related to the dryers. Ron had a true gift of gab, helpful for selling ideas and products and listening to what his customers told him about their needs. He knew how to meet and talk with farmers about options for developing more profitable harvests. Over the years, these skills continued to sustain his success.

Grain dryers had become the new rage in agriculture and Ron earned the distinction of being the largest national distributor of dryers from 1971 to 1977. At the helm of his own company, he worked even harder selling and servicing dryers in North and South Dakota as well as Minnesota. Some folks said he borrowed $5000 to start his career in agriculture and turned it into a fortune.

Within Ron's personal records there is information suggesting he knew people who resented his success and may have plotted his downfall. One document was a notarized statement by a man from Clondorf, Minnesota, dated December 1, 2003 about a man, "Bill" who had attended an Alexandria Beetles baseball game on June 9, 2003. He left the stands to smoke and began a conversation with another smoker, eventually asking the man what kind of work he was in. Bill reported the man responded he had been a head jailer for over twenty years in Douglas County, at which time Bill asked if he had ever heard of Ron Steen. The man responded in the affirmative, and said he was on duty the night Ron came into the jail, adding, "They railroaded that man." When Bill asked what the man meant, he said,

"He was so strung out on drugs he was incoherent and in really bad shape, babbling he thought he may have shot someone." When Bill asked for clarification related to the mention of "drugs," the man said Ron did not smell of alcohol or of smoke. When Bill asked what the man meant by "railroaded," the man reported that he believed the shooting was accidental or at worst unintentional given the state of Ron's behavior, adding Ron should never have been charged with 1st Degree Murder, and that it should have been Manslaughter or less. When Bill asked the man why he thought Ron was charged the way he was, the man answered, "Well, there's a lot of people that would just as soon he be out of here for good." When Bill asked what people, the man simply said, "Just some people." Both men returned to their seats and never spoke again.

What piqued my interest in finding this document was the fact that Ron had mentioned this incident to me more than once during our conversations. Initially, his comments to me about this situation did not make any sort of impression in my mind, whereas finding the dated and notarized account of this conversation added significance to what had been reported to me. Ron was a master researcher and obsessively collected information important to his interests or personal situations related to health, business and legal issues.

Before the night that changed his life, however, life for Ron was good. Ron was a natural kibitzer, a born salesman, energetic, likeable, a businessman with down to earth business acumen. He also liked taking his clients to the local Holiday Inn in Alexandria for lunch where they could talk business and close deals. He lived for the sales, and he had the bankroll to prove he was good at it.

Unfortunately, Ron also had a history, inherited from his mother since the late 1970's, of what was identified as episodic periods of depression that included agitation, anxiety, and briefly reported psychotic symptoms. Aware of these mental heal issues, Ron would probably have been the first to admit that his endless energy for business and success was paired with neglecting his young family and his own physical and emotional health while focusing all his time into making his new company grow.

Eventually, his business pace and related challenges took a toll on his marriage, and his wife to divorced him in May of 1981, twenty years to the day after their wedding in 1961. Ron also shared with me that his having a brief fling with a red head also contributed to the split. The red head called Ron's home one day, Ron's wife answered the phone, and that was the proverbial last straw. Ron accepted what happened and moved on, basically because his wife had left and wasn't coming back. However, some of his comments over time hinted that his marriage ending left a lasting scar on his heart. He never spoke ill of his wife, but rather, only shared his deep regret at missing out on his children as they grew up because he was so engrossed in his career.

With time and unexpected business challenges, some of which smacked of shenanigans or mischief by his competitors, Ron began to exhibit outward signs of his inherited mood disorder. Perhaps these displays were also related to or combined with his outgoing personality. Ron reportedly could be challenging to have as a boss. He was competitive, liked to be right, and at times came across as dismissively arrogant. But amidst it all, he was a hard worker and thrived on it. He once shared a photograph with me of his standing with one foot on a haybale in front of numerous sales trophies and awards he had won. When I commented on the number of trophies in the photo, he chuckled, "I loved selling those dryers, and I sold a lot of them. The farmers were great to talk with and I gave them good service, people like good service." In his heyday, Ron sold and serviced thousands of grain dryers, along with drumming up thousands of trips, deals, and new accounts. Then, a variety of problems began to emerge.

In 1979 **DRYMOR** launched advertising efforts attempting to discredit competition, like Ron's Transmatic products, as well as discourage those who might want to be Ron's prospective employees. For instance, one ad noted, "First the service people came over to **DRYMOR** because of less problems...then the salesmen came over because they didn't have to lie about the price, capacity, service, delivery, full savings, etc. Plus, they don't have to go to court to get their commission!" This latter statement was based on a situation in 1978 when three of Ron's sales associates sued him related to back pay. Apparently, there were confusion and hard feelings as to whether a promised 15% was related to the employee's sales commission, the margin difference, or the selling price. Unfortunately, it become revealed that Ron, despite all his financial and business success had been so busy selling farm machinery he had little time to pen written documents detailing employee compensation.

In Ron's collection of personal papers there is a copy of a 1978 Echo Press newspaper ad for **DRYMOR** that noted, "Farmers Beware! Only **DRYMOR** has a unique patented design, "Controlled Air-Flow" and saves 30% on Fuel." The ad continued, "Some of the orange competition (which referred to Ron's orange painted dryers), has changed the name on their dryers and are claiming 40% fuel savings. Skunks are black with white stripes and have a strong odor. If you change the name, they're still black with white stripes and have a strong odor...Farmers Beware!! If they lie about fuel savings, they'll lie about capacity and retail prices. "Beware of imposters, DRYMOR-Number One."

Because the disgruntled employees sold grain dryers for Ron in the same vast network of small towns, news of problems within the ranks traveled far and fast through the countryside. After a beginning that included DRYMOR Farm Fans and Ron's Transmatic Big-R company working cooperatively an agreement that had both businesses prospering, with one supplying dryers and parts and the other selling and maintaining them, clashes arose in the form of misrepresentation of the costs of dryers, followed by buyers complaining and not wanting to pay what was owed.

Dryers varied in price from $1300 to over $7000+++ depending on the features included. In its peak of operation, Transmatic reportedly could rent and lease or sell a minimum of 200 dryers yearly in addition to selling additional models and products each crop season. In the context of small town Minnesota and the Dakotas, Ron's Transmatic grain dryer business was akin to a gold mine.

Complicating the picture was the fact that Transmatic sold Farm Fan dryers, motors for the dryers, augers, bins and tanks and used grain dryers, and some dryers were trade-ins. The process by which Farm Fans provided dryers to Transmatic included trucking the dryers to Transmatic where they would be inspected. Eventually Transmatic determined that they had not received all the dryers purchased, and problems arose accounting for these dryers in the inventory. Additionally, Ron had designed a bin for the dryers and planned and paid for a fabrication company to build the bins. The bins were never fabricated, and Ron did not get his money back. He claimed he had money due him.

Even more, there were delivery challenges due to the sprawling territory covered by Ron's company. There were parts and servicing of the dryers that were delivered by small airplanes in some cases due to the distance of need. And there were challenges with the ASC, an agricultural lending body that advanced loans secured by farmers buying the dryers. Sometimes loans and/or payments were held up because of differences noted in pricing invoices for DRYMOR Farm Fans vs. Ron's Transmatic products. For example, Ron's pricing for a dryer included freight, set up and warranty; not so with DRYMOR.

One huge problem involved transport kits which were owned by the dealer, Transmatic. Ron had literally hundreds of transport kits and many salesmen who had problems keeping organized records. Sales of dryers were one item, and transport kit sales were another, as these kits still belonged to Transmatic, unless paid for by the buyer. If the sales person sold the transport kit along with the dryer at no additional cost it caused a loss to Ron's company. At times, Ron felt people were stealing from him, a sentiment reciprocated by his competitors, which at times, mirrored the feelings of how the competitors felt about him. On the other hand, Ron's price for a dryer also included freight, set-up and warranty.

Some of these mounting problems between **DRYMOR** Farm Fans and Transmatic also smacked of cronyism, if not worse. For example, **DRYMOR** Farm Fans were manufactured in Alexandria, and the company employed a lot of local workers; this was the home-town company. So, when Ron wanted to build not just a storage building for his dryers, but an office complex, the city was reluctant to give a boost to anything that threatened **DRYMOR** and nixed it, leaving Ron with a farm-house style building for an office. Begrudgingly, Ron accepted the city's decision because he had no choice, and eventually he decided the farmers felt more comfortable doing business in the farm-house office. Always, Ron pushed through business challenges and remained undaunted.

Eventually, Ron's grain dryer supplier in Indianapolis, Indiana abruptly ended its relationship with Ron without explaining its reasons. Adding insult to injury, when he went to visit the company, they personally gave him back his check for $250,000 for new dryers and said the business relationship was thereby ended. Ron's interpretation of this situation was that other distributors were envious of his success and slandered his name. His ability to sell dryers in certain parts of Minnesota in December of 1979 fell dramatically due to the ending of the Indiana supplier. Still, he would continue with his business endeavors until 1983.

In August of 1981, during a period when Ron was once again involved in litigation with Farm Fans and was relentlessly demanding additional discovery to shore up his case, Farm Fans made a motion that Ron undergo a mental evaluation by a psychiatrist of their choosing. Of course, Ron objected, and the evaluation was never ordered or conducted. The court also denied in part Ron's request for additional discovery, denied Ron's request that DRYMOR Farm Fan's balance sheets and cash flow statements be made available to him, reserving this viewing only to Ron's attorneys.

There was much back and forth deliberation and argument related to Transmatic Big-R owing DRYMOR Farm Fans Inc. for attorney's fees and vice versa. Court proceedings would note that each company won and lost various judgements against each other.

In April 1983, a St. Paul attorney forced Ron into a settlement wherein dryers could **not** be rented or sold related to an indemnification clause. Indemnification involves the "duty to make good any loss, damage or liability incurred by another." If one party (the indemnitor) causes a problem and the other party (the indemnitee) gets drawn into it, the first party agrees to be responsible for the problem on behalf of both! Added to this reported disappointment was Ron having to wait five months for an evaluation of his business worth by a Nebraska attorney only to discover the report excluded some crucial data for an accurate accounting of the worth of the business and loss in damages.

Frustrated, Ron hired a "powerhouse" attorney, from Minneapolis, by the name of John Cochrane, to bring an antitrust action against DRYMOR Farm Fans. Reportedly, in the beginning, Mr. Cochrane claimed the case was worth "millions." Ron telling friends and family he had been told the case was worth 20 million dollars-if not three times that much. Trial was set for the spring of 1983.

Within Ron's collections of letters there is an "Affidavit of Fact:" signed by attorney Paul Breyer who met Mr. Cochrane with Ron on December 22, 1980 in downtown St. Paul, Minnesota. This was a "preliminary meeting to consider Transmatic Big R Save $ More Corporation's potential lawsuit against Farm Fans Inc and others. The "others" included "a list of more than twenty persons or entities, starting with Farm Fans Inc, its officers and the Farm Systems Inc and its principles...and additional litigation to be pursued against the local newspapers, DRYMOR and its Principles and agents, Douglas County, the City of Alexandria and the Douglas County Attorney, for allegedly mishandling of lawsuits brought on by former employees." It was mentioned in this note that this information was "entered into the corporate book according to corporate law to authorize the hiring of the Cochrane Law firm." And, as such, Ron felt that he had covered all the bases, was going to have his day in court getting back what he had lost from the hands of so many who had colluded against him and be restored to a state of respect that he felt he deserved.

However, Mr. Cochrane would later demand Ron settle for considerably less money than had been initially discussed. In return, Ron felt betrayed that he had invested four years of gathering information for what was supposed to be a legal win for him; with a trial date of April 1983, the settlement conference was set for the day before the trial.

In the end, the actions initiated by Ron against Farm Fans for violations of the Sherman Act, Clayton Act, Minnesota Antitrust Law and alleged fraud and misrepresentation, conversion and misappropriation, interference with customers, employees, and breach of contract by reason of Farm Fans termination of Transmatic were dismissed. The parties were told they had to bear their own costs and disbursements.

Ron was shocked by the ruling. For him nightmares began when he awoke in the morning and continued during the day. Large amounts of capital were involved, and the losses added to his growing stress of not knowing what was going to happen next, when, and to whom. Unequivocally, the legal battles were taking a toll on his already shaky mental health, priming him to snap.

To make matters worse, one of Ron's attorneys, Mr. Breyer investigated some of the terms and found that **no** insurance was available to protect Transmatic against losses it might incur because of its agreement to indemnify Farm Fans for any claims arising out of dryers sold or rented by Transmatic. Ron's legal team also found that because the settlement permitted Farm Fans to withdraw its warranty, the Farm Credit Service would not finance farm purchases of theses dryers. Ron decided not to sign the settlement papers, with Cochran telling Ron he had to sign, or he would no longer represent him; still, Ron refused to sign.

During this time a comment was offered within an exchange of business correspondence that Ron was "not so much bothered by the settlement figures as he was by losing the opportunity to have a jury vindicate him in his dispute with his competitor." He wanted to be seen as having taken the high road. His self-perception was that he was the honorable party in this deal, not the one who made any mistakes; not the one who missed seeing any of the possible roadblocks or ways around them.

In 1985 Ron hired yet another law firm to bring forth a new-law suit for damages, which again, was unsuccessful. When the insurance company learned they were on the hook for the indemnification clause, they cancelled

Ron's policy, and Ron couldn't get premise insurance or any kind of insurance to re-establish himself in business. Subsequent bouts of anxiety and depression, some with suicidal ideation caused Ron to be hospitalized. Being obsessive can make you a person a hard worker, detailed to a fault, persistent, highly responsible and tenacious in the face of challenges, but the drawback can be not knowing when to quit. The toll on Ron paralleled the disastrous outcome with Farm Fans and consumed him. He became bogged down in negativity related to what he had expected to happen, depression over what did happen, and agony in the face of not being able to do anything to change either. There were weeks of emotional ruin, an endless vicious cycle.

Some of his business associates and advisers, did understand Ron's stress and saw signs of what seemed like a change in his mental stability. One letter dated August 13, 1985, from Lawyer Robert F. Bartle, of Nelson and Harding Attorneys at Law in Lincoln, Nebraska told Ron after they met with him that "the lawsuit against Farm Fans and any affiliate of that corporation is over. The Eighth Circuit Court of appeals has ruled that you were competent to enter a settlement with Farm Fans, and that, indeed, you did enter an agreement with them. I see little to be gained in pursuing that former course... you need to understand that it no longer makes any difference whether Farm Fans treated you fairly, or for that matter, whether they should have paid you more money. The only question which remains is whether you have a viable cause of action against your former attorneys based upon negligent representation." Of course, these were wise words offered in an attempt to assist Ron in stopping his obsession about things that were over. This professional cared for Ron; the problem is that people upset with outcomes are not as able to let go of their pain, even though to those outside of the pain this seems so logical. When one is obsessive to a fault, the only option is to try harder to win, not to give up or give in.

Mr. Bartle outlined one avenue of recovery out of three possibilities, that had the best chance of prevailing. He suggested Mr. Cochrane, failed to represent Ron properly the settlement conference, and failed to determine a workable and meaningful settlement agreement with Farm Fans. Mr. Bartle was honest in noting he did not want to mislead Ron in "expecting some sort of "pot of gold," along with telling Ron that "to have a strong case, they needed a strong plaintiff or client to work with." He added, he did not believe that Ron was "strong enough" to endure the strain and emotional stress of a deposition or other aspects of trial preparation." In other words, he was trying to tell Ron to let go of the entire Cochrane situation and move forward in another direction and let go of the painful past.

At about the same time, in December of 1985, Douglas County Hospital records documented the rocky course of Ron's mental illness and repeated hospitalizations. He had been to the emergency room at the Alexandria hospital 11 times the previous year, with the last time in December of 1985. Beyond this, Ron's personal records note he had a history of variable moods that prompted him to seek medical help beginning in the 1970's related to what was then seen as episodic anxiety and depression.

By the mid-1980's, his pattern would be to stay a day or overnight in the hospital and then demand to leave. His variable diagnoses included a "depressive episode" versus a major depression, possibly a reaction to a specific situation," like his overwhelming business pressures. He was noted as experiencing exhaustion, rumination/obsession with business problems, intermittent and fleeting visions of shooting or hanging himself, and extreme anxiety related to anticipated financial losses. The combination and timing of these distressing business challenges intersecting with Ron's descending mental state grew to critical significance as the pattern of his symptoms repeated with increasing frequency.

Unfortunately, humans can be both blind and vulnerable to our self-destructive patterns. Ron had no awareness that it was he who was falling apart; he was focusing elsewhere for both the source of his problem, and the solution. As such, while he was in the midst of an impending life changing disaster, he never saw it coming. Within the next three weeks, during a state of psychosis, Ron would ultimately act in a manner that would change his life, forever. People say they would like to be forewarned of such an impending disaster, but would they actually heed the warning signs?

It was clear Ron's business issues were having a significant impact on his mental health. What was less clear, however, was how Ron's state of mind played into what would become the defining event of his life: the shooting of his friend and lover, Margaret Brown.

1986 The Turning Point in Time

The only good thing that happened during the time Ron's business was painfully unraveling was that some friends introduced him to a woman named Margaret Brown on Labor Day, in 1984. At the time she was 32, divorced, and the mother of three children; Ron was 38, divorced and also had three kids. Mutual friends knew that both Ron and Margaret had lived in Mora Minnesota at one time and guessed that the two had other things in common. Margaret had a history of problems with alcohol and being the victim of domestic abuse; Ron had his history of emotional problems and insomnia. Their divorces behind them, both had healed to the point that meeting someone new who was fun to be with, someone who made them feel special again held great appeal. Initially, no one was planning on getting serious. It was just nice to have someone special to meet with, talk about things, go out to dinner with and share companionship.

The matchmaker friends prided themselves on introducing Ron and Margaret, and they loved to comment on how easily the new couple hit it off as they congratulated themselves for seeing traits in Margaret and Ron as individuals that made them click as a couple. Being able to talk easily together, sharing a similar quirky humor and their enjoying the same music and interests had been noted. Friends remembered Ron telling them that his meeting and knowing Margaret "was the happiest time of my life, the time of my life when I had the most fun." As a couple they were described as relaxed, listening to and emotionally supporting each other.

As a single parent without much support, Margaret had financial challenges. She also wanted to better herself and add to her education. It's unclear what Margaret knew about Ron's financial situation. There were some comments in earlier records about her knowing Ron at one time having had his own business. Margaret was described as the more cautious one about getting into a serious relationship, which is not that unusual for a mother with three kids who had been through one relationship involving domestic abuse.

Good and true friends, even the ones who date each other tend to try to be helpful. In some cases, this was noted as Ron reportedly encouraging Margaret to cut down on the number of beers she consumed and Margaret, in turn, voicing her concern that it wasn't healthy for her children to see Ron taking "drugs" which is what she called his prescribed medications for his nerves and emotions. Friends commented on the level of honesty between Ron and Margaret and the fact that they could talk about their own and each other's respective problems, even joking about them at times, without appearing to get offended or take what was said as personal. Relationships take time; second relationships are no different and may take more time due to individual baggage and personal mileage.

Margaret's main complaint was that there were times when the medication Ron took, "knocked him out for hours, or at times an entire day." Her solution was to hide the pill bottles she found, throw the medications in the garbage, or flush them down the toilet. Ron reportedly tried to cut down rather than go without his medications, later admitting he felt like he had to have them to help him cope. He resorted to stuffing bottles of pills between the mattress and box spring on more than one occasion and finding otherwise creative hiding places around the house. His secrecy about medications he needed in order to remain functional was like a silly game. While they voiced "concern" to each other about their respective use or abuse of substances, they also seemed to agree, neither of them was perfect.

When Ron and Margaret first met, Margaret was on welfare, living in a trailer, and attending school for hotel/motel management. It was no secret that Ron helped her out with some extra money, and shared meat and other food from his freezer with her and her kids. Ron owned two homes, the official homestead on Lake Miltona and another home in the Woodlawn area of Alexandria. Ron was not working for the two years they dated but he always had money, and Margaret must have found some needed relief in his support.

For fun, Ron and Margaret spent time at Jim and Judy's, a local favorite, where they played pool, had beers, visited with mutual friends, and talked about their future together. Ron also enjoyed Margaret's three children. In his relationship with Margaret's three kids, Ron would comment he had "missed out raising my own kids because of what I saw as the demands of my job; there was work day and night and weekends and holidays."

He reported he had "been so busy working, that the first thing he knew his kids had grown up, graduated from high school and were going their separate ways." Margaret's three kids took easily to Ron, and often asked him if they could go along with him to the weekend rummage sales and farm auctions he attended. Ron was delighted, by their interest. They would all drive off for a day at sales and come home talking about and sharing their treasures. Ron said he loved their company and especially liked it that they actually asked, if not begged to be with him. With Margaret's kids it became clear what a great teacher Ron could be. He knew all sorts of commonsense information about things, and he passed on his belief that it is never too early to learn how to dicker and bargain, and how to not pay too much for a desired object.

In October of 1984 Ron, Margaret, and her children moved to her newly rented home in Alexandria. At Christmas time in 1984, Ron took Margaret and the children to his grandmother's home where she made little blankets for the girls' dolls, and Ron took Margaret's son hunting. Ron was also present when Margaret's son needed reconstructive chest surgery. Growing closer with each new shared experience, Ron and Margaret continued with their relationship of love and support; fun and hope. Even in stressful times, they hung together; at one point they went together to Meadowbrook Women's hospital to terminate an unplanned pregnancy. When Ron received one of his successful legal settlements from his business lawsuits in 1985, he and Margaret picked out wall paper for the kitchen, dining room, and other rooms at the Lake Miltona home. They also talked about possibly moving to California or Arizona and starting a new phase of life together.

On the evening of January 14, 1986 Ron and Margaret and Margaret's two daughters left at 5 p.m. to go to the house of Margaret's friend,

Lynda, on Lake Miltona so one of the girls could get a permanent. As was their custom of doing nearly everything together, both Ron and Margaret went to the drugstore that afternoon to pick out the permanent. As Lynda applied the permanent, Margaret, Ron and Lynda drank beer and talked. The evening was reportedly pleasant for everyone. Ron, Margaret and the girls headed back to Margaret's home around 10 p.m. in the bitter cold, arriving at the house a few minutes later. Margaret and the girls went right to bed. Ron stayed up.

Reportedly, Ron talked often with Margaret about what he called his 'nervous disorder,' referring to his problems as "mental stress, mental exhaustion." He tended to minimize, or flat out deny that he had an actual mental illness. In the beginning of September 1985, Ron's medical records noted his reporting intermittent "visions of suicidal conditions, hangings, driving recklessly into trees, or off some bridge abutment." He described these experiences as making him "really nervous that something was going wrong, along with reporting he had momentary urges of "just rolling the Suburban! But I couldn't do that with the kids and Margaret along! I was really nervous.'"

The night of January 14, 1986 was one of the nights Ron experienced a siege of one of his "nerve spells." According to the police report he had voiced " 'feeling anxious and having racing thoughts all day.' " He claimed he " 'only slept a couple hours a night for the past 2-3 days.' " After the drive home from the permanent, Ron was reportedly truly suffering. He needed his medications, noted at the time as including Stelazine, an antipsychotic prescribed to be a sedative with another reference citing Mellaril, a similar antipsychotic, Elavil, an antidepressant, and Valium to reduce anxiety. The drugstores and grocery stores were all closed. Could he find some loose medication somewhere in the house?

Ron tried to watch TV. He reported being " 'wringing wet with sweat.' " He went outside to sit in the Suburban to cool off. In the icy cold vehicle, he re-read pages of the December 1985 Douglas County failed petition to civilly commit him as mentally ill, which was still in the glove compartment. The petition had failed due to lack of evidence to support Ron being a "danger to himself or others." However, Ron's doctor felt he needed inpatient psychiatric treatment to control his symptoms, based on his frequent calls to his physician related to what he described as, " uncontrollable anxiety."

On this particular evening in the cold Suburban, Ron read the pages of the petition as he held them in his shaking hands. The words, "danger to self or others" echoed in his ears, and exhausted his reasoning, it was impossible for him to stop thinking of the words and what they meant.

He reported reliving the angst of a not-too-long before incident on a Sunday noon when he called his doctor for help because he hadn't been able to sleep. Dr. Kulman, wasn't at the clinic, nor was he at his home when Ron tried him there. He mentioned to the receptionist on the phone, who was trying to find Dr. Kulman, that he was " 'seeing these suicidal visions and things like that,' " which prompted the person who took the call to contact the Alexandria sheriff's department. The sheriff drove to Ron's home, broke down the back door and entered. Ron told the Sheriff that he had just taken one Unisom tablet, but they wouldn't believe him; an ambulance was called and took Ron to the hospital. At the hospital the staff made Ron vomit and then put him in a room where he said he worried constantly, about "all those dollar figures...they were really bugging me because I knew it cost a lot to be in the hospital... and they kept me for nine days." This documented and reported behavior, along with how Ron was interpreting his situation is often times reported by patients as they attempt to understand or grasp the peril of their disintegrating thoughts. In some cases, people try to couple their confusion with another non-threatening event, like the cost of hospitalization, as though in the midst of their internal despair, they are still trying to report normal associations, which to anyone present does not make any sense.

Ron also remembered that the sheriff's department deputies entered his house in the fall of 1985 and removed all his guns while he was at the was in the hospital. After he got discharged, he went to get his guns back, and as soon as he found the pistol that he usually kept in the Suburban, he put it under the front seat. He always kept the Ruger cased and under the front seat of the Suburban. Ron had been around guns all his life. He was a hunter, liked to shoot at targets and was a good marksman. He prided himself with his gun safety methods.

That evening in the car, as he re-read the papers related to the December 1985 petition, which had occurred only a month previously, he questioned whether he could ever actually harm himself by hanging...despite his fleeting thoughts of doing this that occurred at times. He had even put a belt around his neck one time but then decided " 'No way... I ruled it out.' "

Next, he questioned whether he could shoot himself. He sat in the cold Suburban...cocking the hammer...and pulling the trigger of the unloaded gun...with the thoughts, " 'You know... could I really do this to myself... as was being said in these papers? I decided...I couldn't.' "

And then he decided to test himself as it related to the portion of the petition that referred to "harm to others." The thought, " 'Could I harm someone else?' became a new obsession. The words repeated themselves and weighed heavily on him to the point that he felt " 'compelled to test himself as to not...being a danger to others.'"

Of that moment of internal challenge, Ron recalled the order of events; "I got out of the Suburban and walked into the house...it was just like there was some kind of an image... or something going up the stairs ahead of me... I walked slowly through the darkened doorway between the bathroom and the bedroom... and I just stood there...my only intent was to just stand there...and rule out that I couldn't hurt anybody...I told myself, 'I'll be okay."

"But suddenly, there was like a sound that said..."Do it...do it." And I remember seeing two flashes in the dark black bedroom...I turned on the light... and Margaret was lying on the bed, facing up. I saw blood on her forehead running down her face...and onto her nightgown... I ran back down to the Suburban. I drove to the sheriff's department as fast as I could." " 'I told them to lock me up...so that's the rest of it...you know... pretty much.' "

At times over the ensuing years, Ron would offer a somewhat differing account, reporting the sense that he "saw myself from above the room...entering the bedroom...seeing someone who I thought was about to shoot me...I didn't know who it was...suddenly, there was like a sound that said... "do it... do it," and I saw two flashes in the dark...the bedroom was all black. I turned the light on and Margaret was lying on the bed face up." Between the two accounts, the verbiage changes slightly, but the essence is unchanged: Ron remembers being in the house, being commanded to act, and finding Margaret dead.

At the time of the murder, Margaret's children were sleeping in the next room. They reported hearing what sounded like two clapping sounds, and their mother saying, "No, Ron, no, don't." They reported hearing someone running down the stairs and a car driving away. The time was just after 5 a.m.

Margaret's son was the first to run into his mother's room. He tried to pull his mother to a sitting position, yet she fell backwards when he let go.

51

He ran to get his older sister and then frantically called their mother's friend, Lynda, to come to the house, telling her Ron had shot and killed their mother.

Ron raced in the Suburban to the law enforcement center and slammed on the brakes. He burst through the front doors. He was described as "shaking uncontrollably, crying, wringing his hands, pacing back and forth, repeating he did not intend to shoot or kill her." He wept uncontrollably. He would spend the night at the jail. The next morning, he was taken to the forensic division of the Minnesota Security Hospital where he underwent a full evaluation. He would be held at the hospital until his trial.

Back at Margaret's house, Lynda was with the children when the first police officer arrived, followed shortly thereafter by the arrival of the medical examiner. The medical examiner would determine that Margaret had been shot three times. There was one wound to the chest, a second scalp wound and a third wound about midline on the bridge of her nose. He determined that most likely the first wound was to the right chest and would not have been fatal if she had gotten to the hospital within a short period of time; the second wound, likewise, was not fatal. The fatal shot was the facial wound which would be described as including "stippling...little punctate areas of gun powder on the nose and both cheeks, approximately 6-7 inches in diameter indicating the wound was from very close range...certainly less than a foot."

That January morning was colder than usual for a lot of reasons. Margaret Brown had been shot dead. Ron had frantically driven himself to the jail and turned himself in as the shooter. Three children had lost their mother. Several families awoke to a nightmare on the bitterly cold morning of January 15, 1986. It was one of those nightmares that lasts even in the daytime and continues...forever.

Even people passing by on the adjacent bustling interstate knew all about the shocking Alexandria shooting and who it involved. It would remain the lead local news story in the *Alexandria Echo Press* from January to the fall of 1986 when Ron was committed to the Minnesota State Security Hospital in St. Peter and thereafter.

The Grand Jury

Ron would be deposed on November 4, 1986 while a patient at the facility at St. Peter. In Minnesota, people talk about someone being "in St. Peter," and folks assume they are at the state mental hospital. There were actually two significant institutions in St. Peter, at the time. One was the highly respected and private American Lutheran Church related liberal arts college of Gustavus Adolphus on one hillside, and the other notable institution, on the other hillside across the highway, is the vast State Hospital campus. If one wasn't college age or college bound, and one spoke in hushed tones about "going to St. Peter," the implication was clear.

June in Minnesota is usually the beginning of summer. The June in 1986 was unusually chilly. At the Douglas County Courthouse, a group of people had been summoned to serve as a Grand Jury and to be informed of their responsibilities related to the shooting death of Margaret Brown by Ronald Steen. A few people entered together, then others arrived in a staggered fashion, solemn in mood and greeting each other in hushed tones. This was supposed to be a quiet part of the world where such events, like murders did not happen. It was as though the sting of winter did not end this year and following the long and bitterly cold winter, it was now a dark and colder than usual spring.

On June 12, 1986, at 9:30 a.m. at the Alexandria Courthouse in Douglas County, the Honorable Donald A. Gray, stood before the prospective jurors. While the room was full of people, they were very quiet and reserved. After all, some folks go through their entire lives without learning about, let alone serving on a Grand Jury for a murder case. This was a new situation for most everyone, except the people who worked at the courthouse.

Hearing the facts about the shooting and death of someone in their community made the incident real all over again. Doubly real was the shock of knowing Ron, a local and wealthy businessman as the person who had caused the death of Margaret Brown, his girlfriend and one of their neighbors. Reality-wise, while the situation was serious, it was also racy in nature; there was the wealthy businessman shooting his girlfriend; money was involved, and where there is money there can be treachery. This was going to be a situation where community members were going to learn a lot more about two of their neighbors. whether they wanted to or not, for this murder was a hot topic. Not that many murders occur in Alexandria; this was a shocking situation. What kind of secrets would they learn about Ron and Margaret, what about the kids, what about neighbors who knew Ron and Margaret personally?

Judge Gray looked directly at the group seated before him and with a solemn voice said, "One of the responsibilities and privileges of citizenship includes serving as Grand Jurors. Your names were chosen from those who voted at the last general election. Some of you will serve as a Grand Jury, others as petit jurors, or the trial jury." He explained if the County Attorney had reason to believe an incident in the community involved criminal activity, the District Judge could be requested to summon the Grand Jury, explaining, "Your job will be inquiry into that incident to determine if a person or persons should be listening to the evidence and determining if a person or persons should be charged with a crime as a result." He added that the Grand Jury "historically has been considered as a sword and a shield of justice, a sword because it was to be the terror of criminals, and a shield because it was to be a protection of the innocent against unjust prosecution. Those important powers obviously create equally grave responsibilities to see that such powers are in no way perverted or abused."

Grand jury members took an oath that said they would "not indict anyone through malice or ill will or because you were angry with an individual or any group of individuals or because you think he or she ought to be punished, although he or she should not be indicted." The group was reminded they had been sworn to refrain from indicting anyone because of fear or favor of himself or anyone else. They were also reminded that the Grand Jury "does not try the case...does not decide whether or not the defendant is guilty or not guilty according to our standards...will not hear both sides of the case... their function is simply to hear witnesses and receive evidence as to a charge of a crime brought by the State and, based on substantial evidence...determine whether or not probable cause exists to believe that an offense has been committed by the person so charged and that the person should be brought to trial to stand trial on that charge."

Those chosen were further reminded that "with its extensive powers a Grand Jury might, unless motivated by the highest sense of justice, find Indictments not warranted by the evidence and thus become a source of oppression to our citizens. On the other hand, a Grand Jury might dismiss charges against those who should be prosecuted. The importance of its powers is emphasized by the fact that it is a completely independent body, answerable to no one except under unusual circumstances to this Court of which it is an arm."

The group was informed, that if an offense is punishable by life imprisonment, "It can only be charged through an Indictment from the Grand Jury." The noted exception was possibly finding Indictments not warranted by the evidence, and thus becoming a source of oppression to the citizens. On the other hand, the group was also informed that a "Grand Jury might dismiss charges against those who should be prosecuted." The message was that the Grand Jury was a completely independent body, answerable to no one except under unusual circumstances, Douglas County Court, of which the group was an arm of the court.

The Judge clarified the difference between a person being charged with a public offense by the issuance of a Complaint vs. and an Indictment. A Complaint was noted as a document filed by the prosecuting attorney setting forth the essential facts of the offense charge that establish probable cause that an act had been committed and the defendant was the one that committed it. The latter, an Indictment was explained as an accusation in writing presented to the District Court charging the defendant with a public offense and containing a written statement of the essential facts constituting the offense charged.

Judge Gray explained the County Attorney, Ann Carrott at the time, would be assisting the Grand Jury. She would be helping them reach their decision based on the finding that what was termed, "substantial evidence," existed that would be admissible at the time of the trial. The grand jury members were told they could consider certain evidence that would not ordinarily be admissible at trial such as hearsay evidence offered as a foundation purpose, and other examples that would be explained to them by the County Attorney if and when they came up during the proceedings.

There were 22 people present to make up the Grand Jury. They were told an Indictment could be found by the agreement of twelve or more of the jurors. If twelve were unable to concur, the foreman would be expected to report such to the Court in writing and any charges filed against the defendant for the offense considered would be dismissed.

The Grand Jury experience involved a lot of new information to be considered by local shopkeepers, farmers and housewives making up the group. Information that could result in serious repercussions for the individual charged with the offense, and possibly serious aftermath for members grappling with their decisions, especially as the case would eventually be the hot topic in their community for a very long time, likely remembered and recounted for years to come. Folks who read about the case in the daily *Echo Press* might have differing opinions; conversations over backyard fences or during conversations at the service and social clubs could reveal other folks' stark differences with the Grand Jury opinions. Being on the Jury was a serious responsibility.

These early realizations were somewhat mitigated by the group being informed that they could, at any time, ask the advice of the Court or County Attorney. The County Attorney would act as their legal advisor. Also alleviating some of the pressure was information as to what the process ahead would include: The County Attorney would present the formal charges one by one, witnesses would be called to support the charges with legal evidence, the only other person present in the company of the Grand Jury besides the County Attorney would be the witness and the court reporter. If security was an issue, a police officer would be present or could be summoned.

Added to the information already presented, the Grand Jury members were told they needed to keep secret whatever was said during the deliberations and how they voted. Nothing was to be disclosed except when directed by the Court. The Indictment was not to be disclosed until the defendant was in custody or appeared before the Court. The importance of this secrecy was explained as, "preventing witnesses from being tampered with or intimidated." The Judge explained this level of secrecy encouraged witnesses to offer information related to the crime in question.

Judge Gray then told the prospective Grand Jury members that witnesses would be called one by one, sworn in and questioned first by the County Attorney, then the foreperson, then by other members of the Grand Jury. All jurors would have an equal voice in determining if an Indictment should be returned, and each juror would have the right to state his or her reason or his or her views. No Indictment could be found unless the required number or 12 members of the 16 or more present, concurred. When a decision had been reached, the Grand Jury would notify the County Attorney who would prepare the Indictment that would be signed by the foreperson who would present the document to the Court without comment to anyone. If the group failed to agree to an Indictment, a "No Bill" would be identified. The Grand Jury on this day was made up of voters with names common to folks who lived in the area, mostly of northern European heritage. Names like, Larson, Olson, Sjoberg, Polipnick, Spanbauer, Nelson, and Roelf, just to name a few. Orville Larson was appointed as the foreperson and he would be the lead person and the first to question witnesses if he felt inclined to do so. He would also be the person to preside over the Grand Jury during their deliberations.

Following the long and detailed explanation of these procedures, jury members were taken to a large comfortable room with a table and chairs and a very large coffee pot. Thank goodness for the coffeepot. The aroma of coffee, the first sip, whether you added cream to it or not, helped normalize the heavy instructions everyone had listened to, and in some manner united them as a group facing a heavy challenge together. The coffee was calming and a pleasant and momentary distraction from the topic of murder and death. A diversion from the seriousness of the day and a caffeine lift to keep moving forward in the process ahead of them. You could hear the shift in the buzz of conversation, from the Judge's monotone directions to people sipping hot coffee and sharing in small talk with each other. Some people were actually even quietly chuckling or laughing about something in the course of exchanges with their neighbors.

When the meeting resumed, chatty conversations ended, and folks got instantly serious. Members of the pending Grand Jury were told they would be considering charges of murder in the first and second degree. First Degree

Murder was defined as "premeditation with the intent to cause the death of the person." Second Degree Murder was defined as "the intent to cause the death of the person without premedication."

Manslaughter was **not** one of the options. Manslaughter is defined as the "unjustifiable, inexcusable and intentional killing of a human being without deliberation, premeditation and malice. The unlawful killing of a human being without any deliberation, which may be involuntary, in the commission of a lawful act without due caution and circumspection. Criminal homicide constitutes manslaughter when it is committed recklessly; or a homicide which would otherwise be murder is committed under the influence of extreme mental or emotional disturbance for which there is reasonable explanation of excuse. I do not know the exact reason this was not one of the options. Typically, County Attorneys want to present a strict code of law to the county constituents, with the most severe sentences, for criminal activity. You might want to remember the term manslaughter, as it will be mentioned by others later on in Ron's story.

Jury members were informed that notes would be kept for recording total votes and to keep track of the witnesses that appeared. Additional reminders were repeated as to the importance of secrecy to avoid the proceedings being fatally flawed. No one was to reveal who testified or what was said, what was talked about in the deliberations, no one was to talk about the deliberations with their family members. They were again reminded that they were not a trial jury; they were only to decide whether there was probable cause to bring charges against a certain person, and what crime was committed based on subsequent information related to premeditation.

Of the several witnesses present to offer information to the Jury, the first witness called was the deputy from the sheriff's department who was on duty the morning of January 15, 1986. He would be the first to respond to the dispatch call that a man was in the lobby of the Sheriff's Department saying he had shot somebody. The deputy slowly walked to the witness chair. He gave his name and described his job as a Douglas County deputy and described Ron's behavior on the early morning of January 15, 1986 as, "very nervous, standing and sitting, rocking back and forth, not wearing a jacket, not smelling of alcohol, repeating the words..."It's just like a dream."

It was so quiet in the room you could have heard a pin drop, or a feather, for that matter. People sat with their heads down at times, perhaps in respect for the seriousness of the occasions, or reverence for the seriousness of their jury responsibilities, or maybe to honor life itself, and how fragile it can be.

The second witness was the police patrolman for the city of Alexandria whose shift on January 15, was from 4 a.m. to 12 noon. He said he heard a first call over his radio reporting a man walking in the front door of the Sheriff's Department; then he said he heard a second call on the radio for an ambulance. He headed to the residence and arrived at the house at 5:22 a.m. He reported there were three kids in the house when he arrived, and a young boy told him, "She's up there," pointing upstairs.

He described walking with the boy through a bathroom that led into a master bedroom where he could see a lady laying crosswise on the bed towards the middle of the bed with her knees hanging over the edge of the bed and her feet on the floor. He said the boy left right away when they got to the bedroom. The officer checked and found no pulse and no sign of breath. He reported observing a large amount of blood around her eye area and down along the left side of her face and on the bedding. A gun case for a pistol was laying on the floor minus the pistol.

At about this same time the ambulance attendants arrived, and the officer said he stood back and let them check the victim. The attendants checked for a pulse and for breathing, then one of them left to go to the ambulance to get a heart monitor to check for any sign of life. There was none.

The officer reported he sent another officer back to the police department to get a 35-millimeter camera to take pictures of the room and things in the room. He stated the medical examiner arrived approximately ten minutes later, pointed out some specific wounds in the head area and pronounced the woman dead. They waited for a neighbor friend to come and pick up the children before they moved the body.

The officer said he remained at the scene to begin the collection of evidence, such as taking photographs of the victim and various rooms upstairs and downstairs and bagging up the bedding. He collected three empty Old Milwaukee beer cans sitting beside an easy chair. He returned to the house later, after the autopsy report came back noting three bullet wounds, with one piece of lead found during the autopsy and one found later under the mattress pad. A third bullet was unaccounted for.

During the subsequent discussion, one of the grand jurors questioned the reason why fingerprints were not necessary with the officer replying, "We already had a suspect, the individual who walked into the Sheriff's Department." Another juror asked the reason the police took a brown leather jacket from the house. The officer noted he had seen Ron Steen several times wearing a brown leather jacket that looked and appeared the same as the one they found on a chair at the home. A third juror asked if there was evidence of a struggle, of which the deputy reported none was noted.

The next witness was the Police Chief who had recently retired but was still employed at the time of the shooting. He was at home sleeping when the called came, early on the morning of January 15. He arrived at Margaret's house at five minutes to 6 in the morning. The ambulance was already there. He said he scanned the murder scene, then went to the Police Station to call an investigator and told the person he would pick him up in a few minutes. He also called someone at the Bureau of Criminal Apprehension (BCA) in St. Paul, noting he had dealt with three previous homicides in Douglas County, Margaret's being the fourth. He executed a search warrant to locate the murder weapon from the 1979 Suburban that was in the Police Station. He described how a vehicle is searched and said the police did find the .22

caliber Ruger single six-shot revolver with an approximately ten-inch barrel with three spent shells and three live rounds of ammunition in the cylinder.

One of the jury members asked how the gun fired bullets. The Chief described the gun as a "single six" meaning it holds six rounds of ammunition, and the shooter would have to pull the hammer back each time before the gun would discharge the bullet. He reported it was not a double action gun, meaning you could fire with each trigger pull.

One of the jurors asked how the officer knew it was this gun that had been fired recently and the answer was that the officer smelled gun powder on the gun. The Chief added, the gun was taken to the crime lab in St. Paul to have testing which is a standard procedure at the BCA. Two projectiles were removed from the scene, one from the victim's body and another found in the bed. The BCA could compare the riffling (grooves and lines) in the barrel and perform other ballistics testing.

Jurors asked for some of the terms he used to be explained. The Chief then reported, "Bullets being projectiles have a core, the part of the bullet that kills the victim." Some jurors wanted to know who removed the bullet from the victim and the Chief said it was the medical examiner. The

Chief then explained he actually received the bullet from another officer who was present at the autopsy. He explained that rifling of a specific barrel imparts signature marks identifiable to that unique weapon as the bullet passes through the barrel during the course of being fired. There are rifling in the barrel that tell if that specific gun fired that bullet if it is not too damaged. Jurors asked about other guns and ammunition found in the Suburban and some questioned the reason a person might carry a .22 Ruger in a vehicle. They asked where the pistol was found, with the officer reporting it had been found under the driver's front seat. After this rather heavy discussion a lunch break was taken.

The first witness after lunch was Ms. Polipnick who was the Douglas County Sheriff's Department jailor/dispatcher. She explained her job as, "Dispatching and jailing any women who came into the jail related to booking, and other needs, such as the dispatching of an ambulance." Her shift on January 14-15 was from 10 p.m. to 6 a.m. She explained on her shift "a man walked in the lobby and up to the window in front of the dispatch office at approximately 5:20 in the morning and said he had just killed a woman."

She described him as wearing dark-colored polyester pants, a light cotton shirt, he was about six feet tall, approximately, 200 pounds, and had dark hair, black hair. When asked if he was wearing a coat, she said he was not, and when asked if it was cold that day she stated, "it was January and Minnesota it was cold." She said she asked Ron his name several times, and he finally answered. When asked what he said to her first, she responded, "he said, I need help, I just killed a woman." He did not tell her who he had killed, and she had to ask him several times, like four to five times without his responding. Eventually Ron stated the person he shot was "Margaret Brown."

When she was asked about Ron's demeanor at the dispatch window, the woman reported, "He was very excited, very agitated, almost incoherent. He was walking around in circles, pacing back and forth." With repeated questioning, she reported Ron finally answered, he "shot her." When the dispatcher asked where his gun was, she said he never answered.

Ms. Polipnick said she dispatched the information to the deputies that were on duty that morning and put an ambulance on standby. She reported dispatching the information to Deputies Johnson and Pipo. She said Ron was in the lobby talking to her for approximately five minutes and at times sat down, then was up and down and pacing. One of the jurors asked her if Ron acted like he was going to leave or try to leave. Ms. Polipnick reported she did not get the impression Ron was going to leave and said she did not feel threatened. "He was just walking around in circles, sitting down and getting up from the chair. He wasn't angry, just extremely agitated, very excited. He kept rubbing his eyes and pacing and walking around in circles."

The next witness was Office Roelf, who had served on the police force for eighteen years. He reported he was called at home at about 5:30 in the morning, He was told there had been a homicide and who the victim was. When asked what he did when he arrived at the Brown residence, he said he, "I went in with the children and a woman who were downstairs and started interviewing them." When asked, he described the children as two girls and one boy, the children of Margaret Brown. He talked to the children, individually, in the living room on the main floor. He did not talk to the youngest daughter because, "She really wasn't fully aware of what had happened, much less witnessed or heard any of it...she was 5."

He said he interviewed the son, about 6:00... 6:30 in the morning. The officer took notes of the interview but did not record it. The boy was 12. He reported the boy told him he had been awakened when he heard his mother say, "Ron, don't, Ron, don't.'" Then he said he heard what sounded like two loud slaps or cracks. He heard someone run down the stairs, and heard a vehicle take off out of the yard. He went to his mother's bedroom,

71

saw her lying on the bed and described her as having "blood gushing from her face." He went to his sister's bedroom, woke her up and she also went in and saw their mother.

The atmosphere in the room after the Grand Jury listened to this officer describe the scene at the family home was especially quiet. After all, most people had kids of their own or grandkids. Children are supposed to be protected from violence, especially violence in their home and especially when it resulted in your mom being killed. It was a terrible event to think about, let alone live through and Margaret's three children were the youngest victims of this shooting. It was almost too much to take in and yet everyone knew they had to press on. What a sad thing for Margaret's kids to go through. Some people shook their heads slowly, some just sat there like they had been stunned and left aghast.

The officer was asked if the boy was coherent and he answered in the affirmative. He was also asked the age of the oldest daughter and said she was "13." He said the daughter reported, "Basically the same information as what the boy said...she woke up hearing her mother saying, "Ron, don't." She heard what sounded like two loud slaps and a short while later, her brother came into the bedroom and told her to get into their mom's room." The officer reported he spoke to both children individually; he also interviewed them again the following day in a room where they were staying with an aunt and their grandmother at the Lakes Motel.

The officer offered additional information such as the older two children reporting the lights were left on in the bathroom just off the master bedroom where the shooting took place. Neither said they had touched the light switch that had blood on it. The boy said he tried to pull his mother into an upright position. She was laying on her back on the bed with her feet on the floor. He said he approached her, took her by both arms and attempted to pull her to a sitting position. When he let go, she fell straight back. The boy did not touch anything else, including bloody towels found in the bathroom.

The officer asked about weapons in the home. The boy described the pistol in question and the case where it was kept. He could describe the gun as a "revolver," and said it belonged to Ron, and that it was usually kept under the front seat in Ron's Suburban. He said he had stayed home the evening before the shooting when his mom, Ron and the girls drove to Lake Miltona for the permanent. He went to bed at 9:30 and was asleep when the others returned to the house.

The officer reported the older daughter said on his second interview that "she was awakened by hearing her mother say "No, Ron, no," and then hearing two loud noises. She said her brother came back to her room after he went into the mother's bedroom and told her to go into the bedroom. She saw her mother lying on the bed with a lot of blood around her face and said she did not touch her mother or anything else. Both children said they heard someone run down the stairs.

The officer interviewed Margaret's friend, Lynda, who came to the family home when Margaret's son called her shortly after the shooting. Lynda said Margaret called her at 10:45 after they got home from the permanent, to report they got home alright, were tired, and going to bed.

Lynda reported it was around 7 p.m. the evening before that Margaret, the girls and Ron came to her home and said they left just after 10 p.m. Margaret brought two twelve-packs of beer. She said she and Margaret probably had "about five each," and Ron would have had "like eight cans because there were six left over afterward." She remembered throwing away 18 empties. She denied seeing or hearing any anger between Ron and Margaret. She said Ron had been pressing Margaret to get married and Margaret just didn't feel comfortable yet with the idea of marriage at the time.

She said Ron was wearing a brown leather jacket, plaid shirt and a brown pair of slacks.

The officer also stated he attended the 8:00 a.m. autopsy performed by Dr. Spanbauer at the local hospital on the morning of January 15, adding this procedure took approximately 2-3 hours. One juror asked if a sample of Margaret's blood was sent to the BCA and the result of the analysis. The officer said there was no alcohol content in her blood. The same was true of Ron Steen's blood sample sent to the BCA. One juror asked how much time had passed from the time they drank the beer and their blood was tested for alcohol. The officer responded, "Probably six, seven hours." Another juror asked if the children knew the gun was in the Suburban or the house that night. The officer said "The children denied ever seeing the gun in the house. They said it had always been kept under the front seat of the Suburban." Another juror asked why reason the gun was kept in the Suburban. The officer reported that "Margaret's son said it was kept there in case they saw some gophers and they could do some "plinking."

The next witness was Dr. Spanbauer, the medical examiner. He reported his educational and medical background and why he moved to Alexandria in 1980 from Rochester, Minnesota, after completing his pathology residency at the Mayo Clinic. He stated that at the time he got the call about the homicide he was at home in bed...it was 5:35 a.m. He brushed his teeth, dressed, and proceeded to the address of the house given to him by the Police Department, the house on Fifth Avenue West.

During his testimony he described Margaret's body as, being positioned, "transversely, across a double bed. She was lying on her back in a nightgown and panties. There was a lot of blood on the bed, on her head, behind her head and to the left side of her head as well as lots of blood on her face, in her hair and on her nightgown."

Further, he reported "photographing a wound on the left scalp area and taking multiple photographs of the body and the room for documentation." A question was asked if it was the responsibility of the Medical Examiner to determine whether death was accidental or not. Doctor Spanbauer said it was his responsibility to make such a determination. He said that after the children were escorted out of the house, he instructed the ambulance attendants to take the body to the Douglas County Hospital Morgue for an autopsy or postmortem examination.

He described how an autopsy is conducted, noting, "It is common to first do an external examination, with written notes." He described Margaret as a "moderately obese white female in her mid-30's, with the external examination noting a scalp wound." After washing the blood off her face, he said he noted, "a second bullet wound just about in the midline on the bridge of her nose and a third wound to the right chest area, below the clavicle, with the exit wound just a little bit lower in the back below the scapula. Of the three entry wounds, there were only two exit wounds."

Now, if any of the jurors were not paying attention, this report of three wounds to Margaret's head may have jarred them to their senses of the more situation that had occurred. She had been shot three times.

He continued, to describe the external examination as, "the chest and abdomen being opened with a U-shaped incision coming down from the shoulder with a longitudinal incision down the middle of the abdomen." He explained that "during this phase of the autopsy, various pieces of tissue can be looked at under the microscope, after fixation and processing, resulting in a microscopic anatomic diagnosis. After the external examination, an internal exam consists of visual inspection of the organs, removal and dissection. This phase of the autopsy can also include samples of fluids.

He explained specific information related to the three wounds included the right anterior chest wound entrance having clean edges, whereas exit wounds have evidence of soft tissue evulsion, which occurs when the bullet exits pulling fatty tissue with it making it somewhat jagged. Dr. Spanbauer noted, "The exit wound in the right back area was lower than the entrance wound and was a larger wound making it obvious that the bullet went a little bit down, entering higher in the chest wall than it exited in the back where it broke a rib. This wound would not have been fatal, but loss of blood would have occurred without quick medical attention."

He said, "The second wound was a scalp wound, a deep jagged-edge scalp wound of the left superior parietal bone in the middle of the scalp. The entrance was noted, as was the exit wound, again with tissue extending out from the wound denoting an exit." A question was asked as to there being a skull fracture at the point of this wound to which Dr. Spanbauer answered in the affirmative. He further explained, "It was a deep-pressed skull fracture with the skull bone broken and pushed down onto the brain. No bullet fragments could be recovered from this wound, but there were many flecks of lead within the bone and on the surface." Dr. Spanbauer explained, "This wound would have been survivable had she gotten to the hospital and had appropriate care, adding. "The wound was potentially fatal by causing reverberation, or a kind of shaking of the brain, and perhaps damage to the brain stem."

He further noted, "The third wound was about the bridge of the nose and a fraction of an inch to the right of the midline, located below the eyebrow ridge. There was no exit wound."

He explained that he "used a long, thin piece of metal, a very thin rod, to determine the course of the wound which was downward through the nose, nasal cavities, through the mouth, down through the back of the neck and lodged at the base of the brain called the first cervical vertebra from which bullet fragments had been recovered." Dr. Spanbauer noted, "This was the fatal wound."

"Cause of death was the three gunshot wounds. The immediate cause of death was likely respiratory failure, that is, the respiratory control center in the brain stem just before you get up to the actual brain where it widens out very likely failed from the traumatic injury."

He further noted, "The wound on the bridge of the nose included a lot of stippling of gunpowder residue on the nose and both cheeks, perhaps six inches in diameter, maybe seven across, indicating this was a wound from a very close range...certainly less than a foot. The tip of the barrel would have been at least no more than a foot from the entrance wound at the time the shot was fired."

Shockingly, as the jury listened to these words, they must surely have understood that the doctor was describing Ron as standing very close to Margaret when this last shot was fired from the gun.

After a brief silence, a question was asked of the doctor as to stippling being found on the other two wounds, he responded, "No, none."

Dr. Spanbauer offered an explanation about the children reporting they heard their mother saying, "No, Ron, don't. Please don't." In his recounting, he surmised, "They could have heard this after one shot was fired...which woke them...along with the fact that she would not have been in any condition to utter any words had she suffered this wound as the first wound; therefore, it being the third wound was more likely."

The jurors listened intently, some looked down seemingly at their laps, and some shook their heads and closed their eyes. Everyone was very quiet. The details related to the children were hard to listen to, let alone comprehend what it had been like for them.

The doctor continued, "The gun used was a small caliber weapon, not a shotgun, a single projectile type weapon." No accidental cause for Margaret Brown's death was noted. Death was estimated at 5:10 a.m. on January 15, 1986.

Jurors asked about Margaret's position to the shooter based on the entrance wound being higher than the exit wound and Dr. Spanbauer responded, "The assailant was apparently higher than she was." Some Jurors questioned if Margaret had any other wounds by her face like she could have been hit. Was there evidence of domestic abuse. Dr. Spanbauer said there was none.

The County Attorney, having no more witnesses, gave the Grand Jurors instructions for their deliberations. She stood in front of the group and with a calm voice said, "Your job is to assess the testimony you have heard and review the legal issues which are twofold: Is there probable cause to believe that a crime was committed? And Is there probable cause to believe a certain individual committed that crime? She added, they did not have to reconcile all the facts of the case since they had not heard all the facts, all the facts would be presented at the trial. She also offered a comment that may have mitigated the jury's fears related to their heavy responsibility. She paused and stated slowly, "There is never total reconciliation of the facts in a case such as this." An understatement.

She continued, "Is there reason to have Mr. Steen go to trial on this matter or not? The options for you as jurors are to return no Indictment in which case Ron would not be charged with any offense or consider the issue of first degree murder or second-degree murder, or Jurors can indict on both first and second-degree murder." She continued, there must be 12 members of the Grand Jury voting for the Indictment. Names will not be recorded, only votes. If an Indictment is returned, the foreperson will sign the Indictment; a different form will be used if there is no Indictment. Once you begin deliberations, you will be sequestered. Remember, a charge of first degree murder is defined as 'causing the death of a human being with premeditation and with intent to effect the death of the person or of another;' murder in the second degree is defined as 'causing the death of a human being with intent to effect the death of that person or another but without premeditation.'"

The group was reminded that there had to be a majority of them voting for the Indictment. Also pointed out was that names would not be recorded as to how they voted, only the number of votes would be recorded. If an Indictment is returned, the foreperson will sign the Indictment, a different form will be used if there is no Indictment. Once you begin the deliberations, you will be sequestered. Remember, a charge of first degree murder is defined as 'causing the death of a human being with premeditation and with intent to effect the death of the person or of another;' murder in the second degree is defined as, 'causing the death of a human being with intent to effect the death of that person or another but without premeditation.' Please let the bailiff know once a final decision is made."

Members of the Grand Jury had a few minutes to get an extra cup of coffee or take a stretch before they sat down to discuss the case. It had been more than a full day. An unforgettable experience. The Jury foreman took notes as each juror offered their comments; many questions were asked requiring assistance of the County attorney at times. No one underreported the heavy responsibility of the group sitting together to discuss the fate of one of their neighbors. When it was over, the jurors parted to their respective homes. Surely their shared serious responsibilities that day would keep them connected on some level for a very long time.

The Jury Decision

On Monday, June 16, 1986 Ronald Lee Steen appeared in Douglas County Court. He was informed of the decision of the Grand Jury returning an Indictment charging him with Murder in the First and Second Degree. When the decision was actually announced, it was an ominous experience for everyone present, but especially for Ronald Steen. One life had been ended, and now another life was going to be changed forever. That's how these situations unfold. As the process moves forward, there are always more victims.

"The above named defendant is hereby accused and charged by the Grand Jury of Douglas County in the State of Minnesota by this Indictment of the offense of Murder in the First Degree, Count I, in that Ronald Lee Steen on or about the 13th day of January 1986 in the City of Alexandria Douglas County, Minnesota did wrongfully , knowingly and intentionally cause the death of a human being, to wit: Margaret Ann Brown with premeditation and with intent to effect the death of the said Margaret Ann Brown.

The next portion of the Indictment read: "Count II charges the defendant with the offense of Murder in the Second Degree and reads as follows:

In that on or about January 15th, 1986, in the County of Douglas State of Minnesota, and more specifically in the City of Alexandria, Ronald Lee Steen did cause the death of a human being to wit: Margaret Ann Brown, with intent to affect the death of Margaret Ann Brown but without premeditation.

The Indictment cited the statutes under which the defendant was indicted and the punishment for each of those offenses. Also listed were the witnesses called before the Grand Jury. The Jurors were told the Indictment would be filed and the defendant would be brought before the Court immediately, furnished with a copy of the Indictment and be arraigned on the Indictment before Judge Paul Flora on Monday June 16. They were thanked for their service. To the reading of the Indictment, Ron responded, "Yep."

He could only respond as such because *that is* what happened. His response supported his report of a frantic drive to the police station on the morning of January 15, minutes after the shooting, his bursting through the doors and telling staff that he had shot someone. Shooting someone causes their death...Ron was the first to admit that fact and he was owning up to his actions.

The Court informed Ron he would get a copy of the Indictment along with his attorney, Mr. Quam. Ron's arraignment would be the same day, June 16, 1986 at 10 o'clock a.m. before Judge Flora. The trial for this matter was set for July 14th, 1986.

At the time of the shooting, Margaret's children became victims. And now, Ron's family became victims. And their burden would be different inasmuch as they would feel the brunt of public opinion for years and years to come. None of this was their fault, but they would be seen as the children of the man who killed his girlfriend. Collectively and individually, they would each feel it, at least for the first few years. Perhaps in some folks' opinion, they would be marked forever. Children left behind in tragedy can in some cases become collateral damage.

The Trial Verdict

There were two phases of Ron's criminal trial. In the first phase, he was found "competent to stand trial," meaning he understood what he was charged with and, the pleas available to him, and he demonstrated being able to meet with his attorney and carry on a meaningful discussion related to his rights and participate in his trial. In the second phase of trial, the five-man, seven-woman jury deliberated over six hours before finding Ron not guilty of first and second-degree murder, specifically "Not Guilty by Reason of Insanity, NGRI." The basis of this decision included his history of mental illness, and the existence of his reported and observed symptoms at the time when Margaret Brown was shot.

Now insanity is an ominous word. How can someone people knew and met in the grocery store, or sat beside at the adjoining table at the Holiday Inn, someone who looked normal, now be labeled insane? How does that happen? The legal definition of NGRI is, that the individual at the time of their crime was, "laboring under a defect of reasoning so as to not know the nature of their actions or that they were wrong." Ron's driving himself to the Sheriff's Department was clear indication he realized his actions were wrong, along with the fact that he had identified himself as the shooter; he had also reported psychotic symptoms associated with his depression and his explanation of what occurred when Margaret was shot.

"Insanity," is a legal, not a psychiatric term. Different states and federal standards contain slightly different worded criteria for determining whether one is "insane." In Minnesota, if a crime involves evidence of death caused by another individual, along with that individual having a history of mental illness or unusual circumstances related to the death of another person, the accused will be evaluated related to his or her "mental state at the time of the offense." What was their original plan and thinking before the event, what did they want or expect to happen, what occurred during the time of the event and what happened afterward; how did they feel, what were they thinking about, and what did they think would happen?

On March 11, 1986 Ron was evaluated at the Minnesota State Hospital in St. Peter, related to his competency to stand trial and his mental status at the time of the offense. The findings included his being seen as "capable of participating in his defense at criminal proceedings," and his being seen as "having elements of a psychotic presentation around the time of the alleged incident warranting the raising of a M'Naughten defense." At this time, it was also noted that "Mr. Steen continues to acknowledge some suicidal ideation and there is considerable concern that these individual harbors the potential for homicidal acts."

References note fewer than 1% of trials include a successful finding of an insanity defense; cases that proceed with an insanity defense include individuals, like Ron, who would spend more time in state hospitals than they would have spent in prison, had their case been handled as a strictly criminal act.

In the above comments the word, "M'Naughten" was referenced. Legal insanity began in 1843 in England with the case of Daniel M'Naughten, a Scottish woodcutter who had an intricate delusional belief system that members of the governing Tory party had targeted him for persecution and had plans to murder him. His plan to protect himself, was to kill the Prime Minister, but instead, Daniel mistakenly killed the Prime Minister's private secretary. Mr. M'Naughten was a man of means and hired an attorney who raised the issue of his insanity. M'Naughten was found to be insane (early version of NGRI). Since Queen Victoria was fearful that insane people might possibly be set free, and therefore pose a threat to the public, Daniel M'Naughten was sent to Bedlam, a psychiatric facility, and subsequently other institutions until his death in 1863. The "M'Naughten Standard" includes the wording previously noted related to the individual "laboring under such a defect of reason so as to "not know the nature and quality of the act, or if he/she did know, he/she did not know what he was doing was wrong." This same standard has continued to be applied since the mid-eighteen hundred to John Hinckley in 1981 and Ron Steen in 1986.

Of course, there are situations where seemingly normal people try to appear mentally ill. Thus, there is always an evaluation of the person to rule out feigning symptoms of a mental illness to alter the course of his trial and confinement. The earliest case related to such a situation was the murder trial of Charles Guiteau, the assassin of President James Garfield in 1881. Guiteau was an eccentric individual who had exhibited erratic behavior and paranoia. However, he was also a capable and intelligent speech writer for the President. When Guiteau wrote one of Garfield's speeches that was not used, he felt betrayed, became despondent, bitter and began to plot revenge. He eventually stalked the President for a month before shooting him in the back at a train station in Washington, DC with Garfield dying three months later, on September 18, 1881.

History would describe Guiteau's trial as somewhat of a fiasco and of great interest, not just because of his crime, but because of his bizarre outbursts and courtroom behavior which were exaggerated bizarre behaviors. Guiteau's testimony was also disjointed, including his reporting he shot the President because 'God told him Garfield was destroying the Republican Party and needed to die to save the Democratic Party." ' Charles was found guilty of Murder in January of 1882. Before he was hanged on January 13, he recited a poem in a childlike voice at the gallows. His case was seen as sparking the need for change within the courts related to the issue of Insanity.

Sometimes people ask how I assess whether the individual I have been asked to evaluate is faking their illness and their symptoms in an attempt to look mentally ill, for sympathy and possibly to mitigate their situation. The answer is "collateral information." People's behaviors tend to be consistent over time. But some have tried to look crazy to escape imprisonment by getting sent to a state hospital; not such a smart move, but nevertheless a move. I remember reading about two brothers, Anthony and William Esposito, 35 and 28 respectively, in the 1940's who shot the office manager of a payroll carrier for a Manhattan linen company. A chase ensued with some bystanders getting shot in the crossfire. Eventually a police officer shot William and when the officer went to check on the injury, William rolled

91

over and killed the officer. Both brothers were caught by a group of observers with the assistance of a taxi driver. When brought to trial, the brothers claimed they were "insane."

In court they drooled and banged their heads on the defense table, made animal sounds, cried uncontrollably and howled like wolves resulting in their being tagged with the name "Mad Dogs." They walked like apes into the courtroom, ate bits of paper and carried on until the jury, after deliberating for only minutes, found them guilty of First Degree Murder and sentenced them to die in the electric chair at Sing Sing. On the way to prison, a brawl erupted between the brothers and the police, with the brothers beaten into submission. For months they engaged in hunger strikes, and eventually, at 80 pounds each, they were carried to the electric chair and executed.

Ron's history noted he had been diagnosed with a mood disorder, depression or a mixed mood disorder including agitation, sleeplessness, at times reportedly appearing to have mildly psychotic symptoms that passed with the inclusion of medication. His symptoms followed patterns of emotional pain and distressed behavior. The fact that he was so successful business-wise is not unusual. People who have mania can work day and night, think quickly, and have endless energy. Ron also had a history of "down times," some appearing to be common to life or worsened by situational stress related to money concerns and business pressures. His local pharmacy had a long listed history of medications that had been ordered for him.

His admitting diagnosis at the Minnesota Security Hospital and eventually the MI and D Transitional Unit was Schizoaffective Disorder, Bipolar Type. This diagnosis incorporated his variable mood presentations and episodic psychotic symptoms eventually treated best by the neuroleptic, named Risperdal.

Ron had a documented history of times when he had an inability, to concentrate, relax, or find relief from he called his "mental suffering." In conversation, he switched from one subject to the next and at times could appear disorganized. He saw the effort by Douglas County to commit him in December of 1985 as demeaning, an indictment of his worth, instead of his mental illness.

Since the early to mid-1980's, he had fallen into obsessing about the specific sums of his financial reversals. He was described as "preoccupied with money he has lost," and cycled back repeatedly to thoughts of an attorney "botching a business deal;" moreover, he obsessed about the worth

93

of his remaining inventory, lamented property taxes, loss of rental income, loss of sales, a competitor "stealing" his business. Reported were his preoccupation and rumination involving numerous attorneys and appraisers who were unable, in his opinion, to properly and correctly make reasonable assessments of his assets and expressed suspicions about some of his religious advisors pressuring him into disassociating with Margaret. Additionally, reported were vague physical complaints of his hands feeling numb and his frequently feeling "dizzy," a recurrent experience of "standing behind this figure; I was outside of my body...I was standing in the dark in a secluded room looking out, and someone looked like me...it was not like myself, for things were going faster than I could think." Comments included his perseverating about "a sense of abandonment, worthlessness, hopelessness...being destitute and alone with no place to turn," along with occasions when he was convinced that the professionals, he hired to help him were in fact attempting to harm him or do him injustice.

State Security Hospitals: Who is Most Secure?

People are familiar with regular medical centers and adjoining hospitals, but not everyone has been in or wants to visit a psychiatric hospital, let alone a security hospital. There is a huge difference between a neighborhood hospital where babies are born, and people go to get stitches. The former are places of healing; the latter, the security hospitals are secure facilities to protect the community from the patients within and to protect the psychiatric patients from their own violent or psychotic behavior. Regular hospitals have a cheerful information desk with flowers and a smiling volunteer ready to tell visitors how to find the room number of the person they wish to visit. In state hospitals, however, each building has a specific purpose and houses certain psychiatric patients. There is a main floor with patients usually being housed in the floors above. When visitors ask to see someone, there will be questions as to the relationship with the person, and visitors will possibly be asked to provide identification, before being asked to have a chair while a direct-care worker is found on the patient's floor to come and escort you to a secure but general visiting area. Or visitors may be informed the person is unable to have visitors at the time. When visitors get to the visiting area, there may be staff standing nearby and cameras visible recording what is going on; there may be vending machines to get soda or snacks. The main difference is that the patient will not be in bed in a typical medical ward. The patient will sleep in a large room where there are many beds, possibly with half-wall partitions between areas. This is a group plan, not a single room option.

The first state security hospital I visited and became acquainted with was Florida State Hospital in Chattahoochee, Florida, where I did my post-doctoral internship. In 1991 when I began my internship this institution was an impressive setting of huge buildings scattered amidst a rolling hillside covered with massive pine, wild dogwood and magnolia trees, and carpeted with a ground cover of deep pink azaleas. It was also hugely intimidating. The memory of the nurses' station when I first visited was that this room appeared more like a harness shop with its rows of wide tan leather belts with padded wrist/arm bands for patients who were out of control; I was also surprised that these patients would also be present at times in crowded elevators that carried both patients' and staff together.

What I would later learn was that the women patients were more frightening than the men. Their inventive attack plans against other women included fights that would abruptly break out in the bathroom. The toilet stalls were approximately six feet deep and did not include doors. So, someone could be beaten by others in a surprise attack with no way out, and little defense. Then there were the reported used sanitary napkin fights that, luckily, I only heard about, as my status as an intern kept me in lectures and interviews instead of controlling people. That was a good thing because the week before I started at FSH a direct care staff had been found strangled with a guitar string and stuffed into a closet.

I also knew FSH to be a bastion of history related to mental health case law with mentors who had the best training to share with me, the neophyte. I was not disappointed. Initially, I was fearful of the large number of patients, the extent of their illnesses, and my proximity to possible harm. I was told to know where people had their hands. With these cautions in hand, I listened. I learned. I still admire FSH. I knew that any state hospital I would later enter in my professional life would not be intimidating, because I had trained with the best. My training included experiences in two wards for patients incompetent to proceed (men's' ward/women's ward), weekly case law lectures, having a year-long patient I saw weekly, mental health lectures by a variety of presenters, working for three months with a forensic psychologist in outlying counties, a stint in the forensic unit where there was a real *Silence of the Lambs* unit, and time spent in Corrections Mental Health Institute

97

where prisoners from all over the southeast section of the United States were sent for treatment. This institution had a death penalty unit, but prisoners facing "Old Sparky" would be taken to Stark, Florida to meet their fate. One of the last individuals I observed being interviewed before my internship ended was Danny Harold Rollings, the man eventually executed for the Gainesville serial killings. His history included his commonly presenting himself as a devout Christian, singing gospel songs, quoting Scripture, and portraying himself as unabashedly and humbly righteous. For the women who fell for that, their lives were in true peril. He did not just kill his victims, he mutilated them sexually. I had seen this overly religious presentation too much and too often to believe it.

By contrast, the St. Peter State Hospital in St. Peter, Minnesota began in 1855 and was the first institution in Minnesota to treat the mentally ill. It also included large building scattered over a rolling hillside of pine and maple trees that showcased the phenomenon of autumn when formerly green leaves turned orange and crimson. Kettles of hawks soared overhead. Then there was winter where everything was blanketed in white ermine. Dangerous patients in Minnesota had their own building, with a newer Security Hospital built in the early 1980's at the top of the hill. While windows included jail bars on thick windows, there had been escapes.

The original mission statement of this institution, like others of the time, boasted lofty aspirational verbiage touting the "provision of services and treatment to optimize the safety of patient, the staff and the greater community." "Visionary" pledges were even more obscure and heralded a plan to "deliver a high quality of services to meet customer needs." "Values," included lofty pronouncements regarding "teamwork, professionalism, integrity, service, dedication, and respect for the individuality and dignity of all persons."

I pondered these lofty and empty-sounding aspirational statements. I would have liked to have met the people who wrote these flowery descriptions for an institution seeped in dark mystery and fear of the unknown. What were some of the problems and challenges during these early years that continued into the future? What was the average length of stay? Who looked out for patient rights; did they have any rights?

Originally established as a treatment center of mental health services beyond that which could be provided to individuals in rural cities, these giant institutions used to house and treat 1000 patients on a daily basis. Over time, newer treatment philosophies suggested people could manage in communities. Also aiding the shift to the community was the development of neuroleptic medications in the min-1950's and atypical neuroleptics with fewer side-effects in the min 1990's. As a result, these huge facilities were divided up, scaled down in size or closed. Buildings were emptied, jobs were transitioned or ended, and services were downsized. What remained were the huge brick or ornate and pillared buildings.

In the beginning of his hospitalization Ron talked about the shooting as "an accident... unintentional" which was...caused by a "toxic combination of medications causing him to be delirious." In 2004 he would liken his behavior to that of former Twins pitcher Jeff Reardon who, was found not guilty by reason of insanity of robbing a jewelry store in West Palm Beach while under the influence of a combination of prescribed medications that reportedly left him "emotionally unstable, hostile and manic, depressed, suicidal, delirious and hallucinating." In this case two court-appointed psychiatrists, along with two defense psychiatrists testified. I remember wondering what it would be like to be in a situation like Ron's and if he thought he would have been better able to manage his situation if he had been convicted and sent to prison. I wished I had thought to ask him about this.

The *Lake Region Echo*, on April 22, 1986 (after the shooting and before Ron was committed as MI and D) included a report by the State Hospital representatives describing treatment for individuals deemed Mentally Ill and Dangerous as "highly effective." Added was the statement that it was "extremely rare for a St. Peter patient to repeat a violent crime once they are released." The hospital's success with such patients was reported as related to "long term surveillance and carefully supervised discharge agreements along with a detailed and individualized program developed for each patient released back to their families in the community." Supposedly Ron's treatment program would include "monitored activities altering the environment to eliminate stresses that could cause problems, family members being thoroughly briefed on the danger symptoms of returning psychosis, and scheduled visits by public health nurses."

Again, as an example of old habits being slow to disappear, shortly following Ron's admission as MI and D, in 1987, Ron again contacted yet a new law firm to continue litigation against Farm Fans. In response he received a letter that in frank terms informed him "in sum and substance, the success of any claim you may have had against attorneys you saw as botching the settlement depended on your credibility as a witness. Given the events of the past few years and your present confinement, any hope or likelihood of a successful verdict has been lost."

Incredibly, similar correspondence dated October 19, 1989 to yet another law firm, resulted in his being told that Transmatic's claims against Farm Fans were unable to be reopened. It was noted that none of the antitrust lawyers in the Twin Cities would touch the matter because they did not want to offend John Cochrane. It was also noted that Ron's commitment to the state hospital was strong evidence he was disabled, and appointment of a guardian would not remove this disability. Ron was encouraged to "move on...work at getting well...forget the past."

Interestingly, one of Ron's psychiatrists also noted within the first few months of Ron's commitment that "the persistent involvement in his legal affairs is evidence of his ongoing competence and intactness...he is able to continue to participate in rather complex legal maneuvers(sic) which have as their goal, ultimately to restrict him of whatever resources he appears to have. If he does not intrude on unit functioning and other staff activities, I feel we have an obligation to allow him to exercise his legal rights."

A year later, another psychiatrist described Ron: "Patient is his usual alert, cooperative, coherent, relevant (sic) self, with no evidence of psychosis." He is currently free of all symptoms of depression or psychosis which led him to commit the murder; understands and is remorseful for the death of his companion." Add to these comments was another entry noting, "Were it not for the legal issues related to the death of his girlfriend and his commitment as Mentally Ill and Dangerous, he might be able to seek discharge."

Another factor feeding his hope of early discharge was a February 8, 1989 meeting of his co-conservators and early conservatorship attorney meeting with Ron's psychiatrists. Topics included the various options for disposition or preservation of Ron's vast assets; like the disposition and or preservation of the grain dryers and related equipment, the motor vehicles Ron owned, the motorcycles and other items of personal property.

The Lake Miltona property housed the 1977 Lincoln Mark V, and a Mercedes; at another property was a Cadillac, at a commercial property were the Harley Davidson motorcycles, 1925 Model 4 Ford, 4-wheel drive Chevrolet pickup truck with a ploy blade and several smaller Harleys. Other automobiles were stored at an Alexandria commercial property including several tractors and boats. Not to be overlooked were the hundreds if not thousands of noted rummage sale items Ron had collected over the years.

Of course, the person who knew the most about these items was Ron. His conservator and his attorney attended a "team review" meeting at the Minnesota State Hospital on March 1, 1989 to ask questions regarding Ron's diagnosis, treatment plan and prognosis. The results of this meeting were noted in a March 6, 1989 letter to the "review team," which spelled out the hospital staff present at the meeting and explained Ron's "treatment plan." This plan consisted of four goals: "1) "That Ron acknowledge his mental illness and acknowledge that his mental illness played a role in the death of Margaret Brown. This would include a recognition that drugs and alcohol played little or no role in that event." 2) "That Ron participate in therapy programs including five hours of structured activities per week for short term goals and ten hours of structured activities per week for his long-term goal." "3) "That Ron no longer be preoccupied with legal matters but concentrate on regaining his mental health."

Included in this letter was mention that the staff continued to be reluctant to make any prediction about Ron moving to a less restrictive setting due to his present poor participation in his programming. They were critical of Ron's attempt to "litigate his way out of the state hospital" and stated they would not support his efforts to leave the state hospital by such means." There was also information that Ron was blunt about the treatment program being "no good" and felt strongly he did not need it. He was cited as asking rhetorical questions of the staff, such as, "What drugs did they put Thomas Alva Edison on?" After all he worked twenty hours a day too."

A Minnesota State Hospital *39 Month Review* dated November 30, 1989, not surprisingly noted Ron remained committed as Mentally Ill and Dangerous with no change in his legal status. Ron was not seen as believing he was mentally ill, and he did not give the impression he could benefit from any therapy offered. He was however, medication compliant. He did not attend scheduled groups or structured activities.

Ron's presence in the hospital prompted a certain amount of curiosity by staff familiar with his history and sometimes flamboyant, if not easily confident presentation. He had a certain arrogance and sense of entitlement towards hospital staff towards whom he also held some level of disdain because he perceived them as unable to understand how his situation and his emotions were intertwined. In short, Ron did not have confidence in the professionals surrounding him and he did not treat them with respect.

105

They, in turn were put off by his demanding nature which included resistance to cooperating with their forms and methods of treatment. They were on one side and Ron the other; each pointed at the other as being the real problem.

Ron's room routinely contained stacked boxes of legal records which he was allowed to have. He poured over these records, wrote letters and made phone calls as though he was conducting normal everyday business. Repeatedly, business people would contact the hospital demanding Ron be stopped from writing letters to them; long lists of names of people he was forbidden to contact either by letter or phone resulted. At times, he would contact people mentioned in newspaper articles, only for these people to respond to these overtures by calling him at the hospital, unaware he was in a mental institution. At one point in time when all the boxes of legal records were removed from his room, Ron demonstrated a sudden and dramatic decompensation that went on until his legal records were returned. For him, these legal records were a form of security: if he reviewed them more, perhaps he could learn what really happened to him and correct it. Perhaps these records were his security to a time in the past when he was completely absorbed in business and being successful. These boxes of documents kept his mind active in an otherwise non-stimulating setting. He understood these records. They kept him intellectually focused.

One particular example demonstrates the lack of trust between hospital staff and Ron. It speaks to the problems that can develop when people assume something without asking questions for clarification. Ron was known for dismissing staff when he tired of what he saw as their inane effort to understand what he was talking about. He also contributed to the brittle interaction with his caregivers, with his own kind of arrogance.

It was a long-standing practice, if not a component of treatment monitoring for nursing staff to pay close attention to patient's behaviors on the unit, including when they were talking on one of the patient phones. As it happened, Ron had several conversations with some unknown person, conversations that were overheard by nursing staff, and comments related to their eavesdropping made their way into Ron's medical record.

When his conversations were overheard, in which he repeatedly mentioned the words, "ten-thousand each," nursing staff developed heightened interest and curiosity. No one asked him about this statement; of if he was in some kind of trouble and needed assistance. To psychiatric staff considering the array of possible meanings of the words, "ten-thousand each," all possible interpretations were problematic. Some of the staff wondered if

Ron was possibly arranging to pay some hitman $10,000 to "take care of" staff who were unsympathetic to his situation. There was no record of anyone asking him if "10,000 each" had to do with a car, motorcycle, or piece of property. Hospital Security was not asked to be involved in this evolving mystery; no searches occurred for information related to "10,000 each" in his writings or in his later conversations.

Weeks turned into months with no clarity or resolve related to the "ten-thousand each" issue. It seemed this comment overheard in the course of eavesdropping was forgotten. However, over a decade and a half later a highly regarded professional reviewing Ron's records as part of a risk assessment protocol, formed his own conclusions about what was occurring and, without basis concluded Ron was involved in a "multiparty conspiracy," a conclusion that conveniently underscored the evidence of "psychopathy, and .(consequently, Ron's) high risk for future harm to others if released, and his being designated "unable to live safely amongst others."

The important issue here is distinguishing between perception and reality, and the awareness of the influence of each notion. Both can be manipulated by information and reasoning. As review of thousands of records revealed, entries of caregivers' observations can be either neutral, helpful in a positive manner, or blatantly misleading.

That was never more true than in the daily accounting of patients' behaviors and interactions within a psychiatric setting, depending, of course, on the individuals in question. What becomes concerning is when people assume, they alone are correct in their appraisals and when others are fearful to dissent; always, it is essential to explore ideas and rule out bias.

The perception of the "10,000 each" comment in the mid-1980s, and its meaning to the examiner reviewing Ron's records in the early 2000's, were both amazingly off-target! There was no malice intended or involved; but that would not be clarified, for the examiner who offered his most bizarre explanation never talked with Ron personally to verify what was meant by the words "10,000 each!"

When I initially read about the "10,000 each" I had no expectations that this vague term could be paired with anything based in reality let alone be used to support Ron's connection with a so-called "multiparty conspiracy," which was a figment of some examiner's imagination.

The notion of perception versus reality became an anchor point throughout Ron's case. Particularly, since most, if not all, of the more current information about him was offered by others through progress notes, treatment program behavioral descriptions and unfortunately in assumptions made by others that were, unsupported by collateral evidence. Partly this was his doing as he was more often than not, dismissive of anyone who represented "treatment" which did not advance his cause. On the other hand, he was not a disruptive patient. He also had a relaxed and friendly side that was not documented in his chart.

Ron would spend his first nine and a half years within various locations of the St. Peter State Hospital system, moving from the Security Hospital down the hill to the lower campus units of the Regional Treatment Center. While he initially did nothing but sit in a chair and watch television, not even playing pool when it was available, later he began attending his required groups and therapy sessions, making friends with some of the patients with whom he shared similar interests, keeping appointment with his designated psychiatrists and other treatment providers and following all the rules.

That did not mean he gave up his continuing focus on his legal matters. That never changed. He continued to review legal information related to his case and he had staff make him copies of information he considered of primary importance. He was a voracious reader, and he continued to write letters to people he felt a resonance with, wanting to compliment them or further discuss some topic of political or legal interest. He also contacted people with whom he had a bone to pick. For me, as a psychologist, when I read these accounts, I just saw Ron as, still working, carrying out his business as usual.

By the mid 1990's, based on his record of good behavior, regular attendance at programs and psychotherapy, along with his agreement with his diagnosis of bipolar disorder and denial of hallucinations delusional beliefs, suicidal/homicidal ideation), Ron was rewarded with unsupervised campus privilege meaning he could walk out of the building in which he lived and roam freely anywhere on campus. His next reward was a transfer to a sister institution, the Willmar state hospital in Willmar, Minnesota where he would live for three years. This placement was seen as preparation for further advancement to in less restrictive settings for individuals working their way towards resumed community living. For Ron, life was looking hopeful.

In response for this change of status for Ron, *The Echo Press*, the local Alexandria newspaper, that originally covered Ron's murder case in 1986, the jury selection process and the trial in minute detail, as well as a 1987 story about treatment for persons committed as Mentally Ill and Dangerous, was now, in July of 1996 headlining a story about Ron about to be "set free," which was inaccurately worded, as he was not going to be imminently released!

Included was a front-page photo of Ron looking relaxed, smiling broadly, and sitting in an easy chair with his legs crossed. This photo was captioned with a description of the interview content wherein Ron reported the death of his girlfriend as "unintentional" and an event over which he experienced daily regret and loss. In the article he would again say he was trying to prove he was not dangerous when the shooting happened, still unable to grasp that this statement made little sense to anyone else but him. He reported his first experience at St. Peter was helpful, and that he felt better emotionally. Moreover, his former history of stress related to business issues and his depression were briefly repeated.

Common to Ron's pattern of interaction, he would later express regret and anger toward the *Echo* story, saying he did not like their choice of the quoted comments they published, and that he was upset because the newspaper story included the word "murder."

In the way of additional backlash, some readers criticized the paper for their concluding that Ron was being "honored" for his criminal acts. The *Echo* editorial page on July 12, 1996 explained that the focus of the story was "crime and punishment," insight into the tragedy, how the man who pulled the trigger was changing elements of his story, what had happened to him since the shooting, whether he was remorseful, and whether justice was being served. And that *was* news."

Placements in Willmar and Duluth

Willmar Regional Treatment Center (WRTC), in Willmar, Minnesota was the next move for Ron after St. Peter. Willmar is northwest of St. Peter, a two hour drive by car. This smaller hospital campus had tan brick housing and treatment buildings set in an orderly fashion through which ran tree-lined sidewalks and flowerbeds. Not surprisingly, Ron was described as easily meeting a new set of fellow patients with whom he shared interests, such as sharing fish stories in an area surrounded by at least ten different lakes. With so many lakes nearby, many residents had tales of catching a lot of walleyes, or the popular pickerel, a fish that was available nearly year round.

As well, Ron continued to engage in group therapy and meet with his caregivers as scheduled. No one reported any problems with him, personally, or with his behavior. His diagnosis at the Willmar facility was still noted as schizoaffective disorder, bipolar type along with a personality disorder NOS (not otherwise specified). At this time, he was taking Thorazine for his history of psychotic symptoms and a mood stabilizer in the form of Depakote as well as the antidepressant, Wellbutrin. The credibility of this diagnosis at WRTC was supposedly a repeated Minnesota Multiphasic Personality Inventory that noted, "no evidence of acute symptoms of psychiatric illness including mood disturbances or problems with reality testing, no evidence of delusional thinking, or other active signs of psychosis."

Because of his progress at Willmar, in July of 1998, Ron was advanced in his treatment to live at Arrowhead House, a halfway house in Duluth Minnesota, seen as a "trial run at eventual community living." A halfway house is like a large family home in a community. People have their own rooms or may have a single roommate. There are meetings about house rules and schedules. Staff continue to document residents' behaviors, interactions, medications, and appointments, as well as share such records with the mother institution, at St. Peter. Even better, at Arrowhead Ron had the added luxury and permission of staff to drive his own car, a used white Cadillac. Obviously, he was trusted as to decision making related to driving and to responsible behavior in getting himself to places he needed to be on time and safely.

He drove for the entire three years he lived at Arrowhead without an accident or a traffic ticket. Such positive behavior was not however, noted in his records at Arrowhead, and I never had the opportunity to find out the reason as this time of his life was long over before I got involved with Ron or his case. He also had passes to drive to visit family members in other parts of the state. And Duluth is a beautiful part of the state to leave, even for brief visits elsewhere. Residents of the city are on the impressive shores and coast line of Lake Superior, surrounded by tree-covered hills, and good people who more than not hailed originally from Northern Europe and had been born into generations that actually enjoyed snow, ice and wind.

While Ron lived at Arrowhead, his only son, Ron Jr. described him, saying, "He was confident and like his former self. He was the best I saw him for years, he was confident and relaxed. He could have sold ice cream to an Eskimo!" With his car, Ron also resumed his customary visits to rummage sales. Moreover, he drove to various places for lunch, to his medical appointments, and to keep appointments with his community psychiatrist.

Of course, old patterns and problem areas were still at hand. On November 21, 2000 Ron's Duluth psychiatrist wrote a letter indicating he was aware of Douglas County Human Services having made comments about Ron not being entirely cooperative or compliant with his treatment plan such as attending Day Treatment groups. This psychiatrist noted, "at this point, Ron was not interested in such programming, and, according to a recent evaluation, day treatment does not appear necessary."

I remembered being impressed with this treatment providers' candor. Finally, someone was making sense related to Ron's individual needs. I had low expectations that Arrowhead would respect these statements, as group home treatment providers are for groups, not individuals; everyone marches together; there are no individuals in group anything.

The good doctor also noted that Ron had been "compliant with taking medication, drug screens, not possessing dangerous instruments or weapons...had not displayed psychotic symptoms, or any evidence of depression, paranoia, mania or other active mental illness." He added that Ron's history included past involvement with psychiatric treatment programs, and that he had not seen any clear evidence that Ron continued to suffer from a psychotic illness, which casts doubt on the validity of statements about his "denial." He added, "it would be appropriate for anyone to deny a mental illness if they did not in fact suffer from that illness. Such a denial is by itself not necessarily a sign of mental illness and cannot be taken alone as a sign of noncompliance with treatment recommendations." To my way of thinking, this professional made a lot of sense in paying attention to Ron's good side. Unfortunately, I did not have a great deal of hope that his opinions of Ron would be appreciated amongst the other psychiatric professionals at Arrowhead House.

This physician further noted the statutory criteria for a designation of Mentally Ill and Dangerous adding, "while Ron had a (history) of a mood disorder and in the past engaged in an overt act causing serious physical harm to another, the only question remaining, is, whether there is a substantial likelihood that he will engage in other acts inflicting serious physical harm," adding "this was a question no one could answer with certainty." He ended his letter by stating, "On the basis of Ron's behavior while I have worked with him, I do not see any substantial likelihood of future harm." This letter concluded that Ron "engaging in 20 hours of programming that was a repeat of past programming had little, value."

I admired this professional's apparent drive to say and do the right thing, even though he walked alone on this path. His opinion and words of wisdom, however, fell on deaf treatment team ears! The staff at Arrowhead could not understand anyone who treated Ron by recommending a treatment plan that differed from theirs. Ron would continue without incident to take his Depakote (mood stabilizer); Wellbutrin, the (antidepressant) and Ativan, (anti-anxiety) and other non-psychiatric medications such as Pravachol, Singular Nitrostat and Albuterol inhaler.

Again, in 2000, this physician credited Ron as being consistently compliant with taking medications and requested drug screens. This physician also indicated he had proposed a reduction in the form of discontinuation of the Thorazine related to Ron showing evidence of a new tremor and dyskinesia hand movements a common side effect of this neuroleptic.

It was not surprising that during the three years Ron lived at Arrowhead, Ron's social worker and case manager felt growing resentment against his Duluth psychiatrist, who had questioned the usefulness of lengthy programming that was basically repetitious. All the professionals involved had been supposedly trained in the behavioral sciences and worked with people who had behavioral issues. Certainly they, as human beings couldn't be biased and have differences simply based on unsupported opinions? Or could they?

All residents at Arrowhead, without exception, were expected to participate in 20 hours of weekly programs that treatment providers adhered to with religious fervor. There were **no** exceptions. Being in previous programming for ten years was not seen as a justifiable reason for not "learning more." While the staff at Arrowhead were not psychiatrists by any stretch, they were part of his psychiatric treatment team and overall care!

119

Perhaps it might have been helpful for the staff at Arrowhead to meet the psychiatrist and discuss how his recommendation for no additional groups could be understood and dealt with. It would never happen. House rules **were** rules to be adhered to.

In reality, "individual treatment needs" was a term used without assurance that treatment professionals understood the implied concept. Additionally, raising the ire of Ron's social worker and case manager, besides his having a psychiatrist who was challenging their programming, were Ron's frequent drives to rummage sales where he collected Elvis memorabilia. In the eyes of the Arrowhead staff, this behavior constituted a "symptom" demonstrating re-emergence of his mental illness (obsessive hoarding as opposed to adding to one's collection of treasured items). This notion took on new energy with his room being designated, a "fire hazard," including large photographs of (several neatly stacked) boxes lined up against a wall. For staff, it was an overly large leap to move from collecting rummage sale items to evidence of actual hoarding symptoms verging on the brink of total mental collapse.

Did no one challenge this notion as extreme? Was there ever a discussion related to a range of ideas about these items? Could residents not

120

be individuals? Could this not be a teaching moment for the future, since Ron had a history of collecting certain items? What happened to working on problem-solving and open discussions with options, weighing of options and plans to deal with this problem, if it even was one? Instead of discussion, review of options and plans of resolve, Ron was given a month to "do something about it."

He did. He got a hitch for the Caddy by driving across the bridge from Duluth, to Superior, Wisconsin where a case worker at Arrowhead told him he could get the best deal on a U-Haul. He drove back to Duluth, loaded everything into the U-Haul himself, despite his recent ER visit related to shortness of breath, informed halfway house staff of his plans to relocate these items to a specified family residence in Alexandria and return to Arrowhead. His records included documentation that Arrowhead staff had full information of his plans to the point of having sent medication with him so that he would not miss a single dose. Everything appeared to be in order.

Co-occurring with this event was Ron's case manager charting him as "missing" his treatment groups. She also noted other "behavioral incidents" to the extent that a case was built against him in what appeared to me to be a growing and heightened example of clinical zeal gone off the rails. Ron would

121

next be charted as "intentionally" missing a meeting with his case manager even though at the time of this appointment, he was at a local hospital ER complaining of shortness of breath. Preceding the ER stop he had spent time at the courthouse reviewing old legal documents related to his case.

Other progress notes entries included a growing list of pejorative examples of noted infractions pointing towards what would become a revoking of his Arrowhead placement and return to WRTC. Surprisingly, documents dated December 19, 2001 from his chart noted the sentence, "Ron has NOT been informed that Douglas County is planning to have him revoked to Willmar Regional Treatment Center,'" the same institution he was at prior to moving to Duluth and Arrowhead House. Did any staff raise the issue of ethical decision making or lack thereof? No one raised the question of this appearing to be a set up in the making.

Ron's records at Arrowhead on December 20, 2001 noted "Ron showed up at Arrowhead House at 4:30 p.m. with a U-Haul attached to his car. He wanted to know if someone could help him move his things. He was told his trip to Douglas County was revoked, with his quoted response, that he "was not going to get a refund on the trailer and was going to move his things no matter what." While this was a foolhardy response to his being informed of the rescinding of permission for this trip, I saw nowhere in his records where any Arrowhead staff made calls to intervene in what was to become a pending disaster. Ron returned the next day on December 21, 2001. Law Enforcement was called and took him to Miller Dwan Hospital in Duluth, rather than WRTC as was noted on the court order. It would take four days to locate his social worker to inform her of his whereabouts.

Staff at Arrowhead would later describe Ron as "spending most of his time driving to rummage sales and eating in fast food restaurants," reporting his "principle downfall was his obsession with rummage sales, accumulating over two years' time a massive volume of "junk" which filled his car, his room and the Arrowhead storage room." Also charted was the information that his being given a "rescindable eviction caused him a great deal of stress that triggered a manic cycle resulting in his needing to be revoked and returned to Willmar Reginal Treatment Center."

Staff would add, that at the time of this revocation he was also describing a belief that he "was wronged by the mental health system and they had been perpetually plotting his legal revenge." Added was a sentence stating, "One of his main goals was getting off medications and he was successful in having his doctor discontinue the Thorazine." Once again, perception was being treated as reality.

Apparently, the Arrowhead treatment team who documented his reported plans to move the Elvis items to Alexandria and return promptly to Arrowhead in Duluth, and who sent medications along with him kept silent, or possibly they were enticed to remain silent to keep their jobs. As a result of this situation, Ron's provisional freedom disappeared. All those years of compliance, cooperation, and progress were, gone in a matter of seconds.

Interestingly, records I reviewed about this situation from Miller Dwan described Ron as, "non-suicidal, not demonstrating aggression, but appearing delusional related to comments about attorneys and accountants taking advantage of him and physicians forcing him to take medication with side effects that concerned him." He reported his medications as "Depakote, Wellbutrin, Pravachol, Singular, Ativan, Nitrostat and an Albuterol inhaler." His diagnosis at Miller Dwan was "disorganized schizophrenia." His diagnosis at Arrowhead was bipolar disorder, an entirely different entity. And where was evidence of the "manic episode" Ron reportedly had demonstrated at Arrowhead related to the trip to get rid of his extra items? It was not apparent in any subsequent documentation.

Miller Dwan staff questioned the reason for his being brought to them, with charted information noting Ron also was "unable to explain the reason." There was documentation that Ron presented as "paranoid and delusional, but not a behavior problem; not suicidal or homicidal." To Ron's detriment, psychiatric staff were quick to perceive behavior as evidence of symptoms, without actually verifying their accuracy by asking the person about the words they are saying or getting verifying collateral information before certain information is entered in the chart. Jumping to unsupported conclusions is normal professional behavior, I guess.

Ron's Arrowhead records in 2001 described his revoked provisional discharge as due to his "failing to participate in required treatment programming, missing follow-up appointment with his social worker, and missing multiple doses of his required medication." Never mind that an added note was that this "*missed medication was a cholesterol lowering medication discontinued by his internal medicine physician.*"

Ron was also cited at Arrowhead as "displaying an inability to relate to his caregivers resulting in deterioration of his sleep and activities, resulting in a labile mood and his becoming impulsive and angry suggesting a reoccurrence of his mood disorder." No mention was made in these same records that there had been discussions with Ron related to a variety of ways these issues could be remedied; no mention was made of problem solving methods other than those of the extreme.

Adding to the egregious unrolling of these events included Ron's conservatorship attorney at the time being a person I came unfondly to refer to as Mr. Black. This attorney documented in a letter related to Ron's revoked discharge that "Ron agreed he should be re-hospitalized and restarted on medication." This attorney was a real piece of work; a true discredit to the legal profession, perception-wise and in reality.

Apparently, no one questioned the non-existence of threats or acts of harm to self or others which has to be present for loss of freedom. Apparently, no one asked about the absence of this threatening behavior in the subsequent proceedings, neither the judge or the attorney; how come the Miller Dwan hospital staff described him so differently? It was like a well-oiled assembly line, well-oiled and twisted.

Also, the guidelines related to revocation of a provisional discharge including, "the patient has departed from the conditions of the provisional discharge plan and is exhibiting signs of a mental illness which may require in hospital evaluation or treatment or the patient exhibits behavior which may be dangerous to self or others" were magically seen as having been met. Suddenly, Ron was seen as dangerous when the day before he had been seen as safe enough to drive his own car to a distant city, common to his driving history of the past three years without a single traffic citation or parking ticket. Neither of the appointed court examiners who would have reviewed this information missed evidence failing to support presence of dangerousness. No mention was made of his psychiatrist writing a letter that credited Ron's treatment compliance and need to not require additional repetitive group programming he had already completed.

Ron's personal documents that I would acquire after his passing actually included a transcript from this Jarvis Hearing which is a court hearing to determine whether the patient is competent to accept neuroleptic medication or needs to be ordered to take it by the court. The hearing was conducted by ITV at the Stearns County Courthouse on April 2, 2002 (approximately three months later, allowing plenty of time to discover challenging evidence). The same two examiners who interviewed Ron were appointed to offer an opinion regarding Ron meeting the criteria for forced neuroleptic medication. Ron's diagnosis was noted by one psychologist as

127

"bipolar disorder, manic," with the second examiner saying the diagnosis was "schizoaffective disorder, paranoid type." The symptoms that warranted forced neuroleptic medication were noted as "depression, and manic periods, currently he is irritable, has an elevated mood with symptoms of grandiosity, delusions, talkativeness pressured speech, distractibility and some flight of ideas. He has been in the hospital with elevated mood and has been grandiose."

When the issue of Ron no longer being on a neuroleptic medication was raised, it was reported that his "community psychiatrist in Duluth tapered him off the neuroleptic in February of 2001 followed by his then starting to experience symptoms of mania." When asked if this professional knew the reasons Ron had been revoked, he reported Ron was "not complying with programming, was at times refusing to take medication, was accumulating many purchases and had an unauthorized trip away from Arrowhead," with all these issues reported as consistent with a diagnosis of mania.

The other examiner testified that Ron had a "major delusion relating to the legal community and the fact he needed a lawyer, but all the lawyers were employed by an agricultural machinery business that were out to get him... there was a conspiracy in relationship to his use of his land, his profits from this land, and to prevent him from selling overstock of machinery."

When Ron's defense attorney cross examined this professional and he asked, "If Ron's opinions about his legal issues were true, would the psychologist's opinion about the need for neuroleptic treatment change?" The psychologist responded in the negative. Ron's reported symptoms were "delusions of persecution and delusions of grandiosity. When the defense attorney asked the psychologist if Ron did own land, and was in fact wealthy, the psychologist stated, "It's my understanding he is quite wealthy and does own some land but that is only through hearsay evidence and I don't have any concrete proof of that."

Obviously, they were in a hurry, did not read the information given to them, did not question what was not included and did not want to embarrass anyone by asking for the missing information.

Ron testified he was unwilling to return to Arrowhead because of staff telling lies about him, which was a legitimate complaint. I had seen him as a consistently very direct person, and one able to honestly assess another's intentions; but he was not aggressive. He remained in WRTC for a year until new searches for provisional discharge placements for him were attempted but unsuccessful. Ron visited several half-way houses and/or assisted living facilities in five different communities without finding a match for his needs.

None being found, Ron was returned to St. Peter when Willmar Regional Treatment Center closed. It was 2004, just short of 20 years since his indeterminant civil commitment as Mentally Ill and Dangerous.

I thought about Ron's situation at Arrowhead House often during the time I spent writing his story. It was a perfect example of a patient being set up to fail, by professionals **not** sharing the rest of the story; the truth of the matter. Sometimes I would contemplate if professionals who twisted client reports ever regretted their actions, knowing that most likely this never occurred. Although many make jokes about the likes of Nurse Rachet from *One Flew Over the Cookoo's Nest* as pure fiction, I, however, am not alone in having met and known professionals who were mean spirited at best and who may have outshone Nurse Rachet.

One of the advantages of good record reviewing is noting inconsistencies, contradictions, and evidence that what is claimed is verifiable or otherwise. Such information, when brought to light can influence trial outcomes. There was no support for Ron having skipped medications for a number of days as suggested in the petition. Never clarified was the reason the Arrowhead director was unable to locate Ron for four days, when he was at the local hospital as she had ordered. She was not subpoenaed to be a witness at his revoked provisional discharge hearing despite her being the initiator of this action. Additionally, support staff were not asked to contribute information. In short, the many mitigating issues related to his revoked discharge were not brought up. There will always be professionals who are silent for whatever reason, when the situation demands they find their voice.

2004 Back to Square One: St. Peter

Deja Vu. Ground Hog Day. Full Circle. Back to square one. Ron was returned to St. Peter on October 7, 2004 and housed in the Mentally Ill and Dangerous Transitional Living unit. This unit, was part of the St. Peter Regional Treatment Center, located on the lower hill below the Security Hospital. This unit, in theory, was the living unit for MI and D patients preparing for their eventual release from the hospital. The key word is, "eventual." I would not have the opportunity to meet Ron in person until 2006 when I was asked by his defense attorney to interview him. Before my interview, it is important for me to review the person's records to understand their case, the ground that had been covered clinically, the person's responses and behaviors, all in anticipation of a recommendation for onward care which can include continued confinement or possible release.

Ron's first stint at St. Peter Regional Treatment Center was nine and a half years, including four years of unescorted walking privileges on the hospital campus based on his compliance with hospital rules. It had now been six years since his provisional discharge to a half-way house in Duluth had been revoked with his subsequent return to the Willmar campus for 33 months until that facility closed. It had been 14 years since he was in the high control unit at the Security Hospital and nearly 20 years since he was designated MI and D after a grand jury determined he should be charged with First and Second-Degree Murder, later found NGRI. I could not even imagine how he felt about returning to the very hospital his confinement began so long before. It must have seemed like nothing really was changing at all.

The Mentally Ill and Dangerous Transitions Building was a two-story brick structure, the entrance of which was lined with wooden benches where patients could sit outside on sunny days and watch the cars and people arriving at the hospital for work. There were many sidewalks connecting the various near-by buildings. Trees and manicured flower beds were everywhere.

As usual, Ron's chart noted his having an established circle of friends with whom he enjoyed talking about mutual interests, like local and national news, baseball, television programs, board games or playing cards; Ron was also a pool pro and at the transitions building there might have been a pool table. He played somewhere on the hospital grounds because his earliest records noted that in his years of hospitalization in the late 1980's and early 1990's, he was initially so depressed that he even declined playing pool.

His typical day after his return to the Transitions Unit was noted in his medical records as beginning with a "careful reading of the newspaper followed by conversations with fellow patients about worldly affairs, politics, visits or calls by friends and on occasion dabbling in business issues by phone or engaging in some topic of research related to his medications, his case, or something he heard about on the news." He continued to have boxes of his legal records in his room where he repeatedly reviewed them. His day was also noted as being full of "receiving calls from friends on the outside and his having a nearly regular weekly visitor," who was one of three lifelong friends. Ron now had what was called "level five liberty," allowing him to walk anywhere on the hospital campus unescorted. This level also spoke to his being seen by staff as trustworthy, a factor that bears remembering.

Hospital activities were routine. MI and D building views seldom changed; cars or state vehicles pulled into and out of the parking lots as staff came to work, or other workers trucked in assorted supplies; sometimes new folks would show up who might be visitors, or new hospital trainees, or patients' family members. Seasons came and went. Maple trees turned from summer green to orange, burgundy varieties morphed into blazing yellow and the leaves on the poplars turned into what appeared to be pure spun gold. Green grass dulled into a flaxen color in the fall, eventually blanketed by soft layers of snow blown into frozen drifts. Rains of spring inspired the hint of green buds on the hillside trees until they filled out into thick forests with the process starting all over again. Staggered placement of white birch amidst giant pines created a contrast on an otherwise tree-bark winter pallet. Kettles of soaring hawks shared the wind patterns high above the rolling hills and made continuous spirals as they kept their vigil on the earth below. This peaceful setting contrasted with the turmoil in the lives of the people who had been committed to a hospital they had to learn to call, "home."

One new twist was that this time Ron had a Treatment Team assigned to him. I was curious to see who made up this illustrious group and hopeful when I found out it included a psychiatric behavioral analyst, primary nurse, program director, psychologist, social worker, licensed practical nurse, primary care physician, county case manager, guardian/conservator, recreational therapist and vocational counselor. Surely this large a group could come up with a plan for Ron that advanced both his cause, and theirs. The trend in treatment in 2004 was that of a "psychosocial rehabilitation environment" where members of a variety of disciplines grouped together to,

135

(as per the patient handbook, to "wield therapeutic influence for the patient's recovery by modeling a therapeutic environment." This team rotated every three months to become an entirely new group of professionals. The actual "leader" of the group was whoever of the professionals volunteered to conduct the meeting at the time.

Ron's treatment team document began with a Bio-Psycho-Social Summary including three paragraphs related to 1) The reason he was originally sent to the state hospital in 1986; 2) His symptoms supporting the diagnosis he was given in 1986; and 3) Assorted statements of charted events seen as relevant from his earliest records and since his readmission in 2004 (meaning someone had reviewed at least some of his records).

However, based on statements from his records that he was, "delusional about not being mentally ill," and "fixated on legally challenging his commitment status," one might wonder how it was that his 11-member team of professionals had not noted any progress he made. After all, a level 5 liberty is a high level of trust. How could he have that level of trust and still be seen as delusional? How could he have driven his own vehicle all over the city of Duluth, south on state highways to Alexandria and elsewhere to visit family without an accident or getting lost if he was actively delusional, confused or unable to think in a logical manner? And why were there no questions like this in his records to challenge his treatment providers with advancing his treatment?

Also mentioned was his "refusal of treatment groups." No mention was made however, that he had participated in treatment groups from 1986 to the mid 1990's without problems and that he did attend the groups initially, reporting none were interesting or helpful to him before he stopped attending them. No reason was given as to the mandatory nature of these groups, what their goal was and the reason they were mandated, if in fact they were. No mention was made of alternative activities, like other group events for patients who opted not to attend one type of group treatment.

The groups the hospital would order Ron to attend, and which he eventually declined after attending them for a while, included "Blueprint for Change," Computer" (he scored 100% on the final), "Health Education-Diabetes," "Refocus and Relaxation," "Frisbee Golf" and "Happy Hour." At best these groups presented opportunities for socializing; no explanation was noted as to their being "mandatory." Certainly, they did not sound like therapy groups to treat mental illness...or reduce dangerousness.

Within Ron's Individual Treatment Plan, I noted a variety of different treatment headings with noble sounding, yet vague, esoteric descriptions. For example, "Educational Services" was defined as "enrichment opportunities to maintain academic skills, foster awareness of current events and ethnic diversity in which the person can pursue specific interest areas through a variety of resources and practice communication." "Self-Management and Social Skills" was defined as vocational services "assisting skill development, providing various opportunities for self-management, social and independent living skills." Individual Therapy was described as "assisting the individual in completing treatment assignments and managing independent requests of staff." Psycho-Educational Group was defined as "supporting the patient's goals as recommended by the team and/or or requested by the patient." Patients were encouraged to have a plan for preventing relapse with journaling and cue cards used to assist in building these skills that included regular updating. These certainly had flowery sounding descriptions, however undefined, and without including examples.

Treatment team plans were reviewed on a quarterly basis and modified based on the team's opinion regarding the patient. All of this "treatment" was done under the larger than life umbrella of "milieu therapy," defined as "staff setting examples, guiding and reinforcing responsible,

138

appropriate behaviors" in patients. Milieu therapy is a very old, vaguely defined therapy that consists of patients sitting in a group with staff present. It is doubtful that many patients have made progressive strides behaviorally from milieu therapy. For all practical purposes, *it is* useless. I was informed that the behavioral analyst, social worker or nurse would write up the summary findings of the treatment team meetings.

However, in my review of these summaries, I noted that, for whatever reason, the treatment team's synopsis of Ron's progress or lack thereof failed to match the separate progress notes written by his psychiatrist; as well, they did not match nursing entries related to his self-care, behavior on his living unit or his interaction with staff and peers. Why was this?

Nor did the team consensus match with the opinion of Ron's psychiatrist, who noted Ron showing improvement in his presentation through past treatment in Willmar. Ron's documented presentation was typically opposite the most recent independent risk assessment comments noting he was seen as at, "low risk for aggression." I wondered the reason for these discrepancies. Were the programs offered based on research supporting their reducing symptoms of mental illness, or was I reading pages of empty therapeutic planning and doomed treatment advancement? My suspicions were piqued but I decided to hold final judgement until I knew more.

For the most part, the nature and tone of the information in the treatment team records described Ron in pejorative terms, basically denigrating treatment advances by others and evidencing his onward need for the treatment programs provided at the hospital. Medication entries described Ron demonstrating a return of symptoms of anxiety when off his medications. There were no entries where his physician documented asking Ron what else was going on in his life when he would complain of insomnia or anxiety or when he would be observed acting anxious.

Treatment teams determined patients' short and long-term goals: the terms, "long" and "short" were not defined, nor was the word, "stability," as noted in the sentence; "The patient will maintain clinical stability on a long-term basis." I guessed that goals would be endless, and once accomplished, if that was actually possible, the completion would prompt a new set of goals. If a patient had goals to work on, further treatment was necessary. If further treatment was necessary, the patient was not ready for discharge. With milieu therapy, the patient is never done being treated.

It was explained to me that the MI and D program director that Ron's team would be made up of 11 different professionals. Treatment focus and subsequent questions raised by the group, if in fact that occurred, would be researched by one of the team members. The behavior analyst would coordinate some meetings and the social worker would serve as a liaison for "external input." She clarified the unit was not a medical model like a hospital but rather a "rehabilitative model to transition people back into the community," with all professionals equally influential within the team. She stated the entire team met with the patient, adding that all members of the team were "available, except for the medical doctor." She did add that all the team professionals offered input into the process, "sometimes, even the doctor." When I asked about the designated physician (either or both the psychiatrist or internal medicine physician) attending the treatment team meetings she reported it was not customary for this to happen and offered no explanation when I asked the reason.

I noted no specific team member wrote up the quarterly report, but all members facilitated input, and the report summarized the collective voice of the team. No physician signed off on treatment team decisions. I was left with less than clear description of a team, with a less than solid direction, and no method of measuring improvement in actual behavior other than attending

141

groups with what appeared at this point to be ambiguous treatment goals couched in flowery language.

Ron was eventually "encouraged" to meet individually with a hospital psychologist which he did. I found this to be inefficient since this therapy occurred twenty years after Margaret's shooting. Therapy for the shooting should have taken place immediately after he was first admitted to the hospital in 1986. To my surprise, records indicated Ron's psychologist had determined the current time was "the opportune time to revisit what occurred before, during and after the shooting in 1986."

Records noted Ron continued to maintain that the shooting was "an accident and he had to intention of killing his friend." These proclamations on Ron's part were documented by the psychologist as "his (Ron) being in denial of his crime and absence of remorse. "Ron shared with me that he had told his psychologist what he could, related to the basis for his being back at the St. Peter campus. When Ron said, in his opinion he currently did not have any symptoms of a mental illness, he was (again documented) as being "in denial" with no corrections as to what "symptoms" the psychologist saw Ron exhibiting. No mention was made in the records of Ron's level of honesty with this psychologist. No mention was made of their discussing their different perceptions of how they were interacting, and what was happening within the "therapy session," other than Ron being noted as asking questions, which were then translated into his being "disagreeable with the therapeutic process."

These sessions must have been torturous for both Ron and his psychologist. Unfortunately, the psychologist did not recognize each hour in treatment as anything less than arguing to see who was right! What could have been said was... "This is how each hour we spend together turns out. What do you think is the problem, and what can we each do about it? What would you like to focus on today, Mr. Steen?" And then after each sentence spoken by Ron I would have said, "Tell me more," and then kept quiet."

During one of my conversations with Ron, he reported that his psychologist reminded him weekly that their working goal was to "focus on treatment, centering on the shooting incident, what happened and why." When Ron repeated his position that the shooting was an accident, he would be asked, "Then why are you still here? Then why have you been hospitalized for twenty years." That is a million-dollar question for a patient in a system where staff limit progress to attendance at certain programming, and the only way to get released is to complete all the programming, even if participation in programming already occurred years ago. Even worse, sanctioned alternative programming was nonexistent.

Ron would show the psychologist letters and reports of past state hospital and community physicians who had documented that at the time they treated him, he had no symptoms of a mental illness. He stated, consistent with documented entries in his records, that his new psychologist would tell him to "Stop denying what is clearly apparent; you have a mental illness." When Ron would ask what symptoms, his psychologist observed in him, the psychologist entered into Ron's medical record he, "was not going to argue... and added that together they needed to develop a relapse prevention plan if Ron was ever going to be released."

When Ron would repeat he had not relapsed in twenty years...hadn't hurt anyone...he would be told, as verified by his hospital chart, that he... "hadn't done anything, for he had...no group attendance, so...how did he expect anyone to see he was better if he didn't follow rules and go to the groups his treatment team said he needed to attend? Ron was charted as reporting he had "gone to groups for years, that did no good," adding people who attended the groups were never released either!"

Now, at this revelation, which the psychologist should have known was the ugly truth, he could have asked Ron, what he thought could be a solution for such a problem, along with remaining silent and listening. And with each moment of silence, the psychologist should have asked again, "What else?" until a dialogue actually took place. I guessed Ron's psychologist was frustrated he couldn't get anywhere with his patient.

Ron described the groups he was supposed to attend, as "Boring...Blueprint for Change is about people being irresponsible; I was never that way and it means nothing. I was a successful business man. I can't relate to anything in the group. I'm sixty-five and the Date Smart group is not for me either. They are all a waste of time."

On the same note, the psychologist summarily documented in Ron's chart, that working with Ron was a "waste of time" because Ron displayed, "no insight into his problems, and remained delusional and paranoid." Ron shared with me that his psychologist called him a "murderer" and said he had to "come clean" about what truly happened, even decades *after* the shooting, despite the fact that he had been found NGRI.

Ron told me that his psychologist said Ron had no empathy for the victim and was unchanged from the time of his admission to the hospital in 1986 to the present day. I never saw in the therapy notes Ron being asked how he thought about Margaret at the present time...Certainly he had embraced his grief and was prompted by empathy to be able to control his emotions when someone wished to denigrate the relationship he and Margaret shared. Had this professional not read the details of the shooting? Simple question such as, "How do you look back on this...Mr. Steen? What did you learn about yourself? Could have redirected the treatment experience for both Ron and his psychologist.

Also, unfortunate, for both Ron and his psychologist was the missed opportunity to explore what significant relationships Ron currently enjoyed and how he maintained those connections. If he had a single act of violence, like the shooting, how had he controlled his emotions before the shooting and after; how did he deal with differences with fellow patients, if he had any; how did he deal with differences in how staff interacted with him? How was it he had no record of other violence over years of time in various confinement settings? Ron had close patient friends with whom he shared his days. He had buddies from his past with whom he continued warm, honest relationships.

I also found it to be of interest as I reviewed Ron's records, that I never saw where any treatment providers asked him about his current feelings related to the shooting and loss of his friend. What did it mean to him to have this tragedy occur? How did he deal with his feelings related to his losses? What I noted was that Ron mentioned at various times that he was not getting help for his emotional problems. Yet, I never saw where anyone asked him what that meant and then listened.

It occurred to me that Ron's seeming dismissal of the shooting event as accidental still did not allow a venting of his personal losses, the death of his friend, the end of his life in the free world, the loss of his status in the community, of his family, of his business interests, and his reputation. How was that for him? No one would ever know the answer. What I wondered, was whether he was attempting to distance himself from what really happened by simply repeating it was all an accident, without talking about the details of this event and what they were like for him. In some ways, his curt explanations that brushed off the presence of emotions related to the shooting may have been the way he did not deal with it. I never saw a reference to his being asked," Well, what was that accident like for you; what losses did you experience, how did you move on, what was the hardest part, who helped you, what was it like to lose everything, lover, friends, business, money,

147

homes, children, your future? How did you go on, and how did you deal with certain reminders over time? What was the most painful part later, after the trial? What is it like today for you to think of it? What is different? None of these questions were ever asked in over two decades.

I considered Ron's long noted pattern of dismissing the shooting as "an accident." Accidents are still traumatic. Did he displace his emotions related to the shooting death of Margaret because it was such a horrendous emotional situation? He definitely was an intellectual person and it would not have been out of place for him to rationalize what happened and move on. But, in that process trying to understand what happened, what were his fears that caused him to sidestep his inner defenses? I never saw these issues addressed or challenged. Perhaps for him the shooting itself, was not only his worst mistake, but a total discrediting of his worth, which in his mind was easier to just "deny" than delve into? Every time I considered Ron's case, I wondered what remnant issues related to this shocking and life-changing experience might remain.

Driving Thoughts

Reading records can be exciting and powerful, and of course, some records can be just utterly mundane. I choose to see my reviews as feeding my curiosity about the case in question, prompting further inquiry and need for answers. This activity can also create doubt. And it can drive one further to gather more information for a well thought out conclusion.

The activity I do nearly as much as reviewing records is driving from institution to another. My driving time to just watch the road and think about what I had read about any patient or learned from engaging with them was invaluable. I learned to challenge my own thinking and decision making and I learned to think of further information necessary towards the process of conclusion and a recommendation. Driving also offered me the distance and space for reflection and an opportunity to argue with myself about my collective information.

One predominating theme related to Ron's case was that the people with the most power and influence had firmly made up their minds about him, despite information to the contrary which to them apparently did not

149

exist. The challenge for each new case provider was to go along with the existing narrative or to tactfully take a new direction, one based on a different interpretation of the record. What experience has taught me is that the powers that be, in Ron's case the multiple treatment groups, had solidified their opinions, and did not appear open to perspectives differing from the one they supported.

Nevertheless, records and opinions can vary for a variety of reasons, not all honorable. In reviewing large masses of records of individuals over years of time, my experience has been one of concluding my own based on the review, reporting it and supporting it. If I sense I do not have a solid conclusion, more information is needed. Sometimes challenging my opinion without mercy is good. What discrepancies exist need to be listed and clarified; differences need to be reconciled, and when records and facts diverge different, questions need to be asked. Cross-referencing pays off: irrational relationships stand out. Personality issues in some cases mislead. Groups of people can miss details and what has been reported, may continue to be reported for no reason other than habit.

Some information may change with time, and other points of fact remain unchanged. My report would begin to be written when I had no more

150

questions to ask of the person or myself. This process can be lonely. It can

also be unpopular.

2006

In the spring of 2006 I was asked by Ron's defense attorney, Ryan B. Magnus, of Mankato to serve as an Independent Examiner on Ron's case. Mr. Magnus' job was to advocate for his client; my role was that of an advocate for the particular mental health statutes that applied to Ron's situation. That meant my role would be reviewing his records, interviewing him, performing a risk assessment and finding evidence, or lack thereof, related to his continuing to meet the legal criteria in question: did he remain mentally ill and dangerous, or did he meet the statutory criteria for release with the likelihood of success in the community with available assistance?

The first question needing to be answered for the court would require examples of Ron's mental state when he entered the hospital compared with his current presentation. Evidence to answer the second question would require specific treatment programming he had completed, examples of his demonstrated behavior consistent with safe interaction with others, as well as the reasonable expectation of the types of programming that would be available to him in a community.

Prior to meeting Ron, I spent hours reviewing his hospital records from 1986 to the present. These 20 years of records amounted to numerous four-foot-high stacks of manila folders that stretched along an approximately 12-foot wall in a room in the Administration Building on the state hospital campus. This room included a large, old, oak, table, a chair, a phone, and a large window looking out on a grassy area of the hospital, framed by a chain link fence. My plan to make the huge task manageable was to review the most current records first and then backtrack to the admission records. To keep the information organized, I used separate yellow tablets for each area of focus with color coded sticky notes attached to copied information within each of these areas.

Red sticky notes indicated pertinent information, blue notes indicated supporting information and yellow notes indicated incidental information that might or might not be helpful. Included within each tablet were circled question marks where I considered the possibility of inconsistency or missing data. A separate tablet was exclusively devoted to questions I wanted to ask Ron personally when we met. These were questions about his thinking and behavior that came to me during the process of this review of his records. This last tablet would help me get to the heart of issues and resolve contradictory information in Ron's records, based either on his noted

153

comments or others' comments about him. For me this is a process akin to putting together a puzzle.

At one point, to test an early hypothesis about the direction of the sheer quantity of information in front of me, I laid out on the big table quarterly treatment reports in separate columns over five-year intervals. What I discovered with this broader view of columns of records with obviously advancing periods of time, was similar if not repeated/robotic wording. I noted that Ron's symptoms from twenty years ago continued to be repeated verbatim, under all major headings, some entries in stark contrast with corresponding recently dated nursing observations of his behavior or comments he made. The most common word in Ron's records was "delusional." This term was mostly applied to Ron's opinion that he did not consider himself to be actively mentally ill, and that he had been taken advantage of and exploited by various attorneys and accountants.

All of the people I interview have been in the legal system for a considerable length of time related to serious violence. I have had cases where my recommendation is that the individual needs to remain exactly where he or she is, in confinement, due to absence of clear change and/or for the safety of the public. In other cases, there may be support for their release. In situations where the balance is close as to my recommendation, I ask for additional records which usually tip my recommendation one way or the other.

The day for the formal interview with Ron arrived, and I too was looking forward to meeting him in person. Typically, I know what the people I am scheduled to evaluate look like from a facial photo in their records. In some cases, I have videotapes of police interviews with them. In preparation for the personal interview I have a prepared list of questions to ask. If I do not hear a clear response to my question, or if the response merits additional query, that also occurs. This process is akin to connecting the dots, as I connect the facts and behaviors of the person over time. It is like tackling a 1000 piece puzzle.

As a prelude to any interview, I will inform the patient that research has actually shown that the most accurate information about an individual is found in their records, *not* an interview. I have found that to be true in some cases with mixed results in other cases. What really helps me the most is reviewing what a number of caregivers have said about the person and seeking to clarify the varying impressions and reports.

In some cases, individuals decline to be interviewed and a report must be written exclusively based on the record. Of course, this kind of situation requires informing the reader that attempts to meet with the person were made but declined. The advantage of an interview is particularly helpful when a person has participated in treatment that is either not part of the original record or noted only in a limited manner. An interview can also add clarity when there is a discrepancy in the records. Ideally, the record and the interview information would be consistent. However, anyone who has conducted interviews understands the variable quantity and quality of available collateral information. Some interviews produce no meaningful or different information than the record. Because of the seriousness of Ron's case, talking with him in person was a must.

My interviews with Ron took place in the mornings of May 3 and May 8, 2006 in a meeting room in the MI and D Transition Building. It was a rather large room, with an assortment of chrome legged, red plastic covered cushioned chairs, and tables covered with puzzle pieces or boxes of games. The room itself was institutional, with beige-tiled floors, and walls with somewhat faded examples of someone's notion of art. The room was quiet with intermittent intercom announcements from the ceiling speaker about programming or lunch. There was also a large window that allowed staff and patients passing in the hallway to observe us but not hear what we were talking about. I noted the wonderful aroma of what smelled like goulash being prepared, perhaps in a nearby kitchen, for lunch. Ron was on time, neatly dressed and groomed, carrying a stack of file folders and papers. He appeared relaxed and had a broad smile.

As I shook his hand, I introduced myself: "Good morning, Mr. Steen, my name is Dr. Linderman. It is a pleasure to finally meet you in person. Your attorney Mr. Magnus asked me to review your case including interview you for possible release. I have reviewed a huge number of records, and have some questions to clarify with you, if you are willing to talk with me. My role is to ultimately prepare a report for the court related to whether or not in my opinion you meet the criteria for release. Do you agree to talk with me?" At this point Ron indicated he was agreeable.

"For starters, I would like to focus on what you can personally share with me about your case as you look back and note changes in yourself over time. Before I leave today, I will also ask you to complete a Minnesota Multiphasic Personality Inventory which is a true/false assessment tool which I will review with you the next time we meet. I will meet with you again in approximately a week to 10 days for a second interview and I will stay in

157

touch with you throughout the process of your case." Having given him an overview, I asked if he had any questions, and further explained my interest in talking with his family if he was agreeable with this request. I explained the importance of his asking questions if he did not understand what I was asking or saying and said I would do the same.

During this first meeting it was Ron who initiated telling me about the recent annual passing of the anniversary month of the shooting death of Margaret. In a lowered and serious voice, he said, "This past January was the passing of another anniversary of when Margaret died. I am reminded each new year of her death and the reason I am here. I think of her every day, but especially in January." He said this seriously and solemnly in a quiet and reverent voice. I wondered about the reality of what it would be like to have remained in a setting that reminded me every day, of the worst situation of my life that took away someone I loved and took me away from everything I knew, and then I mulled about the feelings I would have if, over twenty years, I was still in the same place.

Consistent with his records, Ron, explained that during the second phase of his trial, his attorney used a mental illness defense and hired two expert witnesses, with his ultimately being found NGRI and committed as

Mentally Ill and Dangerous. He came across, in alignment with what I had read in his records, as someone who appreciated details and including them in his conversations.

Unexpectedly, during this first interview, just as we were getting acquainted, one of the unit direct-care staff knocked on the door and said I had a phone call. I was not expecting any calls during this scheduled interview time, but since I was a single mother, I excused myself briefly in case my secretary was calling me with an emergency. When I answered the phone, an unfamiliar voice snapped, "Who do you think you are talking to my client without my permission?" I asked who this person was, and the man said his name and informed me he was Ron's attorney.

I then informed him, "I have a court order signed by Judge Battey to interview Mr. Steen today, and you, sir, are not the attorney of record."
He snapped back, "Nobody wants Ron released, not his doctors and not his family, so what do you think you are going to do about it?"
I replied, "That sir, remains to be seen." He wanted more information, but I did not owe him anything, so I simply said, "Have a nice day, sir," paused, and politely hung up the phone. We never spoke again.

I did not have good vibes about this man beginning with this incident, and I pay attention to such feelings. I have and will continue to unfondly refer to this attorney as, Mr. Black, because from this beginning point, his intent felt dark and evil. Ron would report this person, darkening his hopes, expectations of honesty, integrity, civility and more, in the form of the fruits of Ron's labors and in an effort to diminish Ron's spirit. This attorney never disappointed my lowest expectations.

The thing that continues to remain perplexing to me, even over all these years, is the fact that only my secretary, Ron, and the MI and D staff knew I was interviewing Ron that day. So, who informed Mr. BlackTh that I was at the hospital on that very day talking to Ron, so that he could call and attempt to intimidate me, and why? What was in it for him; what was his stake in the game? Over time I developed an unmitigated disgust for him.

After the jarring interruption the phone call, I returned to my interview with Ron, already developing a sense of the larger context of the case. Before being interrupted by the phone call, I had noted Ron presented himself as relaxed and friendly, able to explain his NGRI situation. When we resumed our conversation and I asked him his impression of what resulted in getting him committed, he said, "I was aware of what was going on. It was not murder .I had no intention to kill Margaret. I think she may have grabbed the gun, but I still don't have a clear thought about how it happened." He appeared somewhat embarrassed by his sketchy memory, as though unfamiliar with how such a traumatic event could remain unclear despite the passage of time, re-thinking it and trying to make sense of something very foreign and bizarre. People who try to make sense of some event in their distant past that was life-changing, and shocking to their usual habits of functioning, frequently report memory disorganization specific to the event.

Ron would repeat he never meant to hurt, let alone kill Margaret; he talked about his own feelings related to the loss of her life and presence. His accuracy or inability to recreate what happened was not relevant to my purpose. He had already been tried and found not guilty by reason of mental illness in 1986.

When asked what he saw as his current problems Ron paused, as though thinking. He eventually stated, "I am still emotional, because of my divorce, my kids going different directions, my past business problems; I look back on the way things could have been, and I think back, I had the largest grain dryer business in the nation. In Alexandria I was caught with a large inventory, paid an attorney a retainer and never saw him for twenty-eight

161

months. I had used up all my cash flow and the bank wouldn't loan me money against my equity. At the time of the shooting I was under the influence of four different kinds of psychiatric medications."

Ron denied a history of head injury, and current feelings of depression, but he did volunteer he had recently requested an antidepressant and antianxiety medication because he had chills like in the 80's and an antidepressant helped him then and he thought it could help in the present. He repeated thoughts about the stress he had been under and remained under for years of time. His presentation, however, was reasonably relaxed and he was easy to talk with; there was no outward evidence of depression nor did he present as distracted by symptoms of psychosis. He denied current problems with his temper, denied crying spells, and denied a pervasive feeling of sadness.

When asked if he felt hopeless, he answered in the affirmative and said "Because of the way this program is set up here, it's like 1986 again. I have a step program. I must go to groups that I don't think benefit me, like Cooking, and Blueprint for Change, which picks apart people's irresponsibility. I can't recall being like that ever in my life, and I don't get anything out of the classes. I completed all the groups early on and earned the right to walk anywhere I wanted on the hospital campus. Then I went to other institutions and did what I was supposed to. Here, I feel like I am supposed to start all over. The classes are boring, it's like being in fourth grade."

Ron came across as more intellectually minded and confident than most patients. His business success was most likely how he acquired his confidence. He was open in speaking his mind when the 'product claims' (the selling features of the group programming) failed to match the actual product (like "Movie Classics" somehow being related to reducing mental illness and or dangerousness). I had no problem understanding his views and his reasoning related to these treatment groups.

Ron denied feelings of helplessness, volunteering, "I am capable of handling things." When asked about feelings of guilt he repeated his comments about the impact of the shooting for him, the loss of his girlfriend and his buildup of extreme business-related stress. He denied a history of suicide attempts, acknowledging he had made comments in the past that he was afraid he was going to commit suicide, but noting that he made no actual attempts. He denied current thoughts of hurting others.

When asked the most difficult part of his confinement he said, "Knowing I was my normal self and I could have continued in business. I have had no communication here with staff about my personal problems, just groups. They focused on the trial and why I was sent here. I never got to talk about my personal problems. They say I am suspicious and grandiose, but when I ask them for examples, they don't say anything. I lost millions of dollars and am still paying expenses for the past twenty-five years. They say I manipulated a psychiatrist to lower my medication, but when I ask them' " Who?' " they don't tell me."

As I listened to him, I recognized that his records tended to minimize how the events he was talking about impacted him on a deeply personal and emotional level, absent opportunities for him to find relief for his feelings of confusion, and his multiple losses; family, comforts, friends, hobbies, normal everyday mundane activities, all were suddenly all gone and replaced, by a hospital routine with its sterile approach to life via groups, programming, schedules, and medical care for his body and supposedly his mind with little or no care for his inner self, to bridge his losses. All of these injustices were accentuated by the pervasive and robotic indifference of a clinical schedule in combination with a set program and expectation that all patients would participate in designated programming, like it, and benefit from it, regardless of their histories and previous programming.

When I asked him the reason, he thought he had been kept confined so long, he paused, and said, "Because it's political and because of the D on the label." The room was very quiet, not a sound, only two people talking about a lifetime of one of them. When I asked if he saw himself as dangerous, he paused, eventually stating, "No, absolutely not." When I asked if he worried about returning to the community after so long a time, he answered in the negative and reported that in his opinion he had gotten along fine in the community during his stay at the halfway house in Duluth.

When I asked him what he meant by his case being "political" he commented on the years of time that had passed, his denied release requests, his attempts in the past and his being required, again, to complete programming that in his opinion had nothing to do with him personally or his particular individual problems. In response, I listened and observed his responses and his manner of responding. He came across as being mentally exhausted, worn out from the void, tired of the endless search for meaning, and bored with the choices.

When asked the chances of his hurting anyone if he was to be released, he responded, "There's no chance. There never were any thoughts of harming anyone. I just wouldn't do it. It would be wrong. When I wanted revenge it was through litigation, but the statutes of limitation have run out now, actually years ago. I'm not happy about what they have done to my life, but I wouldn't harm anyone."

The words, "what they have done to my life hung in the air." How does someone manage to shift his entire thinking from personal periods of success, albeit with setbacks and political games to days of complete lack of stimulation and purpose? I could only imagine how that could make a person deeply solemn, and very alone. I actually felt he deserved credit for not going crazy in the process.

When I asked his current attitude about the shooting in 1986, he said, "I'm so sorry it happened. I should have never gone in the house with a loaded gun. I didn't feel like myself. I wake up today and every day and know my being here is because of the shooting." When asked what he would do if he thought he was experiencing new, subsequent. emotional problems he said, "If I had crying spells and felt sadness that didn't end, I would go to a doctor."

When asked to explain what caused the revocation of his provisional discharge in Duluth, he said, "At Arrowhead I had my own car and drove everywhere, there was no alcohol, no trouble, no aggression, I never missed a dose of medication, but I was accused of not taking my medication for eleven days in December. I don't know where they got that." I thought about what I had reviewed about the situation at Arrowhead as a whole when his conditional release was rescinded. In my mind I quietly agreed with him that he had been set up, but for a different reason than he mentioned. I suspected the Arrowhead staff resented Ron having convinced his doctor to withdraw support for his attending their version of mandatory groups. There was no evidence in Ron's records that his doctor and the staff at Arrowhead talked about their divergent views as to group treatment or came to some kind of understanding/resolve what house meetings Ron would attend, separate from the "groups" conducted.

Ron reported that three months before the Willmar State Hospital closed, another discharge was being planned for him. He volunteered he had visited, "several halfway houses in Spicer, Atwater, Litchfield, New Ulm and in Willmar but they were just dumping! One of them was okay, but it would cost $4000 a month for assisted living and then you had to pay separate for the day program and that would have cost $7000 a month in all. I wanted a direct discharge and the staff at Willmar didn't petition for it, so I was sent back here, to St. Peter. I have been before the Review Board three times in twenty years. I didn't realize I needed a court appointed attorney and that I could have petitioned them every six months. I wanted a direct discharge-- because if you just have MI and not the D, you can live in your own home if you have one, and I do. I have assets." He added, "I would see my doctor, take medication, have case management; I would agree to anything to have my life back."

When I asked him what he was currently most angry about, he stated, "Being confined here right now. I went through a whole cycle of people who kept breaking promises. Now I have no optimistic views because even if I do everything they ask, like all the programming, nothing will happen. The patients here have been here for years and years. Participating in programming has not changed anything."

I heard him express his hopeless resignation, which is the way someone could logically feel after working hard but the carrot was always a little higher in the end, and then there would be another end that would be set in place. How was this process therapeutic? How was it that the path to accomplishing treatment was a single road to be traveled in a specific black and white manner. The individual was no one in particular, and yet the

168

individual represented everyone. Of course, there had to be order, but how was this kind of order, therapeutic? Where was the voice that asked, "How are you today as an individual? What is on your mind? You look sad and tired today, what is going on? How many kinds of change and recovery could there be? The look on his face told me he was long overdue for a real conversation about his emotions and how he felt about a lot of things, including who he had become as a person at that point in his life.

One of the comments I noted in Ron's records was that some staff charted him as "lacking insight" as to his mental illness. When I asked what the word "insight" meant to him, Ron said, "Its having knowledge of your whereabouts, conditions, like your illness." When asked what insight involved, he said it was, "knowing what to expect from the results of doing something. I had to know whether a deal was good or not, I had to make projections and know how much money to take in." When asked how his insight about himself had changed from the time he was committed in his mid-forties to the present, he said, "I was so wrapped up with business, I neglected my wife and kids. After I lost my business I sat back and thought of what I should have done but didn't do. But you can't reverse it." And I marveled at his frankness. If some staff person who judged Ron for not having insight had heard what he said, would it still miss the mark of acceptance?

When asked what he would do if he were to be discharged, he said, "Probably live in one of my houses in Alexandria, or maybe in a condo in Willmar. I would find a new psychiatrist, continue with prescribed medication and follow my physician's orders." If he had problems with his emotions, he said he "would see a doctor like I have always done."

Ron had no problem with my talking with his family for their input into his situation. And to make matters even more interesting he told me about life-long friends from childhood who he continued to talk with on a regular basis, with one of them routinely visiting him. He said I could also talk with each of them and gave me their names and phone numbers.

My plan was to gather and review additional collateral information, and then see Ron again for further questioning and to observe whether his demeanor and responses remained the same or varied. The time between interviews adds a good sorting factor to the information; it also allows people to relax a bit and be additionally forthcoming.

Following this first interview, Ron completed the Minnesota Multiphasic Personality Inventory, a 566-item true/false instrument that includes validity scales covering defensiveness, exaggeration, lying or misrepresentation, embellishment of symptoms and then a personality profile tapping depression, anger, anxiety, psychotic symptoms, sociability and other personality features. One of its purposes is to use it as verifying the person's presentation as to their mood, mental organization, possible hidden anger or psychotic symptoms.

The drive home was a welcome change of focus. I had sensed my reaction to Ron's records and now I had talked to him in person. Holding off on a final opinion until all stones have been overturned is a cardinal rule to follow. There was rest of the family to talk with and perhaps Ron's lifelong friends.

My initial impression based on the content of Ron's records in comparison with his presentation was that there was a gross disconnect between who he was in 2006 in contrast with how he was described in his medical file by his treatment team. It also seemed reasonable to assign him the greater responsibility for creating the rift between himself and his team of professionals at St. Peter. He had been dismissive to some; others had approached him with mixed results, and his usual position was to see them all as the collective enemy. Their position as noted within his records was that he

171

was defiant and lacking in insight. Perhaps both had grounds for their opinion. Oddly enough, I did not note in his records at St. Peter that anyone had contacted the Willmar Center to compare or contrast how this treatment center who took him around to possible community placements perceived his success and advancement towards freedom. That could have been a really helpful piece of information for the St Peter treatment teams to chew on.

Collateral Information from the Family

My plan to spend evenings during the upcoming week calling Ron's adult children changed when I called Ron's oldest daughter. She declined returning my several calls, and eventually her husband contacted me explaining she did not trust anyone calling about her father and wanted to talk first with an attorney before she talked to me. The husband also reported that their family had been taken advantage of, and treated dishonestly, so many times while taking care of Ron Sr's affairs over the past twenty years, that the entire family was wary of anyone asking them about Ron.

When I contacted Ron's son, I was immediately drawn to how much his voice resembled Ron senior in the style, syntax and manner of his speech. Like Ron Sr, Ron Jr. was intelligent, personable, and demonstrated interesting conversational skills. He used unique words that made what he said more interesting. For instance, in one instance he talked about his father "parlaying" a situation to his benefit. During our first phone conversation, we talked for over an hour. He lamented his father's situation, noting he was 24 and in the Navy in 1986 when the shooting occurred. At the time he returned home he visited his father in the Security Hospital.

He shared that initially he was upset his father was not doing more to get out of the hospital, adding his father had been told by someone familiar with such situations, that "no matter what anyone does, you are going to be locked up for at least five years." He stated he eventually stopped going to visit his father as often, "because of where he was at, the security checks, people listening to our conversations. He also noted the 3-hour drive from Alexandria to St. Peter took a toll on his day. Ron, Jr. denied knowing his father to be an aggressive man and said, "What I've noticed in my father is that he never even voiced wanting harm to happen to anyone, like the people who stole from him, or ruined his life." He denied his father having a drinking problem, and at the time said he and his two sisters were all supportive of their father.

Ron Jr. also commented that no one from the hospital had ever called him in twenty years to ask for collateral information about his father. He stated. "We've been before three judge panel hearings and we always had disappointment after disappointment. There would be times when it appeared like there were deliberate attempts to derail the release. This has been a twenty-plus year nightmare for all of us."

He added, "Several people have not worked in my father's interests. Some of them have been attorneys, and some have been accountants. They have stolen property and sold it. We have paid $30,000 and $50,000 retainers to attorneys who took the money and then said they couldn't do any more to help us. One attorney told us "the day he got his license to practice law, he got his license to steal". When my dad talks to doctors about his lawsuits, they think he is grandiose and delusional. His psychiatrists see him for fifteen minutes. It's disturbing that they always go back to the beginning and reaffirm what someone else said in 1986."

When asked what his father told him about his mental illness, Ron Jr., stated, "My father doesn't believe he has one. I think it's a pride issue because he came from nothing and then became a successful businessman with little education." When asked if his father had ever made delusional statements, Ron Jr. answered in the negative; when asked if he had ever seen his father acting psychotic, Ron Jr. answered in the negative again, and volunteered "When he talks to doctors about his lawsuits, they don't understand that some of the cases he was being sued for had possible treble damages."

When asked about his father's problems, Ron Jr. said he had seen his father depressed before the shooting and added, "The same week of one lawsuit he got divorce papers and he had two and a half million dollars of inventory. That's what led to the nervous breakdown."

He described his father at one time accepting a diagnosis of bipolar disorder and said, "That made more sense than his having paranoid schizophrenia because I never saw him like that. He reported his father had accepted the bipolar diagnosis at Willmar, and even read the Patty Duke book about her experiences with the disorder, adding again he thought there was a connection." "I remember at one time he purchased twenty-seven cars over a short period of time, and then said he was going to resell them. There were a lot of spending sprees."

Ron Jr. also reported that some of his father's land was sold, and he and his older sister went to court to claim that the attorney and accountant who sold the land were in the wrong because Mr. Steen's property could not be sold while he was under a conservatorship. Ron Jr. reported "the judge threw the Minnesota Statute book at me; it hit my foot. Then the judge, accountant and attorney all removed themselves from the case." He said that his sister was then made Ron's conservator again, adding, "The judge wouldn't give it to me because he said I was scamming which is what I had accused the accountant and lawyer of doing."

Ron Jr. added, "Because of all these things we have all become very suspicious of people. Our whole family is this way because of the criminal activity of people who got involved with my father in professional roles. There just hasn't been an end to this nightmare; treatment providers and people would talk to my father and he would be honest and then they would say he was grandiose and delusional. My father has been in this all alone."

Ron Jr then admitted, "We kids failed him in not trying to help him get his legal rights. It's been so over whelming for the three of us that our father's life has become our life. Every time we found someone to help us it would turn backwards on us. My father is not the sick individual they have made him out to be. He does need medication, and when he is on medication, he's more passive and doesn't talk so much about the past. In Willmar he looked ill and wasn't properly medicated and talked at times about suing us kids. The last time, just before he was sent to St. Peter, they also changed his medication."

When asked about his father's experience in Duluth, Ron, Jr. said "That was the best I've seen him ever. He had his own car and his own freedom. He drove to my sister's and visited, and he came and visited me. He was confident and like his old self."

When asked what he knew about the revoked provisional discharge he stated, "He got railroaded. He had been going to rummage sales and his room was so cluttered they said they'd send him back to Willmar if he didn't clean it up, so he got a hitch put on his Cadillac, got a U-Haul in Wisconsin, loaded up his stuff, dropped it all at the house here and returned to Duluth. He had permission to bring the stuff here and somehow, they turned up with the fact that he was unaccounted for. When he got back, they told him they were revoking his provisional discharge."

Summarizing the injustice his father had lived with for years, Ron Jr. noted, "My father is in situation where he's damned if he does, and damned if he doesn't do something. For instance, they criticized him for not doing a journal, but they've already misinterpreted his thoughts. What would they do if he put it in writing?" After spending so many hours sifting through repetitive paperwork, I enjoyed Ron Jr's refreshing directness.

When asked what he knew about his father's trial, Ron Jr. stated, "I think there is a misunderstanding about how the trial ended. He was found not guilty by reason of mental illness, but he's been treated by some as a guilty killer. He reported there had been two people in Douglas County who committed murders, were found guilty, went to prison and returned to the community." He questioned why his father couldn't do the same. Ron Jr. noted he was "in anguish not doing more for his father and said there was an added but different kind of anguish when nothing anyone did seemed to be helping. Ultimately Ron, Jr. called his father's case "a miserable situation any way you cut it."

Eventually I was able to talk with Ron's oldest daughter who reported she had been appointed her father's conservator of his person and guardian of his estate in 1992. She indicated she had never been asked to sign any document for Ron to receive neuroleptic medication, and voiced surprise that a Jarvis petition hearing had been scheduled for May 18, 2006, "because he's been compliant with taking medications." She volunteered her father's medication was "lowered consistently prior to the times he was scheduled before the Review Board meetings as though the hospital wanted him to fail."

Since Ron's daughter spoke of a "Jarvis petition," this is a good time to clarify exactly what that means. This type of petition is executed by the hospital and sent to the court indicating a neuroleptic medication (Risperdal, for example) has been ordered for the patient by his psychiatrist, including a note about whether or not the patient has been compliant/cooperative in taking it. My experience more than not included the psychiatrist checking a box claiming "patient had refused this medication" precluding successful treatment of his/her illness. My experience more than not, was that the nurses kept track of any refused neuroleptic, and my first stop when I was asked to interview a patient related to a Jarvis petition to force such medication, was to check with the nurses as to "the number of times this medication had been declined or refused," with the answer typically being, "none." That was also true for Ron. Now, in case some patients are seen as "potentially" refusing this kind of medication, a backup person, usually a relative/conservator will be asked to sign for the patient...that way, even if the patient refuses, the medication can be given. In Ron's history I observed the presence of documents related to past Jarvis petitions, however, I never noted his having a history of refusing this medication, even though at times he voiced questions of it helping him.

What is of interest, are the connections in both Ron Steen' and Homer Jarvis' case histories.   Homer was a patient indeterminately committed to the Minnesota Security Hospital in March of 1977 as mentally ill and dangerous. Homer shot and killed his sister but had been convicted of manslaughter and served his time, later being discharged from his sentence. During his civil commitment he was involuntarily treated with major tranquilizers/neuroleptics. The issues with Homer Jarvis included the fact that his diagnosis was unclear. At times he had been diagnosed with paranoid schizophrenia, with his record indicating he had a paranoid state but no hallucinations. His medical record included different physicians noting a mixed list of varied symptoms and diagnoses. Homer denied that he was mentally ill and reported a belief that hospital personnel and the court were conspiring to indefinitely commit him and treat him with what he thought were medications that were poisoning him. His record noted he had good self-care skills, was intelligent and that he had no evidence of being violent. But he had been a "difficult" patient, in that he refused treatment programming, group and individual therapy, and or psychological interviews; he was described as "caustic derogatory and sarcastic to staff."

Homer's doctor was Dr. Levine, hence the name of the court case: "Jarvis v. Levine." The ultimate issue was whether state medical personnel may forcibly administer neuroleptic medication in non-emergency situations to a committed patient who refuses consent without prior court approval. As a result of this case the court refused to leave the decisions solely within the discretion of medical personnel and established pre-treatment judicial review

181

procedure to be used before the imposition of "intrusive" forms of treatment for a non-consenting patient. I was involved in hundreds if not thousands of these reviews and have horror stories related to what patients reported to me about what their doctors did and did not ask them related to their illness, their symptoms and their need for and medications. And I reviewed as many charts noting that physicians would record patients as refusing neuroleptic medication when nursing records *noted no refusals.* I talked to physicians who apparently noted patients were incompetent simply and perhaps wholly because they had a mental illness.

One Jarvis petition had been initiated for Ron by Douglas County on May 18, 2006. It was withdrawn due to Ron ultimately being determined as competent to make decisions related to this type of medication. I also noted an earlier similar petition dated April 18, 2006 for authorization of forced neuroleptic medication for Ron, by one of the hospital psychiatrists, indicating, "Respondent has exhibited behavior demonstrating a clear refusal of treatment of such frequency and duration as to preclude effective treatment," for which there was absolutely no evidence. This was the territory I covered every week for years and years of time.

Hospital records noted, "Mr. Steen has never refused his neuroleptic at the MI and D unit since his return to St. Peter in October of 2004." Ron's oldest daughter reported she had made herself available for Ron's quarterly review meetings in person or by phone for years but "half the time I am lucky if I get a copy of the paperwork even though I ask." She volunteered, "I have doubts at times that my father has a mental illness. We have never felt we could confer with anybody about anything. A year ago, I asked the Douglas County social worker to tell me five ways they had helped my father over the years, and she just looked at me."

Ron's oldest daughter also shared with me that, "Old issues continue to dominate the review meetings. My father has offered comments that have consistently been interpreted negatively." She added that her observations about the way her father had been treated were "sad," and said she thought it helped that her father is "determined not to die there."

Ron's youngest daughter was in her teens when the shooting occurred. She reported sympathy for Ron, and concern related to whatever his current issues included, while also noting she had distanced herself from his situation due to her own family and personal problems and demands. She said she had not talked to her father for four years, not because she did not care about him but because her job, a divorce, and her inability to deal with all these issues and her father's situation were too much.

Ron Sr. also gave me permission if not ordered me to contact his lifelong friend, Orlyn Ristow; Ron and Orlyn had known each other for fifty five years. They had talked daily since 2002 and they remained in regular contact excluding the seven years when Orlyn lived in Missouri. Orlyn reported Ron had "never been an aggressive person, he was only aggressive in his business, he took a $5000.00 loan and turned it into millions. He blames himself for the family breakup. He was the only kid in his family and they were poor." Orlyn denied the Ron had a history of drinking problems adding, "we used to eat out together and he wouldn't even drink socially."

When asked his opinion about Ron's situation, Orlyn said, "I've seen copies of his medical records; he says something, and St. Peter turns what he says around. He had to ask for medication for depression recently on his own." As to the trial outcome, Orlyn described it as "rigged. Once I went to Douglas County to look for a trial transcript and when the court house people found out whose transcript I wanted and that I was a friend of Ron's, they said there were no records and Ron never had a trial." They only showed me a file about his commitment. It should have been a mistrial or at most he should have been convicted of manslaughter."

When I asked Orlyn if Ron offered unusual comments during their conversations, he answered in the negative. He volunteered, "Ron has so much on his mind. He goes into so much detail. Once he started to write a book and he had 400 pages, but it was confiscated. Up there at the Security Hospital they thought he was sick when he wanted his medical records. He got a bum rap. He realized he shot Margaret and didn't know what was going on. Nowadays a lot of people say they have adverse reactions to medication."

A bonus for me was a telephone call out of the blue following my first interview with Ron. My secretary said I had a call related to Ron's case and when I answered, it was a long distance call from William (Bill) Ristow, Orlyn' s brother and another of Ron's childhood friends who lived in Alaska.

Bill said he had known Ron since they were in 7th grade and that they had hunted and fished together many times. He had been calling Ron every weekend for the past year and a half since discovering Ron was back at St. Peter. The last time he saw Ron was the summer of 2005.

Bill denied Ron having past drinking problems and said as an adult when he was married and had his three kids, he never saw Ron take a drink. He talked about Ron being a big Elvis fan and said for a while, Ron "took on an Elvis persona, long sideburns, longer hair, he owned a bunch of cars, like Lincolns and Cadillacs. He had been poor and when he hit the big time, he bought those cars. Ron was what you could call eccentric about Elvis. A lot of people are eccentric, but they aren't crazy."

Bill said he had worked at Cambridge State Hospital in Minnesota after graduating from high school and volunteered, "I recognized over the years that if you have a mental disorder you can cover it for a while but eventually it shows through. Ron never exhibited any kind of disorder when I have talked with him. There would be times when Bill would arrange conference calls between Ron, myself and Bill. They would be impromptu and out of the blue; we never talked about Ron's case, it was just chit chat and history.

Orlyn, Bill, and Ron were truly forever-friends; supportive to the end, encouraging each other; reliving their great memories of long ago and laughing again at all the experiences they shared. They were closer than brothers.

As regards the hospital never contacting Ron's family for collateral information about him, what could have been discovered was comparative information about what Ron was like before the shooting. The answer might have been that he as a workaholic who, in the course of being successful, accomplished the moving of mountains, mountains of dried grain, so to speak, and that over years of time and miles of traveling and closing deals evolved into a multimillion dollar business. It also could have come to light that Ron was sociable, friendly and helpful to others.

While he sounded like a patient with classic "grandiosity and delusional beliefs," for him, his comments were neither. Unfortunately, the hospital staff did not realize this difference and comments about Ron, within his medical records would continue, over years of time to describe him as "delusional and grandiose." Lastly, Ron's hospital records noted he was "estranged from his family." Maybe he was estranged from a few family members, but not all his family. And then he had friends that were stronger than family. How in the world did the hospital staff think he could have been so successful if he did not have people skills?

After interviewing Ron's family by phone while I was at home, talking with his life-long friends also by phone at my office, reflecting on this information while driving to, rather than from St. Peter was the order of the day. Needless to say, this case was growing in interest and had lots of twists and turns.

I pondered how relationships are formed within our families, and how some relationships with strangers take shape and how it is that some relationships are enduring and last forever, while others are more transient. I was impressed with Ron's gentlemen friends and what they had to say about their shared past and current connections. Fractured ties within Ron's primary family were sad, but perhaps expected. Thoughts about all the ways the shooting had altered many family connections was also a reality. I thought about the changes that occurred in seconds of time, lasting forever. Standing out to me was the strength of Ron's connections: who stayed faithful to him and who parted ways. I could understand his youngest daughter just having too much on her plate. I thought about Ron losing his life but keeping his lifelong friends.

My second interview with Ron included my going over the results of his MMPI-2 he had completed and offering him a chance to ask questions he had from the initial interview. For all his years of stress during his confinement, Ron presented himself to me as managing his emotions well. He obviously was eager to talk about his situation and more for apparently being listened to for what he wanted to say. I learned to see his somewhat haughty side as the result, possibly of his having challenges trusting others. And with his experiences, that was understandable.

Although my job was not that of evaluating the staff, what appeared to keep Ron and his treatment staff at odds were the words they each used towards and about each other and the implied meanings they each apparently entertained. Ron bristled when staff talked down to him because he was intelligent and resented being regarded as ignorant. He in turn was honest about not enjoying the groups that staff were invested in conducting supposedly to get people "through treatment." In each case, they needed to understand each other, but to do so seemed like either Ron or his treatment team would have to give in and neither wanted any of that. On both sides there was no conceding, no surrender, no compromise.

The Rest of the Story

In addition to reflecting on what I had learned from his friends and family, I also needed to complete an exhaustive review of Ron's records at St. Peter, Shantz and Bartlett Hall, the MI and D Transition Unit and the infamous Unit 800. I needed to complete a review of these records in case there could be information related to risk that could be brought up in pending court proceedings. So far, I had seen none. Experience has taught me not to tempt shortcuts. The last thing I wanted to hear in a full courtroom was, "Dr. Linderman, did you notice this damning report of the respondent within the last page of the last assessment? Oh, you did not know this existed? Is it not your responsibility to review all the respondent's records, not just the pages that support your opinion?"

The pace was quickened by my thumbing through years of daily patient flow checklists in which nurses had checked Ron's medication compliance. There were records related to safety issues, behavioral problems that arose and comments he made related to such issues. There were quarterly reports related to his functioning over a period of months of time, copies of daily psychiatric progress notes and copies of letters he had written or received.

Also available were the earliest records dating back to the mid 1980's noting his successful compliance with treatment at St. Peter Security Hospital, his subsequent freedom to walk on campus, the transfer to Willmar, and the return to Willmar after his revoked provisional discharge at Arrowhead. At times I felt overwhelmed with the review process, taking in of vast amounts of information and my making notes to add to my growing outline of the case. What kept me excited was the amazing story unfolding before me and the growing number of examples I was finding relevant to his case and the questions I needed to address.

For example, under the heading of "Cognition," Ron would be charted as "displaying a distortion in reality;" whereas under the heading of "Safety," he would be described as "having adequate impulse control" along with "compliant with all prescribed medications and treatment, rarely requires prompts to complete treatment;" yet in the same monthly progress note during the same time period he would be noted as "lacking motivation in treatment." Under the category of "History of Mental Illness" there were sentences noting "patient is not a reliable historian because of the degree of

191

his psychosis," with subsequent comments in the same time frame noting, "denies any problems at the present time, denies side effects to current meds, denies he is mentally ill, linear thinking; no evidence of psychosis; good grooming, no ideas of reference." There was no statement where conflicting descriptions had been noted and clarified.

Under the entries noting "Distortion of Reality," Ron was described as "angry, paranoid and grandiose; delusions center around his legal issues, he continues to make unrealistic demands of staff and threatens them with litigation; decision making ability impaired related to his delusions." In many instances, the word "delusional" did not include specific examples of his so-called delusions, or when examples were noted, they failed to meet the *Diagnostic and Statistical Manual of Mental Disorders* definitions of either bizarre or non-bizarre beliefs.

Delusions (according to DSM-5, the diagnostic and statistical manual of mental disorders), are defined as "fixed beliefs not amenable to change in light of conflicting evidence. They may include a variety of themes such as persecutory, referential, somatic, religious, grandiose. They may also be "persecutory" in the belief that one is going to be harmed or harassed by an individual or an organization. Grandiose delusions would include an individual believing that he or she has exceptional abilities, wealth or fame. Delusions are deemed bizarre if they are clearly implausible and not understandable to same-culture peers, and do not derive from ordinary life experience. For example, a bizarre delusion is the belief that an outside force has removed his or her internal organs and replaced them with someone else's organs without leaving any wounds or scars. An example of a non-bizarre delusion is the belief that one is under surveillance by the police, despite a lack of convincing evidence. The distinction between a delusion and a strongly held idea is noted as "difficult" to make and depends on the degree of conviction with which the belief is held despite clear or reasonable contradictory evidence regarding its veracity."

Under the heading of "Perceptions," Ron's records noted: "denies voices, paranoia and thought control, delusions of reference, says he is involved in litigation that is confidential but has something to do with "wrongdoing." Within the heading of "Assessment," over long spans of time Ron was noted as "needing to increase his understanding and acceptance of his mental health issues by reviewing and revising his relapse prevention plan and journal about his mental health issues," which Ron would summarily voice being a violation of his privacy. He was noted as disinterested in Weight Management and Cooking Skills with conclusions noted as his continuing to demonstrate," "limited insight...but does maintain behavior at all times." He was cited as "refusing to work for minimal wage, denies relapse symptoms, denies that Relationship Skills and Blueprint for Change are helpful to him."

It became clear from reviewing Ron's records, in conjunction with collateral information of his business and relationship issues, that Ron's moods changed with situational or environmental stressors, something common to all of us. Even with a steady diet of Risperdal, Ron demonstrated mood shifts but they did not appear to be prolonged common to a biological depression or mania. His mood shifts typically paralleled what else was going on that mattered to him. There were times when his presentation was narcissistic in nature, or at least assuredly confident, and I contemplated these features underscoring his strong senses of self and refusal to be beaten down, which on some level, kept him from going truly psychotic in his confinement.

Narcissistic personality disorder features include an individual having a grandiose sense of self-importance and entitlement; such people can be haughty, arrogant, self-absorbed and overly confident. However, had Ron not possessed the ability to be undaunted by setbacks he would never have been able to go on, most likely to last nearly three decades of confinement without

194

losing his mind. The challenges to his not meeting an actual Narcissistic personality disorder included his demonstrating empathy for others as well as his not having a history or current presentation indicative of exploiting others.

What puzzled me was the notion that if he had not changed at all in two decades, how was it that he was provisionally discharged for three years, trusted enough to purchase and drive his own car to appointments and drive home to Alexandria and return to Arrowhead? If there had been no nuance of change in his presentation and behavior at St. Peter over the past two years, what changes during treatment were suggested or implemented? At times I questioned whether the primary goal was actual treatment or if basic management of the patient through endless confinement was the entire goal. I knew that did not make clinical or ethical sense.

I was reluctant to see this as a warehousing issue, but it definitely came into my realm of consideration, and often. Warehousing is a term used to refer to patients who basically become warehoused; they are treated like things and not people due to long periods of confinement and often find themselves unable to return to society to make it on their own. Basically, such people entering long term care and never leaving; they are put on a shelf in a large warehouse and forgotten. This is a terrible notion, but it happens:

people go into programs to be healed and instead become helpless to make decisions or take care of themselves. Sometimes they know it and yet become dependent on others for all their care and decisions: they are like objects on a shelf at a warehouse.

Related to the course of his medication management in the 1980's Ron was initially prescribed Thorazine (an older antipsychotic) to which was added Depakote and Wellbutrin a mood stabilizer and antidepressant respectively. Beginning in the 2000's, he began to receive the newer, atypical neuroleptic, Risperdal, which moderates and controls agitation. This is also the type of medication that can be added to an antidepressant in patient s with persistent depression or agitation unchanged by taking an antidepressant alone. His more recent records included the doses varying from 1-3 mg. depending on the psychiatrist who saw him. With the low dose of 1 mg. he was described as having a "calm demeanor and interacting with others." When a new psychiatrist would see him, the dosage would be bumped to 3 mg. and he would be described as "groggy." There were times when I interviewed him when it was clear he was on the higher dose.

Then there were the stretches of time when the Risperdal would be discontinued, or the dosage varied by his treating psychiatrists. His records would include charting entries that he "failed to show evidence of an active mental illness" with the Risperdal reduced or discontinued, only to eventually note he was again showing symptoms heralding a re-emergence of his psychiatric disorder with Risperdal re-started.

The repeating scenario playing out in the records was that of a new psychiatrist in the merry-go-round of changing treatment teams every three months, teams that would increase the dosage, and the psychiatrist who treated him in the next three months would then reduce it. This pattern began in the later 1980's and continued to the mid 2000's just prior to his ultimate release. Perhaps as a result of the inconsistencies in his prescriptions, Ron was a master researcher of medications, resources, procedures and his rights. He spent hours educating himself about Risperdal and he knew that if he refused this medication, it could be forced on him via a Jarvis Petition for involuntary administration of neuroleptic medication.

I engaged in these same discussions with different patients on a monthly basis and my testifying in court involved relating their competency to consent to medication or treatment to the judge. I also listened to other psychologists and physicians including psychiatrists offer similar information during trials. What was clear was that many of the physicians working in psychiatric centers did not demonstrate knowing how to interview patients do determine their competency to consent to neuroleptics. I was once in the midst of an interview with a patient when the physician asked if she could briefly interrupt us. She entered the room and said she was about to move to another building and wanted to know if the person was willing to take the medication she had ordered. That was it, without any named medication or other information. The person answered in the affirmative and the doctor left, thus illustrating the accepted norm of, "no-hassle consent." More often than not, patients would volunteer to me that no one had ever educated them about their neuroleptic medication. Others shared their appreciation for being involved with the educational process of a competency interview.

Under "Barriers to Discharge" (circa mid-2000s and onward) was the repetition of Ron's diagnosis and symptoms originating in the mid-1980's. Ron's goal was noted as to "maintain clinical stability on a long-term basis." Short term goals (after 20 years of confinement, no less) were cited as "acknowledging and accepting his mental illness, signs of relapse and symptoms, review and revise his relapse prevention plan, community health maintenance plan, and crisis prevention plan, invest in treatment by addressing denial of his mental illness, denial of his crime: and lack of motivation."

Under the heading of "Dangerousness" were entries noting, "no insight into problems, continues to report delusional beliefs that he does not have a mental illness, threatens to sue staff for holding him here without reason, refuses treatment groups including Current Events, Harmonizing, Movie Classics, Frisbee Golf, Money Management and Job Skills." Obviously, this was a repetitious pattern related to differences in opinions. There were no examples of overt dangerous acts.

One day, out of the blue, Ron was suddenly informed he was being moved from the MI and D Transition Building to Bartlett Hall, a building nearby, reportedly because there were "fewer stairs" for him to walk. The real reason I suspected, was a behavioral sanction related to his declining to participate in the groups he had been assigned to attend as part of his treatment. What this move did, was take him away from his buddies, the guys he commiserated with daily; it upset his routine for sure. He could not leave the building to visit his friends, and they in turn could not enter his building to visit him. Then when he continued to resist attending these groups, he was further moved to Shantz Hall where he lost all his freedom of movement and was put on a plan where he had to "earn" trips to the canteen and walks outdoors by completing assignments.

Sprinkled amongst the entries of his treatment records were many references to Ron calling treatment program facilitators, "idiots," and claiming the content of the treatment groups was "fourth grade information." While both claims may have seemed true to him, these examples continued to be noted as his "narcissistic tendencies," which are unchangeable with or without medication. Such unbridled bravado can be a double-edged sword: on one hand it can make someone a funny man to friends, and on the other hand, make someone look disruptive in a hospital setting. Narcissism in patients or staff is not conducive to a healing atmosphere.

Another vexing list of entries in Ron's records were the ones associated with his habit of telling his treatment providers, like his nurses and social workers, that he hoped they had their liability insurance up to date because the day was coming when he was going to sue the hospital for the improper care he received. None of these statements added to his popularity, and in turn staff would chart entries of his being, "delusional, paranoid and threatening." The word "threatening" in a state hospital record gets attention and it can get a patient put in restraints. Ron's records over twenty plus years noted no actual acts of overt aggression to anyone, including other patients or staff. Threatening to sue someone did not count, as "threatening," but this comment was plentiful in Ron's medical record: it was always important in his case to read the next sentence which usually clarified he was threatening to "sue" someone.

Most apparent were contrasting descriptions of how Ron was perceived and treated in different ways at different state facilities by different professionals. At the St. Peter campus, the second time around, his personal presentation was described consistently as more negative and critical than it had been when he was first admitted then discharged to Willmar. At Willmar, even and after he was returned to this facility on his revoked provisional discharge he continued to be described in gentler, more encouraging and helpful terms.

One common finding in my experience reviewing medical/psychiatric records was that physicians' entries made clear that fact that they, in general, did not read previously charted nurses' notes. Nurses have the most contact with patients over any block of time, interact with them in different kinds of situations, and can offer helpful information related to behavior(s), patients' levels of cooperation or lack thereof, mood states, confusion or psychosis. For physicians to neglect reading nurses' notes for comparison of their own impressions was, in my opinion none other than foolhardy. I found the nurses and their chart entries to be extremely helpful.

The area of "Diagnosis" for Ron at St. Peter especially, was constantly in flux beginning in 1986, with cells of treatment providers seeing their diagnosis as more accurate than those of previous teams and multiple physicians offering multiple differing diagnoses or some diagnoses in contrast with previous opinions. This range of differing diagnoses spoke to a combined mixture of mood and thinking challenges, the latter noted as schizoaffective disorder, with noted interjections at various points of time that "Ron has demonstrated no evidence of psychosis, depression, mania or other symptoms of mental illness. This lack of diagnostic orderliness persisted over decades of time.

Moreover, related to diagnosis, in Ron's personal records he had letters from different consulting psychiatrists over time, who varied in their diagnosis of him. On January 22, 1992, Dr. James A. Halikas, at the University of Minnesota wrote about his evaluation of Ron on January 13 of 1992. Dr. Halikas was Professor of Psychiatry and Director of Chemical Dependency at the University.

Dr. Halikas indicated, "Often these notes use psychiatric diagnostic terms to characterize Mr. Steen, but in their descriptions of the data and the interaction, the behaviors they cite reflect conflicts over power and control, and freedom of action within the confines of the Security Hospital. For example, there is not cited evidence of hallucination or delusion which might be agreed upon by objective observers, not invested in controlling his behavior and subjugating his will."

Dr. Halikas noted he had evaluated Ron in the past related to a Jarvis Hearing, and also for a separate Three Judge Panel hearing. Prior to that he was Ron's consulting psychiatrist for 14 months from January 1986 through January 1988. Dr. Halikas' reported professional opinion as of January 13, 1992 was that "Ron has no evidence of a mental illness or defect that would force him to be kept in any state hospital or facility against his wishes...in short, I find no current evidence of any psychiatric diagnosis in this man."

Additionally, Ron had saved a letter dated July 10, 2000, that was sent to his social worker at Douglas County Human Services and her supervisor, by Peter S. Miller, M.D. Psychiatrist at the Human Development Center in Duluth. Minnesota. This letter was sent after Ron had been taken by the police to Miller Dwan during the time he was living at Arrowhead house and temporarily left the area to move some of his items to Alexandria before returning to Duluth. Dr. Miller noted it took a "great deal of effort to even find out what the terms of Ron's Provisional Discharge were at the time even though he noted "In some way I was expected to be responsible for carrying them out." Dr. Miller noted Ron was "very compliant...but all of his providers believed that after a lengthy period of time there was no further need for these services."

Dr. Miller then noted on page 2 of his letter, that, "after recent consultation with his psychiatrist from the Regional Treatment Center, I can find little or no evidence that he has a psychotic disorder requiring antipsychotic medication. Thus, it is difficult to assert that he had ' "no insight and basically denies that he does have a mental illness at that time," 'since the exact nature of his mental illness has not been well described from a point of view of clear diagnostic criteria. He legally did qualify as having a mental illness at the time of his accused crime, but that alone is not sufficient to constitute a diagnosis of an ongoing disorder at this time."

Lastly, Ron had within his personal records, a copy of a ten-page November 2, 2006 report of a Risk Appraisal completed by the State

Operated Forensic Service department of the Minnesota State Hospital. In a document headed,

"Addendum A: there was noted a number of bulleted statements including the following:
"From admission through October of 2004, Mr. Steen was without psychotic or manic symptoms. His belief that the MMPI was forged is noted but this does not appear to a bizarre or impossible fixed, false belief."

From "January to May of 2005 Mr. Steen demonstrated no objective signs of mental illness; he was deemed delusional about not needing treatment and not having a psychotic mental illness."

From January to October of 2006 numerous entries were noted related to his being seen as "psychiatrically stable with his antipsychotic medication dose being decreased," his discussions related to legal matters appear grounded in reality," with "no signs or symptoms of psychosis or mania."

Overall, it was concluded that although, "Mr. Steen has not shown any overt evidence of psychosis for many years, he continues in the very same stance that he has since long before I first came in contact with him; it is appropriate to lower his dose of Risperdal at this time."

Further conclusion was that, "Whatever symptoms of psychosis he may have or may not have shown in the distant past, it is clear that these symptoms are no longer present, and I don't believe there is any need to continue antipsychotic medication indefinitely in an asymptomatic patient."

Another complex issue made in reviewing Ron's records, along with collateral information touching on his business and relationship issues made it clear that his mood was impacted by situations outside of the hospital, especially situations involving finances. Again, what seemed to be missing, was that rarely if ever, did I review records where his psychiatrists or other staff asked him what was going on in his life, with his family or his friends, or with his investments and finances.

One time after Ron's Risperdal was again discontinued, he was described as "becoming increasingly absorbed in a pending legal situation, spending 3-8 hours a day reviewing legal documents and 2-6 hours a day on the phone." He was also described as "displaying pressured speech, poor sleep, being argumentative and difficult to redirect in conversations, offering grandiose delusional statements such as talking about firing one of his attorneys." He had been charted as "irritable" and "angry." This would have been a time to ask what else was going on his life, if for no other reason than to have a human being kind of conversational connection. Based on the entries in his chart, no one ever asked him what was going on when he was noted as appearing "agitated" or "short in his conversations" ...

The most egregious example of this questioning related to what else was or was *not* happening occurred on March 26, 2007, *after* the Petition for Ron's release had been filed. A copy of my report/recommendations had been included in his chart and the issue of his potentially pending release, should have been known by all his caregivers. Ron was transferred to the infamous Unit 800, that part of the hospital reserved for the most dangerous and out of control patients. This was the ward of the damned; the worst of the worst. People were never discharged directly from this ward. He would be lost here, invisible, beyond reach except for maybe his attorney getting active and that could take time. Patients were afraid of each other in this ward; it was dangerous.

Unit 800 is described in the State Operated Forensic Program as, "the most secure unit of the hospital. Clients are usually transferred to this unit due to behavior which threatens the safety of others. Examples of such behavior was listed as physical aggression toward others, fighting, attempting to elope, starting fires, severe property destruction, having items considered to be contraband and dangerous to others. You will remain on this unit until you demonstrate the ability to remain free of behavior that is dangerous to yourself or others. Added was, "this unit does not plan for clients to be discharged; this unit is one of the most heavily staffed of all Forensic units, requiring a four-person minimum per staff." Other information noted this unit "served up to 21 men, 18 years of age or older, the patients who reside here carry a wide range of diagnoses or mental illness, the majority of the persons can read and write, they all have exhibited property destruction, threatening behavior and/or assaultive behavior in the recent past."

The pending transfer to this abyss was charted in Ron's personal records as "being in place for his anticipated arguing and resistance to restarting the Risperdal." However, Ron did not resist, and he did not argue. He simply asked that his attorney be informed of where he had been transferred.

However, his medical record on March 26 when he was sent to Unit 800 specifically noted, "increase in paranoia and mania...litigious and oppositional behavior. Then, very rapidly it was noted that following his Risperdal being re-started April 13, 2007; he was discharged back to his "re-motivation unit" on May 2, 2007. This was a very quick turnaround. My takeaway was that these entries appeared orchestrated to accomplish something else.

Ron shared with me what had happened. Ron's lawyer (Mr. Black) who was supposedly assisting with Ron's conservatorship related to his sizable assets called him one day, out of the blue, informing Ron that all his money was gone, and he was broke. This kind of news would be shocking to most people, maybe even to Ron's psychiatrist. But for Ron, such information was devastating and sent him into a tailspin. If his psychiatrist or other staff had asked him what had upset him that day perhaps some actual problem solving could have taken place.

The drive home after reading the last of Ron's history and seeing other patients at the state hospital was its usual well needed break. I picked up a chocolate malt at Burger King and headed south. So far, there was no mention of Ron being aggressive to anyone, ever. Also, not evident was information noting his requiring seclusion or restraint or emergency medication related to out of control behavior.

His history over more than twenty years was that of no outbursts and no aggression. The only records yet to reviewed were those written by state experts as requested by the hospital. The hospital expected an objective report by these experts; unfortunately, some experts tendency is to write for the person paying for the report. But, perhaps I would be surprised and inspired by their findings.

I have also been asked on numerous occasions to serve as an "expert." I once heard an expert defined as, someone who does not live and work in the local community but rather, is from somewhere else and therefore in a position to perform a role that is seen as needed. It is expected that "experts" are thorough, and objective.

The Other Experts' Reports

The last significant records I reviewed included two separate independent psychological evaluations related to Ron's level of risk ascertained by psychologists outside of the hospital system. I knew these professionals, one rather well, and the other by his reports. I was eager to read what they considered as important and what the content would be of their reports.

One was a risk assessment of Ron in 2002 requested as part of the Minnesota Supreme Court of Appeals Panel (SCAP) following Ron's revoked provisional discharge from Arrowhead House in Duluth. The purpose of the evaluation was to determine whether Ron's "recent history and status" justified revocation of his provisional discharge and transfer back to the Willmar State Hospital. Ron had filed a Petition for Rehearing and Reconsideration with the Minnesota Supreme Court Administrator claiming his former attorney (actually, Mr. Black) at the time had misrepresented his willingness to remain a voluntary patient in Willmar, as Ron reported he did not think he needed to be in a Regional Treatment Center and wanted to return to a Provisional Discharge status.

The psychological examiner noted up front that Ron's request for reinstatement of the provisional discharge should be denied. He reported Ron should "remain at a Regional Treatment Center until he has attained a level of genuine insight into his psychiatric illness, need for multiple treatments and has genuinely engaged himself in multidisciplinary treatment involving medications and intensive psychotherapy." Noted were the statutory definitions of a Mentally Ill and Dangerous Person as well as the Criteria for Transfer from an Open Hospital while under commitment as a Mentally Ill and Dangerous.

The expert performing this psychological evaluation acknowledged *he had not been provided with Ron's records* from the Minnesota Security Hospital, Willmar Regional Treatment Center or Arrowhead House in Duluth for review. No records were reviewed noting Ron driving his own car for three years, without absconding, without missing appointments, and with community reviewers, stating he had completed years of programming that did not need repeating. I have to add, that no one "provides examiners with anything that they do not ask for. In truth, examiners may have to ask more than once before eliciting the necessary information.

The examiner added he had traveled to Willmar the morning of the August 2002 interview and spent four hours reviewing accumulative records and that a sizable box of additional materials had been sent containing most of the early records that Ron requested to be reviewed. It was also noted that the interview with Ron lasted three hours. Ron's daughter and a former brother in law of Ron's were present and expressed wanting to speak to this psychologist about their concerns, with this conversation declined by the psychologist out of a reported concern their presence might "contaminate the interview process and outcome."

Considering that not all the collateral information had been ordered or requested by this psychologist, or was made available to him, and that no additional individuals familiar with Ron were interviewed, this was not a situation that was in Ron's best interests. Certainly, if there was a situation that could be counted on to "contaminate the outcome," this could be it.

Some statements in this expert's report were in contrast with the facts of the case. A couple of these errors included the once again reported use of alcohol by Ron that was inconsistent with his behavior as described at the jail immediately after the shooting, and the fact that no blood alcohol level had been determined as present in his system. The alcohol issue was old and

213

inaccurate news. Nevertheless, the conclusion of the report was eloquently stated and without hesitation: the report supported the revoked discharge and the need to keep Ron in a confined setting due to his "ongoing dangerousness."

The risk appraisal report noted that past and current psychological testing results were not relied upon in isolation from other information. Supposedly, the evaluation included a variety of sources including "records, personal contacts, the person's history, results from a variety of tests and questionnaires and whatever independent data was relevant and available."

The results of Ron's new MMPI-2 conducted at the time were included and noted as "underestimating antisocial and manic behavior." The report further noted that his assessment -taking style "tends to come from individuals who have antisocial personality features."

The words "antisocial personality features" can be the kiss of death to any individual to whom they are attached. This type of personality disorder includes individuals who lack empathy, have engaged in repeated examples of reckless and harmful behavior towards others and have histories usually of repeated arrest related to their criminal behavior violating social norms. Such people do not have the capacity to change: the term "antisocial personality disorder" represents individuals who are at high risk for aggression. However, in Ron's over 20-year history at the hospital there was not a single example cited of his actual physical aggression towards anyone. Also missing in his case were customary life history factors seen as precursors for a diagnosis of anti-social personal disorder including contact with law enforcement beginning at age 15 and onward, with a record of continued and frequent arrests.

The report by this metro expert also noted, "There is a strong possibility that his physical problems are feigned and manipulative and that he is presenting medical problems to avoid difficult life circumstances or to gain compensation." No example of physical problems that Ron might have feigned were noted. An additional comment was, "individuals with similar profiles were from nonclinical/normal populations and included their using physical problems to manipulate others." It was suggested that Ron "may be attempting certain behavior for secondary gain; that he displayed a pervasive lack of insight; had poor judgment ad difficulty benefiting from his previous experiences and was a poor candidate for intervention because of his denial, defensiveness and lack of psychological mindedness."

Ultimately this evaluation identified Ron as meeting the criteria for diagnoses of bipolar affective disorder, delusional disorder and mixed personality disorder based on his "reported beliefs that his competitor and multiple attorneys acted to deprive him of multiple assets and business opportunities related to their viewing him as a community nuisance." Noted were Ron's showing this expert letter he had from certain professionals who favored Ron's opinions.

The opinion was offered that "the primary concern in support of his remaining an ongoing danger to others was his single violent act nearly two decades in the past which led immediately to incarceration/hospitalization followed by a prolonged period of secure institutionalization and monitoring. His prolonged and perseverative preoccupation and anger with a "*multiparty conspiracy*" threatening to harm **MSH** staff during a psychotic episode," all seen as speaking to, "potential for additional violence."

Surely, this "*multiparity conspiracy*" couldn't mean the eavesdropping of the concocted hit man telephone conversation from records in the mid 1980's related to the words "10,000 each" buried in Ron's early records? Could it be that this unverified and uninvestigated myth without subsequent threats or reports of even threatened harm, mischief, or investigation by law

216

enforcement, let alone hospital security, had now, twenty years later become transformed into a legend and lynchpin of Ron's potential for additional violence?" Based on these finding along with the entire contents of the risk report the recommendation to the Court was unhesitatingly to withhold Ron's liberty.

When I reviewed Ron's massive collection of his personal legal papers, the phrase "10,000 each" did take on a variety of possibilities. At one point in these notes related to his litigation efforts Ron mentioned "10,000 each." However, these were "$10,000 payments for each of his attorneys. It seemed strange, if not ludicrous that mental health professionals had apparently never just asked Ron what the "10,000 each," meant. Perhaps they asked, and he said it was confidential which he often said when he did not want someone meddling in his affairs.

Another noted expert psychologist who assessed Ron, reported Ron was boasting he was going to sue the hospital for "$10,000 per day of his confinement." The bottom line irony would suggest that when so-called mental patients use such words, they might represent something sinister or delusional, but when professionals decide it must mean "hit men to kill the staff," and a risk assessment expert labels it a "multi-party conspiracy," it makes perfect sense.

So as not to leave any doubt related to Ron's risk status, an additional follow-up risk assessment was completed within the next year by the Minnesota State Hospital Forensic Services department. For whatever reason, perhaps training purposes, the hospital psychologist doing this assessment had a co-signing supervisor. The supervisor could, therefore oversee the report and would be expected to catch irregularities is such were apparent.

The author of this risk assessment report noted the use of assessment instruments common to the process such as the Hare Psychopathy Checklist Revised and the HCR-20: the former was a checklist for psychopathy; the latter was a risk assessment tool based on a person's history, clinical issues and specific factors related to risk as rated by the evaluator. These instruments require special training and understanding to aid in their findings. Both include accompanying testing booklets and guidelines for gathering helpful and credible scores useful in assessing risk for future violence based on past violence and several other characteristics of the person's history and present status. If an assessor fails to follow the guidelines, the result is not credible, and the person's level of risk can be skewed and the report unhelpful.

Only another psychologist would be able to tell if the guidelines had been followed based on the wording of the report or comments made about the risk score in conjunction with the instrument's findings. A psychologist keenly familiar with the record of the person assessed would also recognize when certain statements about risk findings were inconsistent.

One of the findings noted in the report related to the Hare PCL-R risk assessment noted Ron having evidence of "conning and manipulation. The reason this was a problem is that the Hare PCL-R defines "conning and manipulation" as "cheating, bilking or defrauding others for personal gain," with specific examples including "passing bad checks, setting up phony businesses using family members for their money," none of which was hinted at or evident in Ron's history. Thus, to identify this item as being significant without finding evidence of the specific definition example noted would not indicate a credible assessor or a credible assessment.

Ron was likewise observed as exhibiting a "failure to accept responsibility for his actions," as noted in his "denial of his crime," without

219

equal evidence in his history that he turned himself in for this crime and his records noted his repeated expressed remorse.

He was additionally seen as having a history of "revoked conditional release," which is a solid factor for future risk. However, the testing manual identified this item as "omitted for an individual who has had no formal contact with the criminal justice system as an adult prior to the current offense." Ron had no criminal history prior to the shooting of Margaret Brown.

Another evaluation available for review in Ron's records included a neuropsychological assessment by a consulting neuropsychologist hired by the hospital. Teat results were reported in an articulate and professional scribed manner. The stated purpose of the referral was "to add information and answer questions about the degree to which cognitive deficits might account for his repeatedly continuing to deny mental illness, need for psychotropic medications and need for a relapse prevention plan."

In this report, conclusions stated that Ron was, "incapable of truly independent living." And they asserted he "will need assistance with family, friends or professional staff in making major decisions and carrying out more

220

complex aspects of maintaining a household." No examples were offered. Records further noted he was financially independent but were not explained in the context of his capacity for independent living, nor was the information included that his financial independence was a result of his savvy business skills.

Findings for "implication for training and education" seemed out of place for Ron who was at retirement age where retraining and further education were not in his range of interests or necessity. Ron was described as having "possible problems with developing approach-search strategies for extracting required information leading to problems in expressing concepts and resulting in ineffective reading." These deficits were further noted as being "troublesome in higher level academics where there are greater demands for conceptual thinking and development of a complex structural information higher hierarchies." The evaluator did add that this last deficit "is just not one of Ron's issues on even a common-sense level."

The report also described Ron as "unable to arrive at practical solutions to real life problems or participate in endeavors of higher education." No explanation was offered about Ron not being interested in advancing his education.

Ron's level of insight and denial of his problems were noted as his having "attentional deficits leading to premature closure on reflection resulting in an incomplete analysis or incorrect interpretation of a situation resulting in inappropriate behaviors and feelings." The example given was Ron's "challenged insight and dis-control (sic) of his behavior over at least 15 years with no evidence regarding a display of harm let alone behavior that could be described as dangerous." The neuropsychologist pointed out that Ron's "rigid thinking and continuing denial of his mental illness, need for medication, and relapse prevention plan were supported by "evidence of prefrontal cortex dysfunction."

The bottom line neuropsychological conclusion was, that Ron, "should not be allowed to operate heavy or potentially dangerous machinery because attention deficits could lead to a number of errors in executing tasks that would not be acceptable in many work settings."

The last report reviewed was one by the state hospital psychologists, a professional in the State Operated Forensic Services department who interviewed Ron prior to his hearing in 2006 after he had spent over two decades in confinement and six years back in the first institution where his hospitalization began. She documented in Ron's record that she spent "30 minutes" talking to him prior to preparing her report. Did he decline to keep talking with her; the report did not clarify the reason the interview was so short. Based on that length of interview time, her conclusion appeared to have been made long before the 30 minute evaluation.

On the ride home, I considered the last of the records I reviewed and the information I had collected. I questioned the legion of treatment team .members he had over time and the pattern of how he had been described. Treatment teams shifted every three months, every quarter, so overall many professionals were involved.

I also considered the possibility that repetition of outdated information had simply persisted as history over years of time. Or perhaps, it was indifference to the patient, although this did not seem sensible considering so many charts and files including the same comment regarding Ron making "no changes," as noted by people with different levels of training.

I questioned whether the treatment team members saw their jobs as merely akin to that of an assembly line: doing the same thing every day in an environment where neither the staff nor the patients changed, left or moved on, treatment-wise or in some cases professionally. For some, it may have been burnout, or perhaps burned out zeal for getting involved with situations and politics that were for all practical purposes, formidable and unending. Some challenges with some people in charge are not worth the guaranteed shortening of one's career or paycheck. No one spoke up. No one apparently asked questions or challenged discussions for clarity or new direction. Perhaps the routine, over time fostered a sense of security in things staying the same.

From my experiences with mental health professionals in a variety of settings, such as nursing homes, community and state hospitals, clinics, VA centers, private practice settings, I could count on one hand surprisingly few instances of a psychiatrist being questioned or challenged as to a diagnosis he made, by a fellow colleague; may have happened, but I never witnessed it. By contrast, psychologists live to discuss if not challenge each other's diagnostic opinions, risk assessment results and case opinions. This difference is crucial.

Keep in mind that many if not most residents of state facilities, especially individuals like Ron who remain in such settings for years, have few outside contacts; the folks they see most often are fellow patients or staff for human contact, support and self-reflection. Families have long ago stopped

224

visiting because the experience was too depressing or frightening. Some immediate family members and friends move away or have died. A rare few have life-long friends who have become a surrogate-like family. Lastly, people in institutions remain hidden from society by HIPAA rules/restrictions and a veil of confidentiality.

Additionally, psychiatry is currently seen through different lenses than in the past. Nowadays there is talk of bipolar disorder being diagnosed in two-year olds. Some PTSD research involving returning veterans finds no more effectiveness in the use of medications like Risperdal, Seroquel or Abiify than that of placebos. Add to this list the incidence of childhood psychiatric disorders. The autism rate from 1960 to 1970 was .5 per 1000 children and now we have a rate greater that one child in 88 diagnosed with a broader range of autistic spectrum disorders (perhaps requiring or needing a broader array of medications). Due to an ever-broadening diagnostic criteria within the Diagnostic and Statistical Manual of Mental Disorders, the 5th Edition's emphasis is to look for behavioral over biological evidence.

New horizons of psychiatric care abound in the off-label use of neuroleptic medication, as one example, for depression and hyperactive/angry children. Out-patient psychiatric care is one of the most expensive if not the

225

longest types of treatment, usually medication dependent and fraught with infrequent teaching of long term problem solving skills except as purported in some television ads.

The cost of in-patient psychiatric care even in state facilities is rising. In Ron's collection of records was information that at the time of his hospitalization the daily cost exceeded $550.00, comparable to a nice room at an upscale hotel with a pool and room service.

The drive home today was quiet time for reflection. I did not enjoy seeing reports by colleagues that I knew that did not match collateral information. Definitely, reports can be shaped to please the payor of one's services. Somewhere within me is the naive belief that people do the right thing for the right reason. I think everyone is familiar with being treated unfairly in some situation and having no recourse other than to accept a painful decision. What made Ron's situation different for me was the length of time it had been going on. I wondered how anyone could be in such a situation without getting angry, feeling hopeless, reading news articles about people who did the same act and went to prison and got released.

If someone is confined for decades, I expect to see records of repeated seclusion and restraint, fights and aggressive behavior, big problems that repeat themselves, demanding advancing measures of control. Instead, Ron's history was that of first participating in treatment at St. Peter in the early years, following treatment expectations at Willmar, participating in treatment in a Duluth until his physician said that after so many years, repeating treatment might not advance the cause further, then being assessed for community placement in Willmar again and nothing when returned to St. Peter for "remotivational treatment." I was unable to see what was re-motivating about his programming. Ron's earlier programming had apparently been renamed or resurrected into new programming that he was declining. This was like reinventing the wheel and hoping people would get excited.

Where was this case heading?

My Report

After reviewing all Ron's records, gathering collateral clinical data, interviewing him and talking with his one available family member, I wrote my report. It was dated May 8, 2006. At the time Ron was 65. I noted in the introduction, that as of January 17, 2006, Ron's Senior Staff Psychiatrist, had identified Ron as "psychiatrically stable...thought processes reasonably linear and goal directed...thought content devoid of psychosis or lethality to hurt self or others. He does not demonstrate any psychotic symptomatology at this time...he has not in this interview's opinion ever demonstrated any psychotic symptomatology whatsoever."

Needless to say, in 2006 Ron was at a different point in time than he was in 1986, when first committed as Mentally Ill and Dangerous. In 1986 he exhibited active symptoms of his mood disorder, including evidence of symptoms of psychosis and required protection related to his illness, as well as others needing to be protected from him. The hospital had been helpful to him in treating and stabilizing his illness to the point that he was able to demonstrate being safe to walk freely on campus. It took nine years for him to be transferred to the Willmar sister hospital to prepare for what was thought of as eventual return to the community at large.

In my 2006 report I noted that throughout Ron's 20 years commitment he had not been identified as displaying open aggression, nor had he been placed in seclusion or restraint for disruptive or dangerous behavior or property destruction. His last noted need for emergency medication was November 27, 1991. He had not been charted as refusing neuroleptic medication since he returned to St. Peter in 2004, and I noted he had not refused neuroleptic medication since committed as MI and D. The only time he did not taking this kind of medication was when his physicians discontinued it.

His 2001 revoked provisional reportedly occurred due to his "failing to participate in required treatment programming, missing follow up appointments with his social worker, missing multiple doses of his required medication, inability for relating to his caregivers resulting in eviction and deterioration of his sleep and activities resulting in a labile mood and reportedly becoming impulsive and angry suggesting a reoccurrence of his mood disorder."

The rest of the story detailed the fact that his Douglas County social worker's list of Ron's "deficiencies" included his "continuing interest in his legal situation...his being held responsible for his psychiatrist discontinuing his neuroleptic, reducing his antidepressant, and stopping his cholesterol lowering medication, even though available records noted his physician commenting on this being acceptable." It became a whole different story with these important and clarifying details.

I pointed out that when Ron lived at Arrowhead House in Duluth, Arrowhead House rules did not allow stopping medication (even when your doctor discontinued it), unless the House approved it. Additionally, records noted he missed an appointment with his social worker, not because he was intentionally skipping it, but because he was at a local clinic with shortness of breath, which he considered a medical emergency. Despite this experience, Ron had remembered to call his social worker.

Since 1986 there were no examples in his records of his engaging in behavior seen as evidence of "substantial harm." While he had been described by his social worker as refusing medical care, I noted he had an established record of cooperating with medical care. While Ron had been apprehended when he returned to Arrowhead after moving some of his things to Alexandria and he had been taken to Miller Dwan Hospital, it was several days before anyone knew where he was. I questioned the reason it took so long for him to be located by state program employees who were responsible for sending him to the hospital after he returned to the halfway house!

Repeated correspondence from Douglas County Department of Human Services pointed out that Ron was not interested in Day Treatment whereas other evaluators, like his psychiatrist in Duluth, had documented Ron was not only disinterested in this treatment but that, equally importantly *"it does not appear necessary...and is probably impossible to complete."*

While frequently mentioned themes in Ron's records included his "lack of insight into his mental illness," his "denial of his mental illness," and his "lack of motivation in treatment," there were also specifically dated other entries noting his "acknowledging depression, but not psychosis while admitting to a history of situational depression and anxiety,' and stating the shooting that resulted in his confinement was "an accident."

Ron's return to the MI and D Transition Unit in 2004, included noted perceptions by his psychologist and the other eleven members of his treatment team that, in general, pointed to a group of people (the team and

231

Mr. Steen) who were unwilling or unable to hear each other, when it came to acknowledging the realities of Ron's situation. The staff at St. Peter continued to say he needed to complete his groups and Ron continued to decline attending them. I pointed out that apparently few if any staff considered, that according to statutory definition 253B.092 "Disagreement with the physician's recommendation is not evidence of an unreasonable decision." Being able to disagree is an individual right.

Repeated statements in Ron's records also included he was "non-compliant with medication," whereas I referenced 12 such instances in 1988, followed by no prescribed neuroleptics from August 1991 until November of the same year when he required re-starting of his neuroleptic. He was reported as not fully complying with his medications in Duluth in 2000 which Ron disputed. His psychiatrist, Dr. Miller, in 2000, supported Ron's position in his November 21, 2000 correspondence with Mr. Steen's attorney when he clarified that "Mr. Steen has been consistently compliant in taking medication and complying with any drug screens. Also important was when Dr. Becker at Willmar Regional Treatment Center wrote on May 19, 2000, "Mr. Steen has not demonstrated symptoms of depression, suicidal ideation, mania paranoia or hallucinations."

Moreover, in my review of Ron's long history at the hospital I was only able to find one instance, January 23, 1992, he had been placed in seclusion reportedly for "threatening " staff, when he "threatened to sue staff or report them to their professional boards." I also reported the long-decades-old hearsay comments about his allegedly offering to pay someone $10,000 each," noting the exact wording in his records was completely unclear as to whom this one would be paid or for what reason. I reported that, at some point, an independent examiner in his July 11, 2005, Risk Appraisal Assessment described this comment referred to, "Mr. Steen threatening to hire a hit man to kill MSH staff." I repeated I had reviewed this situation with Mr. Steen during my interview with him, and his response to the bizarre claim was that it was, "ridiculous."

At the same time, I acknowledged Ron had been critical of treatment staff and had voiced what could be seen as unappreciative statements along with threats to sue them all in the future. Various interpretations had also been offered to common themes regarding his reported financial concerns, including his questioning how well his daughter was handling his money, with progress notes describing such comments as being "paranoid." I commented that for an individual such as Mr. Steen, who in reality had sizable assets, his concerns related to his finances were understandably rational.

The MMPI-2 Ron completed during my evaluation of him was valid, with evidence of consistent responding in both front and back portions of the inventory. His validity scores noted a moderate level of unconventional experiences, feelings and behaviors, like persons intensely involved in social or political issues or in persona who have adjusted to experiencing chronic problems. Elevated clinical scales were noted as similar to his numerous past MMPI-2 results, none of which were elevated to extreme levels. His most elevated scale was scale 3, representing an individual noting somatic complaints sometimes in response to conflict, one who sees oneself as intellectual, well socialized and well adjusted. Elevations on scale 3 also are common in individuals defending against or coping with an intolerably painful situation by using other defenses to shift their mental focus onto something less negative or even naively positive. His two other slightly elevated scales were on depression, and a scale noting neurotic tendencies.

There were no elevations on scales that would indicate delusional beliefs, a formal thought disorder, or paranoia. He had a slight elevation on scale 7 consistent with his tendency to be moralistic and overly meticulous. I noted in my report that at the time Ron completed this inventory he was taking Risperdal, an antipsychotic used to treat bipolar disorder and irritability.

My diagnosis for Ron, at the time based on the DSM-IV-TR (Diagnostic and Statistical Manual for Mental Disorders, Fourth Edition-Text Revision) was that he had Dysthymia vs Depression NOS (Not Otherwise Specified) and history of bipolar affective disorder, mixed, currently controlled. I did not note an actual Axis II personality disorder. While Ron had be identified as having a schizoaffective disorder, (meaning the person has a concurrent display of thought disorder symptoms, like hallucinations or delusional beliefs) along with mood disturbance, such as an agitated depression or mania), I saw it as questionable that an individual in their late 40's would be first identified with a formal thought disorder, generally speaking, whereas this age group would be more often diagnosed with the onset and identification of bipolar disorder.

I considered his having somewhat paranoid/delusional beliefs until I talked with his family and friends and listened to their interactive experiences with Ron. It was also apparent that as family responsibility managing his assets increased, their own suspicions and mistrust of others began to exhibit in themselves. The emotional and mental pressures Ron experienced related to legal setbacks and business disappointments from the late 70's to mid-1980's appeared to be unappreciated by others, and difficult to accurately factor into what constituted his "stresses" at the time. Now they expressed a new kind of empathy for what he had been going through.

As to my opinions related to the MI and D discharge criteria: I did see Ron as *"capable of making an acceptable adjustment to open society, no longer dangerous to the public and no longer in need of inpatient treatment and supervision."*

His history of community adjustment prior to the 1986 incident included his becoming a competitive, ambitious and successful businessman, who had no criminal history and no history of alcohol problems. He had been married for twenty years, had three children, went through a divorce and re-established another meaningful relationship; he had no history of juvenile problems with the law, no history of educational or behavioral problems in general.

His early adjustment to his 1986 MI and D commitment included times when he was described as "argumentative," but by 1994 he had apparently tamed his demeanor to the point he was given unescorted/unsupervised campus walks and was described as "responsible" in his behaviors. Also, in 1994 he was noted as agreeing with his diagnosis of bipolar disorder, not seen as verbally abusive or physically assaultive and was exhibiting regular attendance in programming and therapy. In 1995 he was extended further freedom in being sent to Willmar Regional Treatment Center and ultimately Arrowhead House in Duluth.

I recounted his successful adjustment to living in society for three years while in Duluth, including his purchasing his own vehicle and driving during this three year period without problems. His treating psychiatrist, Dr. Peter S. Miller noted in July 10, 2000 that "It took a great deal of effort to find out what the terms of his provisional discharge were, even though in some ways I was expected to be responsible for carrying them out. Mr. Steen was very compliant in support services including day treatment, but all of his providers believed that after a lengthy period of time there was no need for these services."

The stated reasons for his December 20, 2001 revoked provisional discharge included: his alleged "failure to participate in a required treatment program, missing follow-up appointments with his social worker, allegedly missing multiple doses of his required medication, reported inability for

237

relating to caregivers resulting in eviction, deterioration of sleep, activity patterns and labile mood and impulsive angry, behavior suggesting recurrence of his mood disorder."

I noted that none of these reasons represented clear and convincing evidence of overt threats or acts of harm or demonstrated dangerous behavior. No property damage was reported, and no evidence existed that police had to be summoned for any interventions of aggressive or out of control behavior. Mr. Steen was not described as threatening to shoot anyone, nor did evidence suggest he resisted transport to Miller Dwan Hospital. Additionally, this hospital did not identify him as suicidal or homicidal at the time of admission nor did they describe him as behaving in a manner to suggest he was at a level of substantial harm to himself or others.

Instead, the hospital on December 22, 2001 questioned the reason he was brought to their facility! He was kept for five days (December 21-26, 2001), with the hospital reporting his having "a long history of schizophrenia...with no old records available...multiple paranoid delusions possibly present, however, behavior organized, and he is not a management problem; at the time of admission on Depakote, Wellbutrin, Ativan, Pravachol, Singular, Albuterol inhaler and Nitrostat."

Further evidence of Ron having adjusted to society included his not acquiring any criminal charges, nor did he break the law or acquire a record of unsafe or improper driving offenses. If he had missed doses of medication, he failed to demonstrate evidence of such in the form of dangerous or irresponsible behavior. Some people might say an individual able to maintain control of their anger and impulses in the face of the series of events converging on him during his revoked provisional discharge and hospitalization at Miller Dwan, could be seen as having more than solid evidence of social adjustment.

His attempts to find another halfway house placement in 2003 were unsuccessful, not because Mr. Steen was uncooperative or exhibited dangerous behavior, but because he did not report feeling comfortable living in the choices available to him and did not want to live in one very expensive facility.

When he returned to the MI and D Transitions Unit at St. Peter he continued to be described as "polite, cooperative, able to express himself, indicate his wants and needs, interact socially with peers, and carry on a conversation with ease." In 2006 his designation was only that of Mentally Ill... not Dangerous.

In Ron's file, documents said he is in need of a "relapse prevention plan." When discharged he would need to identify a clear plan to "purchase a condo, get a new psychiatrist, take whatever medication his doctor prescribes and see his physician for health problems," which he has always done. He would need to recognize emotional problems in himself in having "sadness and crying spells."

Some entries note his "needing to invest himself in treatment...by addressing his denial of his crime." However, documented comments from his treating psychologist (January 17, 2006) include his being quoted as saying, "Sunday was the twentieth anniversary. It was a long time ago...there is not a day that goes by that I don't think about that being the reason I am here." Ron did not deny the shooting incident, but what he remembers was different from the recollection of others. Retrial of his 1986 situation was not the issue. What was germane was his current display of safe behavior in the community, which he had demonstrated since at least 1994 when he first walked freely on campus.

He had been identified as needing to "address his denial of his mental illness." However, in March he asked his physician for an antidepressant and antianxiety agent in response to his awareness of his moods. His records noted he asked his psychiatrist for someone to talk with about his "emotional problems." In the past he has denied having a mental illness common to the opinions of some of his treatment providers. Other times he has disagreed with treatment providers describing him as psychotic. He talked about his history of "situational depression," and to me he said his diagnosis was "schizoaffective disorder bipolar type." I repeated the phrase within the 253B.092 statutory criteria noting, "An individual disagreeing with his physician is not evidence of an unreasonable decision."

As to his *no longer being dangerous to the public:* Ron was at a level 5 liberty level which allowed him to go into the community and to go anywhere on campus unescorted. At WRTC he was allowed weekend passes to visit family. In 1995 he was transferred to WRTC to prepare for extended freedom in a halfway house which he was granted in 1998 including his living successfully in the community for over two years without demonstrated anger, harm, dangerous behavior or driving offenses as he drove his own car to appointments.

His revoked provisional discharge did not include evidence of clear and convincing acts of substantial or serious harm, or danger to self or others, or evidence that he was going to shoot someone. He has had episodes of alternating moods for decades and it was possible that these cycles would continue throughout his lifetime based on the fact that he had been diagnosed with what was seen as a chronic mental illness. To generalize that every time he was depressed, irritable, stubborn, manic, or even seen as psychotic automatically meaning that someone is going to be harmed, let alone killed, was not supported by his behavior since at least 1994 when he was given free campus access, if not during the entire 20 years of his commitment.

Ron had in the distant past (1990's) threatened to sue people or turn them in to their professional boards. He had declined to participate in groups or work for minimum wage. He had been repeatedly identified as lacking insight, being delusional, grandiose, or paranoid, and yet he has not shown himself to be harmful or dangerous. The constant in Ron's 20 years of confinement is the absence of his acting in a manner that had substantial likelihood of harm or dangerous behavior. His last noted that had seclusion date was for six months from November 1991 until May of 1992 due to symptoms excluding overt evidence of aggressive or dangerous behavior.

Current risk assessment scores indicated low risk on the HCR-20, a non-psychopathic score on the Hare PCL-R, and an MMPI-2 profile being neurotic in nature and lacking evidence of antisocial personality disorder.

References noted the annual likelihood of being killed by a seriously mentally ill individual not taking his or her medication are difficult to even find. One reference from 2003 Handbook of Forensic Psychology noted it was approximately .0000036 or 1,000 out of 273 million Americans.

Regarding the idea that he was *no longer in need of inpatient treatment and supervision:* I noted Ron's history included approximately thirty years of some level of depression/hypomania on an intermittent basis, along with the likelihood that during the rest of his life this emotional pattern was likely to continue. I noted, however, that there was insufficient evidence to support his continuing to need the level of treatment or supervision he was currently receiving in a secure treatment setting.

Before he was discharged from Willmar Regional Treatment Center, a second provisional discharge was in the works when he was returned to St. Peter, simply because he was not comfortable in the choices of community living conditions available or their cost. I pointed out he was perceived and

243

charted more positively in his records at Willmar, whereas in St. Peter he is consistently characterized in negative, pejorative and critical terms and his comments to staff were interpreted as "paranoid, delusional, and lacking in insight."

Meetings with his psychiatrist were listed in his records as lasting 20-30 minutes. I noted in December of 2005, when he asked for someone to talk with about some "emotional problems," he was told to talk with "the psychologist, or his one-to -one-nurse Barb." His chart included mention that he commented that "ten minutes with the psychologist or five minutes with the psychiatrist were not enough." His chart then cited him as "not meeting goals, not attending assigned groups or being present with minimal verbal participation, and reporting groups were not of interest to him or beneficial."

Ron's Individual Treatment Plan noted he was, to "maintain clinical stability on a long term basis," with neither term, "clinical stability" or "long term" within the context of his chronic illness defined or explained. I also noted he was described thusly: "Understands complex ideas, is free of neologism, speech is non-pressured, expresses wants and needs, oriented to person, place, time and situation, had a strong work history, is able to read and write, is independent with ADLs (activities of daily living), free of assault since admission, no chemical dependency history, financially secure."

Time-wise it had been two years since his return to St. Peter; five/six years since his revoked provisional discharge in 2001/2002; twelve years since he first received free campus access in 1994; fourteen years since his time spent in the high control unit 800 following his arrest/charges; and twenty years since he acted in a manner for which he was found NGRI, with no subsequent display of harm.

While programming certainly held a level of importance, Ron was free to walk outside the hospital in 1994, long before he participated in his current programming. Necessary for program completion per se, to be seen as the exclusive, standard for release, would require evidence that no longer being deemed 'dangerous to the public' was directly related to the mandated programming he was mandated to attend. I noted no documented or cited discussion related to possible conflicts of interest or complacency being in any way contributory to an individual appearing to remain indefinitely stuck in the system. Frankly, I found no evidence that the amount and quality of his current therapeutic contacts would be unable to be met in an outpatient setting in a community considering his main programming needs had been identified as, weight management and cooking skills.

As regards the item: *Specific conditions to provide a reasonable degree of protection to the public and to assist the patient adjusting to the community:* I suggested Ron meet certain criteria:

First, he would need to meet with an outpatient psychiatrist and Ron and this treating professional have a therapeutic alliance: in the absence of this feeling of alliance, Ron should be free to change doctors: Next I suggested Ron being required to follow the medication ordered for him. Moreover, he should be required to secure a qualified doctoral level psychologist competent in cognitive/behavioral therapy, to assist him in coping with his emotions and live/embrace the present rather than dwelling in the past. Beyond this, Ron needed to remain law abiding and free of evidence of "substantial likelihood of harm as defined by threats or overt acts of harm towards self or others. Equally important I stressed that future hospitalization, if necessary be least restrictive unless he clearly and convincingly met the criteria for commitment as mentally ill. Finally, I urged that Ron avoid access to fire arms and alcohol.

In conclusion I *recommended full and immediate discharge from his civil commitment as mentally ill.*

I noted "years of his life have been occupied in seemingly unnecessary "treatment," particularly since the revocation of his provisional discharge, if not before. I offered I was unable to find one shred of evidence to support keeping him confined for one more day, let alone weeks or months. He has demonstrated safe and successful transition for years and years of time." This report was sent, as usual, to Ron's attorney and the court handling the case, Douglas County.

Actually, sending off my report to the powers that be was not just offering my opinion, it was showing how I arrived at them, how I supported them in an effort to make my process transparent. That is what dissenters attack; your opinions and how you managed to arrive at them. I was comfortable with what points I emphasized and the conclusion I reached. I also knew that after the reports are submitted, then further decisions are made and at some point, there will be a formal meeting to make sense of differences. That is the good part of our system. Sometimes your side wins and sometimes it doesn't. Everybody takes their turns. Hopefully goals and services become advanced and people feel heard.

I learn more about the mental health system with each case, which is the point in "practicing" one's profession. It is never ending. Hopefully treatment practices can advance. When I am driving to institutions where residents have been there for decades, I wonder who is helping them, if it is possible to advance their cause; how are they managing if their life experience can only unfold within the confines of a never changing walls and restrictions?

Surprise!

To my total dismay and shock, a month after submitting my report, when I was reviewing Ron's records, I noted a copy of my report in his master file with some of my statements highlighted, yet this case had not yet been heard. My report was a private professional document sent to Douglas County Court, and it was available only to Judge David Battey in Douglas County at the time, and Ron's defense attorney, Ryan Magnus. I knew Ryan Magnus would never send my report to the hospital, so, did someone at Douglas County do this? The big questions that were never answered: included who did this, and for what reason?

When I realized my report, was in Ron's main chart, I shared with him that this was highly unusual, improper, and could possibly result in some challenges for him. He said he thought some of the staff's actions towards him were intended to goad him to lose his temper. He also reaffirmed his renewed effort to not let that happen.

Within a month of this report appearing in Ron's medical chart, Ron was moved from the MI and D Transition Unit to Bartlett Hall, for "re-motivation!" This move was explained as including "fewer stairs for him to walk." What about his now being isolated and separated from his hospital friends, with no patients allowed to visit other units? In yet another month he would again be moved to Shantz where he was additionally put on a strict behavioral program: no program attendance/participation would result in no outdoor fresh air breaks or "pop-breaks."

I worried for Ron's safety in what had become a tricky system for him. He was blunt enough with his comments to make some people mad and want to retaliate against him. While he had survived treatment machinations before without going crazy, he was older now and less resilient to such games or challenges. In some ways he was the pseudo-object of professional group bullying, although I had never seen such a term used in relation to long term confinement, let alone "treatment."

I would remain fearful for Ron for another two years. I had been through too many clinical experiences of seeing what nasty behavior can do to a person, too many years of dealing with people playing games. There was nothing I could do about the atmosphere in which he resided other than stay in touch with him when I was in his building.

I knew my report would stand in contrast to his existing records. However, I also knew from reading a mountain of records, that there had been other professionals in Ron's history, long before, who also questioned the basis of his diagnosis and confinement.

His community physician in Duluth poignantly noted that "someone not reporting a mental illness could hardly be seen in denial, (of the symptoms of a mental illness), if that was their experience." The reality was that there were fewer professionals with this line of thinking compared with the legions of treatment providers in the state system.

I do not mean to sound virtuous. Writing a report consistent with the longstanding status quo at the time would have been much easier. Such a report would not have invited criticism, with no pending court hearing to be challenged by the opposing attorney. I considered the possibility that Ron was in a situation where the deck was basically stacked against him by default. If he complained of anxiety or reported he was unable to sleep, these descriptions were translated into his demonstrating symptoms of his mental illness. If he denied symptoms that the staff thought he was exhibiting, he was documented as delusional or lacking insight. Truth be told, some of Ron's personal characteristics had been self-defeating in medical/psychiatric settings. Such as his being strongly opinionated, arrogant and disdainful of others.

Clearly refusing groups reaped some nasty consequences, which were not accounted for by the Patient Bill of Rights. Unless patients were dependent on staff, including providing the "right" answers to treatment queries, they failed to be seen as making treatment gains or progress. The part in the Patients' Bill of Rights about providers' respecting patients' individual differences or opinions, seemed like ideals that held little meaning in actual reality. Perhaps needing to be added to the list was the right of patients to have routinely updated treatment programs based on evidenced-based research.

Windshield time, the nearly two hours between St. Peter and where I lived in southern Minnesota, was my cognitive reorganization time. The standard conclusion about Ron was not easy to accept, but that was my problem; there was nothing more I could do on any single issue of Ron's case. At one point in time I had been an idealist, crash program-reduced to a hard-core realist. In the face of the chronic injustices that had been heaped onto Ron, my realism was verging on cynicism. Hospitals were supposed to be places of healing, staffed by compassionate healers. However, I had to accept this was the ideal, unfortunately not always the reality.

I remained concerned that my report had been copied and entered into Ron's chart. I had never in my career seen this happen. Was it to let his treatment providers know someone was recommending Ron's release so that it could be blocked? Was it just to offer a "heads up" related to Ron's case? Looking back, I wish I had asked more questions, including calling the Douglas County Court Services to inquire how it was that a report for a yet unheard case had been sent to the holding institution?

But, then, the report had been in Ron's file for a few weeks before I was aware of it, so it would be a late complaint. Interestingly no one, such as Ron's caregivers commented about it to me. Perhaps they did not even notice it. Perhaps the charts were not read that often, only entries were added; no one assessed progress. It was bizarre. It never had happened before, and it never happened afterwards. The only time witnessed such a thing was in Ron's case.

The Issue re: Dangerousness

One of the most significant differences between people who are hospitalized in community hospitals and those in state hospitals is the existence of some dangerous aspect in their history. Perhaps they attacked others in the midst of psychosis, or they had killed others related to voices commanding they do so, or perhaps they had been victimized one time too many, and they were going to end it one way or another. I had a habit of asking staff who were familiar with the individual I was about to interview, if the person in question had engaged in recent dangerous behavior towards others. It did not matter what setting they were in, jails, group homes, treatment centers. Did they recently exhibit dangerous behavior? If the answer was yes, I would ask for some adjustment to the interviewing accommodations. The available choices were a plexiglass interview room, staff presence in the interview room, or, at a jail I could sit on a chair outside a private cell and talk to the person through the bars. If the situation was too bad, I could reschedule. Always, I was conscious of my own safety.

There were some individuals whom I would be interviewing who exhibited what I call spooky behaviors. While I have never seen this adjective in diagnostic reviews, it is an innate skill that in my profession, can keep us from getting pummeled or worse. This innate skill can also be like a lantern in a dark forest, in sensing deceit or worse in some folks, a sensing of something that is out of place or wrong. It is like looking at a deer in the woods who is calmly eating, only to suddenly stop, look around, pause and then dart away. Self-preservation is a good instinct to have.

Some people I talk with are subtly distracted, vague in their responses, or have a history of being unpredictable and acting out in violent ways as well. In most situations my interviews were visible on monitors, in some cases staff were present nearby, and in other cases there would be more than just me talking with the individual, so we outnumbered the person. In some situations, the person's attorney was present with me. But if I started to get uncomfortable when I was alone with someone, I would excuse myself, end the interview and say I would be back another time.

I have only had two attacks so far in my career. In one situation a female patient in Florida threw a folding chair at me (fortunately, she missed), and another time, a female patient grabbed my hair when she was walking by me in her padded room (this was my fault, for she was walking around naked but covered with a hospital gown, singing the alphabet song). She was quick

255

and ,staff who were present were on her in a flash. Both of these instances were necessary lesion I never forgot.

Dangerousness is one of the main issues that causes people to remain confined in state hospitals. Some of them are so dangerous, for a variety of reasons not all their doing and they will never be able to leave. It sounds strangely abstract, but dangerousness can be measured. This is a not a necessary process for people who have a history of demonstrating repeat acts of overt aggression towards others over time, but which is helpful related to patients who are confined related to their legal status, say related to commitment. There are assessment tools developed by multiple companies each year for this very purpose such as manuals, hand-outs, training programs and certificates of completion to participants.

Risk assessment is big business. Institutions housing individuals with dangerous behaviors are eager to demonstrate their programs can reduce dangerousness prior to release; thus, rating tools are used to note progress or lack thereof in patient charts or prisoner files as dangerousness is assessed in multiple settings. Training programs are plentiful, so professionals can learn how to assess risk, touting the advantages of certain instruments over others as to accuracy. There are short term and lifetime risk indicators. There are risk factors exclusively for sex offenders versus general violence. And there are mitigating factors for risk, like aging, and treatment completion. As well, there are records for individuals noting their risk is never changing.

While science is portrayed as anchoring the assessment of risk/dangerousness, differences in levels of training and experience can cause variance in inter-rater reliability. In most cases, training different levels of professionals with different population management backgrounds becomes an institutional goal in determining risk.

Historically, the most robust predictors of future violence include: high scores on both static (non-changeable things like sex, criminal history including post treatment re-offense, diagnosis of antisocial orientation or personality disorder, evidence of psychopathy) and dynamic risk factors (changeable through treatment, like impulsivity, anger, substance abuse). With time and some types of treatment it is possible that the combination of factors that make some people dangerous, can change.

In the case of civil commitment, like Ron's case, there is legal criteria for a person both entering and exiting a facility. Not being seen as dangerous can depend on the person's behavior over time in various settings. The problem is that we all know of people who spent a lot of time locked up and did not really change at all. So, one wonders about the accuracy of assessing a person's ability to lie about an issue or pretend to change in a certain artificial environment.

The construct of "dangerousness "and its determination has existed since ancient Rome. The Romans separated responsibility and irresponsibility for one's actions into two categories: those who were accountable and those who weren't. Thus, the idea of non-compos mentis, no possession of mind. In the 1700's people who were not seen as "normal" and who acted "crazed" were seen as fitting into a notion like that of a wild beast with the term "wild beast" included in a judge's charge to the jury of a trial in the early 1700s.

The 1723 landmark case was that of Edward Arnold who wounded a lord based on the belief that this man was persecuting him Edward's neighbors and family repeatedly talked of his fits of rage and nicknamed him "Mad Ed." At the time a notion of a "wild beast" standard had become a popular way to describe mentally ill individuals who acted in some out of control manner ending in the harm or death of family, neighbors or strangers. At a time when there was little actual care for the mentally ill, such individuals

258

would be shunned by their family and neighbors or forced to leave and live elsewhere. Since such confinement of such people was limited and unhelpful at best in solving the problems they presented, the "Wild Beast" metaphor for their behavior sufficed to warn others of their unbridled and sometimes unprovoked harm.

As the conditions of mental illness became better understood, the actual construct of dangerousness started to take on a variety of definitions, generalized as the propensity to be uncontrollably violent towards others without consideration of one's actions or responsibilities. Later it would be categorized related to the severity of one's actions, from degrees of assault to murder, to reflective types of dangerousness related to the actions being sexual rather than limited to physical aggression with or without a weapon or involving threats of harm. It is also important that such ratings or scores related to dangerousness are consistent with records related to the persons actual observed behaviors. If there are inconsistencies, these must be explained and clarified.

Dangerousness is defined as a general context related to an individual, with such behavior within civil and criminal contexts having specific and lengthy criteria. In Ron's case, the designation of MI and D included evidence to support lethal harm or death to another in combination with a designated mental illness and other caveats as previously mentioned.

The first generation of predictions of dangerousness occurred during the 1970's with determinations ultimately seen as inaccurate/wrong, two out of three times. These decisions were based on the practice of psychiatrists, and only psychiatrist, reviewing the diagnosis and arrest records of the person in question without a face to face interview and when the concept of differential diagnoses was yet unknown. As such, the failures in accuracy contributed to a growing public consensus of being wary of psychiatric assessment and opinion.

The second generation of dangerousness predictions occurred in the 1980's and fared little better in the ability to predict future dangerousness despite the addition of short-term assessment. This resulted in curiosity about what happened or failed to happen in psychiatric evaluations that resulted in such poor track records of prediction.

By the 1990's researchers focus on the assessment and measure of static (unchangeable) risk factors noted in follow-up data of individuals who repeated violence towards others (factors like gender, current age, age at the time of first offense, age at the time of release, type of violence, violation of conditional release, relationship stability and positive peer relationships.

Ron had been noted as specifically "not meeting the criteria for dangerousness" in 2006, twenty years after he entered the state hospital. He may have met this criterion before 2006 but had not been formally assessed. One persisting problem was, if he was no longer dangerous, what about his mental illness merited his continued confinement?

His records in 2006 failed to identify any active symptoms of a major mental illness such as psychosis or threats of harm to himself or others. Of particular interest is the context he was in, including many, many professional care givers who interacted with him every day for years.

The generally known frequency of individually violent acts in an average community during the early 2000's was 2% with 10-12% of violent behavior at the time secondary to the influence of a major affective disorder such as bipolar disorder or schizophrenia, 19% involving drug abuse, 25% involving alcohol abuse and 35% involving use of more than one substance. The general rate of violence at the time was 50-75% higher for a person with more than two psychiatric diagnoses AND co-occurring substance abuse AND either a major thought disorder or a major affective disorder.

As to Ron's specific criminal act at the time it occurred, the *2005 International Journal of Forensic Mental Health,* cited research involving "Recidivistic Single Victim Homicide" noting a prevalence of 1-3.5% for such an event. An earlier 1999 study noted women killed by their significant others totaled 0.96 per 100,000 deaths. These studies noted limitations related to the paucity of research in this area and time constraints for follow-up data. The frequency of murder of an intimate other in Minnesota was even less frequent.

Only a few professionals were documented as challenging or questioning the extent and/or severity of Ron's psychiatric symptoms over time. Even after the 2006 statement in his records that his dangerousness to others had been "managed," the category of "Dangerousness remained a component of his active medical record.

Examples of comments in this section included repeated mention of the death of his girlfriend being "accidental" and related to what he considered a "medication induced psychosis." He would be additionally described as exhibiting "unresolved precursors for dangerous behavior such as a "lack of insight into his illness and need for medications." As I have noted, the long-term goal related to "Dangerousness" was to "maintain clinical stability on a long-term basis."

Twenty years had passed, and this was still the goal! This, despite his March 29, 2007 MSH Individual Treatment Plan noting he had "maintained socially acceptable behavior and has been free of assault since his offense," thereby shedding the "D" part of his MI and D designation.

It was times like this when I questioned the possibility of staff burn-out. Who could be with mentally ill patients day in and day out, some with great needs of varied care, for your entire career, without considering, 'what do we need to do to enhance this patient's confinement experience?'

Eventually, entries in Ron's 2006 records would note his brief participation in groups entitled, "Blueprint for Change," "Computer" (he scored 100% on the final), "Health Education-Diabetes," "Refocus and Relaxation," "Frisbee Golf, and "Happy Hour," with the face value of such groups being opportunities for social skills training, at best. There was no reported or supportive research that these groups "treated "anything, definitely not dangerousness. No mention was made as to his 2004 assessment at St. Peter when he was assessed as being "low risk for aggression."

The reason I offer this information, is because this would be, and is, a commonly noted behavioral marker in state hospital patients; dangerous patients are the crux of treatment populations in state settings. However, the programming in Ron's unit was not cited as having credibility, research-wise, for reducing dangerousness.

Instead, it was a highly behavioral unit, limited to food treats to inspire compliance. The most basic of behavioral sanctions/perks were meant to encourage patients into adhering to "treatment goals," as established by the staff. Compliance and respect were expected. Non-compliant patients had to face endless boredom; little to no fresh air, few to no treats.

While risk can be assessed and measured, I did not see risk level as a standard chart entry in patient records for Ron or anyone else. Rather, risk appeared to be subjectively assessed and commented on by certain professionals based on their personal opinions and then entered in his records. Towards the end of Ron's hospitalization, when new experts were brought in, risk assessments were conducted on him related to psychopathy, with other scales used to describe his level of "risk" and in what areas.

Staff opinions appeared to vary related to Ron's programming/risk and the particular unit or ward in which he resided. Some staff may have resented Ron being savvy and knowing his Patient's Rights. And the different institutions in which he resided at various times also rated or discussed his risk and likeability in vastly different terms. When he was confined in St. Peter from the years 2004 onward, his records described him less favorably compared with his first living on this same campus following the shooting.

This did not make sense related to what he had accomplished the first time he was transferred from St. Peter to Willmar and onward to Duluth. Moreover, before returning to St. Peter in 2004 he had looked at living arrangements in the community, without finding a match he liked. To be considered for living outside of the hospital, he had to have made progress as to *not* exhibiting being dangerous.

As an outside consultant whose report promoted his release, I had to discuss this topic about Ron with the staff. I truly think the staff thought they were noting everything relevant in his record including his risk level for release. I also considered that the years of time in an unchanging setting might have fostered a mountain of complacency. No one was changing, staff or the patients; year after year they remained the same until, to the weary eyes, residents started to blend in with the wall tiles.

The psychiatrist on the unit who early on had wished Ron well in his bid for release, said he needed to remain "neutral" to the wishes of the treatment team. Another psychiatrist told me that he was not going to get involved with Ron's release efforts because he was planning on retiring from the hospital and did not want his involvement with Ron's case to negatively impact his retirement.

I was stunned. For a second, I considered questioning what he saw as his professional ethics. As a physician was not his job to assist patients to get better, so they could be discharged? I wanted to ask him if he had any qualms about remaining silent. I wanted to ask him to explain how he saw himself as a healer when he was basically turning his back on a patient he had stated in the records did not evidence danger to others.

Instead, being unable to respond to what I perceived as his lack of courage or integrity, I simply remained silent, full of regret. I believe that there are certain events or moments in our lives when we are at moral crossroad. If we take s some of these patient activities reduced dangerousness or had desirable outcomes? Instead, being unable to respond to his lack of integrity, I simply remained silent

And so, the groups were pushed, and Ron pushed back by attending them once or twice and then declaring that he was done with the groups, based on his reported patient's rights, and his not seeing the groups as being helpful to him.

At St. Peter, "Dangerousness" was a designation staff ascribed to patients, and it was a designation that only staff consensus could remove. Some patients, like Ron, had not exhibited dangerous behavior for years. It just didn't seem to matter.

If risk remained unmeasured, the backup plan in theory appeared to be to simply keep (some/many/most) patients there forever. Alternately, staff would make a list of activities, like "Harmonizing" or "Movie Classics" and make participation in them the way to demonstrate residents are not dangerous. followed by more hoops to jump through when, again, some reason was discovered to stall release. Eventually, patients often became unable to be released. They had lived so long in institutions they had no ability to be re-integrated back into their communities. Where were the questions about how some of these patient activities reduced dangerousness?

Continued "Treatment" Failures

Ron eventually declined groups at Shantz Hall following his stint at Bartlett Hall and would be charted as "challenging his patient's rights; obsessing about his case/situation; showing disrespect for hospital rules and staff; lacking insight into his psychiatric illness; and being in denial of his treatment needs" (again and again as already noted in his many past records). The consequence for these behaviors was to take away his fresh air time, and then his "pop breaks." His response was to send a note to the staff pointing out that as far as his no longer getting "pop breaks" he "had saved over $90 the preceding six months and had lost some weight." So much for "operant conditioning," a learning process through which the strength of a behavior is modified by reinforcement of punishment.

When I read about these seemingly endless situations in Ron's records, I struggled to see the staff not discussing ways they needed to improve the programming to make it instructive rather than punitive. I could imagine the staff lining both sides of the conference table listening to the "pop break" issue being discussed, their eyes glazing over from boredom. Still, I could not imagine how not a single soul interjected, "What is our purpose and plan to prompt helpful change? How about a checklist of other behaviors that speak to cooperation amongst patients and programming? Who wrote this rule about "pop breaks" in the first place and what was the true goal?"

More strange treatment examples were actually documented within Ron's medical chart. At one point when Ron requested his Risperdal be decreased, which was denied, the psychiatrist noted in the record, that "as a result of Ron's request to decrease this medication, it may be in fact, reasonable to increase the medication should he continue to demonstrate such poor insight!"

Shantz 1 West was a building surrounded by high walls and razor wire. When I would decide to see patients there, I would stand away from the building at an outer fenced perimeter and push a buzzer to alert staff. Then I would be asked by an unseen person to state my name and purpose, and seconds later a loud unlocking sound would occur ant I could open the chain-link gate to enter. There was a control area where I would present my identification, I would be shown an area for my coat if I had one, and non-necessary items (purse, keys) would be stored in a locker. The patient I was scheduled to see would be escorted by a direct care staff to where I was. The meeting rooms were adequate and included large windows so anyone passing could observe what was happening. Staff were accommodating and pleasant.

Ron's opinion was that the assessment resulting in his move to Shantz was "not an independent assessment but one copied from previous records." He said when he requested to see a social worker, sometimes he would get a visit, other times there would be no response. He asked for a physical exam prompted by new medical symptoms he noted, yet none was forthcoming, so he called the patient ombudsman. When he repeated a request to see a physician related to disturbed sleep from "pain" he said he was experiencing, there would be no response. The not so subtle behavioral message was, "When you go to your groups your requests will be acknowledged."

In addition to no "pop breaks" or fresh air time, a new requirement for Ron was to report how he spent his $5.00 allotment each week. Money issues were strictly monitored, including his once being written up for "exploiting" a fellow patient to whom he had given some stamps by informing this patient of the monetary cost of the stamps.

Rules and Guidelines at Shantz included patients being "expected to follow individual schedules." Failure to attend scheduled groups, classes and activities were noted as resulting in a "C" restriction. Patients were notified they needed to be signed out on the board and they needed to wait for 5 minutes by the board before an activity. Patients who arrived at the door after the staff escort had left would not be escorted to their scheduled activity. Patients on restrictions would not be able to leave the unit for leisure activities including evening or weekend activities, kitchen use or the canteen. One noted example of Ron's "unreasonable behavior" was charted as his approaching the nurses' desk in the morning and asking if he could get mail he failed to pick up the previous afternoon with the rule being repeated that, "mail is only distributed at a specific afternoon time."

What stood in the way of Ron getting fresh air was his (again) failing to attend the "treatment groups." His canteen visits were restricted when he failed to attend certain classes, like "Wellness," Harmonizing, "Happy Hour" and "Movie Classics." When he failed to attend he would be described as "unable to redirect his energy into constructive activities," which indicated he required increased monitoring. In other instances, his "failure" to follow his treatment plan was seen as evidence of his "paranoid ideation and denial of his mental illness."

Another requirement was patients' sharing written journals of their thoughts or facing loss of freedom. Ron's longstanding reason for not journaling was that such information was "confidential" and things he wrote could be used against him. Which was absolutely true. At one point he was charted as having contraband in the form of excessive cash on hand ($320) carefully sheltered within the pages of a book, reportedly to give to an unidentified family member in need. It did not help when he would get into discussions about his behavior with staff and refer to them as a "defendant" and their having a conflict of interest.

Special Review Board Hearings: Special or Unusual?

The first step towards release of a mental patient from a state institution is a formal meeting before the Special Review Board (SRB). This Board is comprised of three members: an attorney, psychiatrist/psychologist, and another member at large, who could be a retired professional with either a law or mental health background or a member of the public. Requirements include the attorney having two years of civil commitment experience, being licensed, in good standing, able to preside over hearings and deliberations and having writing skills to summarized information.

The psychiatrist/psychologist also needs to be licensed and a have a history of practicing in a clinical setting in the state; no specific forensic experience is noted as necessary. "Being familiar" with mental health issues is required and the word familiar is undefined. I noted that for "a two year period of familiarity" within a mental health or civil commitment area, unless one had a professional specialty such as forensic psychology, it would be most unlikely that you would experience the range of issues related to a patient designated as mentally ill and dangerous. "Familiarity," without a more expanded definition such as "experience and a working knowledge of mental health case law, including a history of evaluating respondents for a range of civil commitment issues and court evaluations, could be problematic to say the least. Never the less, these were the standards set and followed.

"Familiarity," alone does not fit with the serious responsibility related to the issue of freedom this board is expected to understand, consider and determine. Ron had met with the Special Review Board three previous times with spans of time in between: all resulted in denial without clear reasoning. I had only read about the SRB. I was in eager anticipation of actually observing how this reportedly time-honored process worked.

On the day of Ron's first scheduled SRB meeting I had the pleasure of meeting three of his long-time friends who showed up to offer him moral support. We introduced ourselves to each other, shook hands, shared how it was we each knew Ron and our hope for what might be able to be accomplished through the pending hearing.

Ron's three long -time easily represented the type of friends that are a circle of connections, tighter than even family. They had known each other since childhood. Fifty years and counting; they were forever friends. They shared with me, perhaps somewhat exaggeratedly, but thoroughly amusing, a few choice stories of their lives, interests and antics related to memorable sports events, car passions, and jokes they had played on each other. For a few brief moments it did seem like laughter was a good medicine.

One of Ron's gentleman friends reminded me of the Marlboro man on the cigarette ads on TV that I remembered as a kid. He was very distinguished looking with his impressive handlebar moustache, western wear and sparkle in his eye, as well as his engaging personality. I recognized his name as the friend who had been banned from state property and I asked him what exactly he did to earn that distinction to which he reported, "I carried a box of legal records from Ron's old room to his new room. They called it contraband and I was escorted out of the building by a guy on each side of me holding my arm. They told not to come back. A few days later I got a letter in the mail that told me I was persona non grata on state property!" Despite this ban, he assured me he was safe to be attending the SRB meeting. The other men seemed to like the notion of his being the Marlboro man and I said if that didn't match, he could have been a stand-in for someone on *Bonanza*, a former popular western series.

Despite my primary and professional connection with Ron, in the midst of this group of his friends, I felt like at least an extension of Ron's his support team. It was truly an experience of split emotions, with the stories of humorous times amidst the serious backdrop of Ron's long and dragged out MI and D situation. No one had forgotten that.

Ron arrived to the SRB meeting room in a blue suit, white shirt and dark tie; he would later apologize to me for wearing white socks with his black dress shoes, noting he no longer owned a pair of navy blue socks. He was escorted to the hearing room by two direct care workers who talked loudly to him like he was hard of hearing and feeble minded. I was taken aback by this observation as Ron was anything but feeble minded; to see him treated like this was completely foreign to me. These particular staff had been familiar with Ron for years; how was it that they interacted with him as though he was intellectually compromised?

Hospital staff started to gather in the large room and took chairs in a huge semicircle facing a large table with a large TV screen as the hearing was held via interactive television connecting Douglas County, the SRB office in St. Paul with us and us with them. The only hospital professional staff included the Minnesota State Forensic Services psychologist who spent a documented 30 minutes talking with Ron, a hospital social worker, his Douglas County social worker, and an IT professional. No psychiatrist or physician ever attended these meetings when I was there. From my point of view, this was surprising. How could there be a meeting of importance without Ron's doctor?

The TV screen was divided into two parts; on one side was a view of the room in which we were siting and on the other half of the screen was a view of a room where the three SRB members would be seated. Also present in a distant location was the Douglas County attorney opposing Ron's release. At the designated time a switch was turned on and both groups could hear each other and interact.

The three SRB members were briefly identified by name; there were a limited number of announcements of the issue at hand. We were invited to present our information following Ryan Magnus' offering what was similar to an opening statement. The hospital representatives followed with their brief statements. The opposing Douglas County attorney said that since Ron was "unable to explain his reasoning for shooting his friend over 20 years ago, there was a high likelihood that a similar shooting could occur again." I was struck by these words. Had he not reviewed the years of treatment reports sent to the county noting Ron had gained freedoms because of his cooperative behavior and more recently, at St. Peter had shed the "dangerousness" designation.

The meeting was scheduled for one hour of time; it started 15 minutes late and the IT connection was lost for ten minutes so the total time discussing Ron's case was approximately 30 minutes. The hearing ended promptly. Considering the preparation and expectation that I had for this first meeting, the shock of it ending before anything was mentioned, let alone discussed in any depth, was outstandingly disappointing.

Additionally, shocking was that such a supposedly important meeting failed to start on time, with no explanation as to the delay. The concluding recommendation was that the proceedings would continue to allow for the gathering of more information. I found it disillusioning that one hour had been set aside to discuss a case that involved a man's freedom after over 20 years of confinement. I understood setting time limits, but one hour, actually less due to the technical difficulties, seemed very short, to present information upon which serious decisions would be ultimately based. Before there was any discussion of the evidence of the day, the meeting was over.

Following the first SRB meeting I was surprised to read in the August 25, 2006 *Findings of Fact and Recommendations*, that I was mentioned in Factor IV, paragraph 2: they stated my name and credentials, and said I had "opined that the history of controlled environment and current programming will do nothing to "prevent harm" to others. This was patently untrue. Thus, I responded with a letter to the SRB Coordinator in St. Paul noting the inaccurate wording, correcting the statement as "current programming is not supported by research as preventing harm," which was an important difference. The standards demonstrated by the review boards so far were dismal. They did not demonstrate that they were truly doing anything for the state, the patient or their own credibility. It was a ridiculous demonstration of getting nothing done as quickly as possible. With the case because they had reviewed the previous board's written notes of the case at hand, or if they were just sitting there listening to what was being said for the first time. The information sent to the board was from the hospital, but no identification of specific records was included as a reference. One of the three new board members was over 30 minutes late, encroaching on our hour of total allotted time, again.

Was this not a serious enough scheduled meeting to warrant a phone call and apology to all present, including Ron for whatever reason this person was late? Once again, I came away from this meeting more than concerned with the process. I was also very curious about these supposedly responsible positions that so far had failed to measure up to even low standards of protocol and far short of what I expected from the stated importance of this Board. Perhaps things would get more organized; perhaps this was just more bureaucratic nonsense.

The November 21, 2006 *Findings of Fact* for the next denial noted Ron's entire history and in particular his reportedly "exhibiting symptoms of mental illness including hoarding papers and other items (the Elvis memorabilia) leading to his room at Arrowhead in Duluth being filled with objects." Ron was also noted as "leaving the State in violation of his provisional discharge plan, to obtain a trailer and find storage." It was uncomfortable to read certain facts mis-stated, apparently related to lack of verification. For example, how this "hoarding" situation was seen as dangerous in the face of his plans to remedy the problem?

It was clear entries included for the board were not based on actual facts, but rather, they were arranged to accomplish a specific goal: discredit the patient. All the comments in the world about objectivity, patient rights, and medical acumen were just hollow words in Ron's case; I was beginning to doubt these lofty ideals were ever ethically applied. These review hearings were huge lessons in disappointment and lost purpose. They were a like the story of the Emperor's New Clothes. There were no new clothes, yet everyone kept acting like nothing was wrong.

Consistently, when Ron declined to go to groups, he could expect some kind of retaliation. Following the first SRB meeting he lost several hours of liberty in exchange for missing groups. By the time of the continued meeting his quarterly review summary noted he had accumulated seventeen liberty reductions over the past few months, which was, "Standard procedure," according to staff.

The last SRB hearing was in December of 2007, the result of customary scheduling changes and inevitable weather problems. The longer the wait, the greater the pressure and anticipated disappointment. Ron remained maturely calm and controlled. The Board consisted of three new panel members who may or may not have reviewed collateral documents or been appraised of what occurred in the other meetings. One member, the moderator, was 40 minutes late for an unexplained reason, so the 9 a.m. meeting did not get started until 9:40 and went to 10:40. Again, the meeting was a disappointment and we all were subjected to people in responsible positions acting completely irresponsible.

The one ray of hope during the waiting time was the support of Ron's friends and their humor. During the time we were all waiting for the missing board member, the IT screen revealed a table with three chairs and two members present with the middle chair empty. Ron's friend, the "Marlboro Man, leaned over to Ron and whispered, "Well, at least they eliminated the middleman." Ron chuckled. I heard the comment and smiled to myself, appreciating the healing power of humor. The sad part was, that nothing about these hearings was impressive or humorous. Who was the watchdog of this system?

Ultimately, harder to take than the uneven hearing process, was the SRB's outright denial of Ron's request for a full discharge. Not surprisingly, familiar old information in the form of long ago recorded symptoms were used in the summary of findings, along with a damning account of Ron's declining to attend treatment groups. The opinion was that Ron "failed to present a persuasive enough case for discharge." The wording was curious; his good behaviors were not persuasive enough, but there were no hints as to what was missing to make it "enough." For years and years, there had been no acts of violence or threats of violence. Again, I was frustrated because it was too vague a decision.

Ryan Magnus had a new approach in mind. He would request a Provisional Discharge which had attached community support conditions, a proposition that differed from the full discharge request, which had no conditions. After a mirror image of a hearing date, new dates, and renewed effort, our energy was met with a denial of even a provisional discharge for the reason, "Failure to present a persuasive enough case."

It was painful to keep losing. Perhaps the SRB was in caution-mode. Apparently, some past problems with the Special Review Board had surfaced from time to time in the *Pioneer Press*, a major Twin Cities newspaper, like a recent one related to the hospital's supposedly recurring failure to track discharged patients on supervised releases. Another story was related to the Board's pending decision to grant the release of a particular sex offender with over two dozen victims, with no reported objections by the same state hospital holding Ron. A third publicized report related to two psychiatrists reportedly falsifying medical records to support and justify their treatment claims for a particular patient.

My apparently unreasonable expectations of the SRB were for them to be objective, ask questions and search out answers. Instead, the process with the SRB was like a mindless assembly line. Their hollow denial of Ron's provisional discharge with claims of a "lack of persuasive information" was an easy and repetitious way to keep saying what they had already said before; no details were offered, such as specific areas where they lacked specific information. This conclusion was also akin to the pot calling the kettle black; this board did not offer "persuasive information" as to their denial! While evidence had been presented related to each of the release criteria, the Board either did not hear it or failed to address it specifically.

As a result, Mr. Magnus petitioned the Court of Appeals for reconsideration of both the denied full and provisional discharge. This was the hoped-for "Hail Mary" pass in Ron's case. The new petition was most of all a turning point in which it was made clear that we were not going away. Higher levels of power and decision making were available; the direction of the case was changing. Ron's case would be heard before a Supreme Court Appellate Court Panel, SCAP.

My driving time following the Special Review Board hearings were just depressing. I was frustrated related to the three professionals supposedly in law and mental health who had jobs to do and couldn't even show up on time, let alone get demonstrate a basic understanding of the case. I saw what they offered as a waste of time and money for sure. After three disappointing demonstrations of their collectively expected skill levels I was done. They were a useless resource. To Ron' credit and resilience, he never complained. He remained calm, enjoyed his friends when he saw them and kept moving on when that was all we could do. With great resilience he seemed to be handling the stress of the situation.

The SRB did essentially nothing, and their reports said nothing. I wondered if families wrote to complain of what was happening to their family members who faced these review boards. Failing to show up on time is not acceptable at the adult level of responsibility, yet lack of punctuality was a consistent problem with every meeting.

I have to say the one ray of hope was the SCAP judges who would hear our case. I knew this system to be more efficient and on target. But it was still a wait and see situation.

The drive home each day was long and empty. I remained insulted that a room full of people (us) had been kept waiting with no explanation, on more than one occasion for a very serious meeting to take place. If I thought writing to someone could or would make things better, I argued with myself that such a defunct system was beyond being understood. These board positions were not that of excellence. What meeting of importance can be conducted in an hour when members are thirty minutes late. It was a kangaroo court situation. A disappointing experience of the state level of expertise. Driving in the rain helped wash the bad taste out of my system.

It was more important to focus on what needed to be said and done next, for Ron's case. I could not fix these Special Review Board people, but I could hold out hope for the SCAP.

The Three Appellate Judges

The Appellate Panel that first heard Ron's case consisted of three middle-aged women judges. As Supreme Court Appeal Panel Judges I expected them to be knowledgeable in the law, unlike our experiences with the Special Review Board made up of lay professionals. To my relief, the three judges were on time and organized. They were poker-faced throughout the proceedings and the mood in the room was serious.

After I was sworn in and qualified as a forensic expert, direct questioning began. I had testified literally thousands of times and felt confident; added to my good feelings was the fact that Ryan Magnus could be masterful in court; organized, on point, not missing a beat. He laid out the case in a manner that was clear and passionate, calm and articulate. He began by asking my role in Ron's case and I stated I was not an advocate for Ron, but instead an advocate for the statutory criteria. I offered information to the court from my evaluation related to whether the person in question met or failed meet the specific criteria being considered.

Ron's history included his first being hospitalized, then provisionally discharged, and finally returned on a revoked discharge that did not include any act or threat of harm. He had been returned to St. Peter where he started in 1986. I reported my review of his many records noting an absence of aggression or violence over two decades despite times when he was described as angry. I reported what I had learned about the treatment programming he had completed long before and the current programming he was expected to complete. I noted no research existed and most likely never would related to Harmonizing, Frisbee Golf, Movie Classics and Cooking having any direct impact on his history of mental illness or lessening his future risk for dangerousness. I noted his being seen as no longer meeting the criteria for dangerousness but continuing to remain confined as mentally ill.

Documented symptoms in Ron's records compared with his presentation over years of time were noted, in my opinion, to be at odds with each other. I recounted the years that had passed since his admission, his last administration of emergency medication, his years of living in Duluth at a group home, driving to his appointments and his current freedom being restricted in retaliation for his declining to attend groups that held no interest for him.

He had been a successful business man and was now required to document and explain how he spent the five dollars he was given each week a requirement which was insulting, and Ron adding these five dollars couldn't even buy him a breath of fresh air, as his walking outside had also been taken away as a consequence for not attending groups. Ron consistently had a list of individual goals to accomplish on his treatment plan. When he accomplished these goals, new ones would be established, and the process would be ongoing with no end in sight.

Ron had been described in some entries as "threatening to staff" which needed to be clarified as his threatening to sue them or turn them over to their professional boards." He had never been physically threatening to anyone over the decades since that one fateful night.

On redirect, I was asked by the attorney representing the Attorney General's office about the need to keep Ron in a controlled setting to assure his taking medication. My response was that the statutes did not support a person being committed or confined or enduring a loss of liberty simply to take medication.

When this same attorney challenged me that if Ron was not confined, he could skip his medication, I noted Minnesota statutes stated it was failing to take medication *and* demonstrating harm to self or others as a result of not taking meds that warranted commitment. I added that, if this attorney was suggesting everyone who was supposed to take medication but wasn't, should be committed, the state would need a fleet of trains and busses to transport this huge crowd of lay people to available state institutions.

My opinion was that Ron should receive a full discharge because he had demonstrated himself as being capable of adjustment to a community. I also acknowledged his need for some services to ease his reintegration into the community. I was thanked for my testimony before returning to my place in the courtroom.

It was then that a most unusual situation occurred. The three judges rose from their chairs, stepped back a few feet and formed a "huddle" with their arms around each other's shoulders, their heads bowed as they quietly conferred with each other. After a brief pause, the huddle broke and the lead judge stated they agreed with the testimony and had decided they were going to immediately advance Ron's case to the Appellate level!

We were so used to losing by this point that we sat stunned by our win! I also noted that Ron, sitting next to his attorney also turned his head towards his attorney, also apparently surprised that for once his case was looking up, at least briefly. He had been calm throughout the Review Board hearings, but then the opinions of the board were never offered live, instead, their negative results came later in the form of a letter. At long last, it felt like a new day for Ron.

In under two hours with this three judge panel, we had convinced them this was a case that needed to be heard in full.

The ride home that day included visions of grandeur as I relived the judges' questions, my responses, the demonstration by the attorney for the state when he confused a person having to be in the hospital to take medication, completely ignoring the reality that throngs of people in their own homes were unable to do this.

The best part to relive was the fact that I had engaged in this same dialogue a thousand times and I had been so ready for it. When I repeated the statutory wording that it was not failing to take medications that was at issue, but also engaging in an act of harm related to not taking medications, the attorney from the Minnesota Attorney General's Office sat there looking lost. It was a point I had been primed for over years of time and when it presented itself again, and finally went well, my only reaction was to just relive it again and again and wallow and bask as I gloated. After so much frustration, we all were ready to savor the rare moments of triumph.

I could not wait to see how this court experience would be written up. However, since yet an additional Independent Expert was now on board this would take additional time...again. My hope was that this new independent examiner, would also see the reasonableness of our position, especially when Ron would be interviewed. The wheels of the court sometimes feel like they are square, since it takes so much time to move forward. I was going to place my hope on everyone except the hospital social worker. I could only imagine how whoever was sent to court to represent their group would repeat what I had been read in Ron's chart related to his empty programming.

The Last Step

The Independent Examiner was to conduct an updated risk assessment of Ron and provide the court with information as to whether Ron's provisional discharge plan had the necessary elements to assist him with adjusting to the community and assuring public safety. This examiner also candidly acknowledged that Ron would have difficulty accomplishing specifics, absent the effort of his treatment team in arranging contacts for him.

As of this time there had been no investigation of appropriate living arrangements/placement settings for him, not contact with case management services in the area and no indentation of a community psychiatrist or other mental health provider who would accept him for treatment. It was further noted that some available services did not offer case management for provisionally discharged adults and fewer communities had a psychiatrist on staff to monitor or supervise Ron's medication.

Such issues constituted the Real Catch 22 for any person seeking discharge from a state institution; without actually getting discharged you are unable to move on, schedule anything, and no one is going to get involved with someone who is "attempting" discharge.

And the biggest problems included no offers of any assistance towards discharge from the state hospital in St. Peter. Neither was there assistance form Ron's Douglas County case manager, who had entered only negative interpretations of Ron's behavior into his records, the St. Peter social worker, or treatment providers who had different opinions but unitedly opposed any and all notions of release for Ron. Without someone to assist him with discharge, he was never going anywhere. No one broke rank.

I pondered this situation over many miles of driving. The energy of Ron's entire treatment team was against his moving on even though he had no acts of overt aggression since his 1986 admission. I found it difficult, to believe that all these professionals and co-workers maintained the exact same opinion and suspected they were united in thwarting Ron's release in any way they could. His own records were used as supporting his risk despite the fact that they failed to specify behavioral evidence of this risk: there were only notations of his declining programming in the last few years, reportedly because he had completed it previously: there were no acts or threats of harm to others to support their claims of risk. How could there be such divergence in this case between Ron and his caregivers. I continue to see it as fear of going against the group; I wondered the reason there were no pages in Ron's records where treatment providers discussed this issue of programming and what it included, failed to include and how it was working.

The hospital social worker said Ron needed "to continue to work on his relapse prevention plan and develop greater health awareness." She did, however, admit that the treatment team had not aided Ron in developing a provisional discharge plan because they did not support his request. She also testified that he had to jump through the hoops to move forward, along with stating there was little probability that what the team wanted Ron to do would further reduce his risk. How can a treatment team's perception of risk be changed when members of the treatment team tell are openly skeptical?

Ron's hospital psychiatrist who would eventually testify, was unable to name Ron's treating psychiatrist on the treatment ward, the stages of treatment in Ron's hospital regimen, or what types of treatment were offered on the various units. Then after demonstrating he was unable to identify any detailed information related to Ron's current treatment program of years of time, he unabashedly claimed, "Ron's plan lacked specificity!" The doctor concluded that ensuring medication compliance was the most important

296

factor for Ron's success in the community. After 23 years, who knew it was that simple? Was the reason the treatment program never varied or required research support because the most important factor for patient success was the medication? It must have been magic medication for sure. He had been compliant with his medication for years and yet was still did not qualify for release. This was sounding like plain defiance of release.

Next, to make his position more confusing, the hospital psychiatrist noted Ron had "probably learned all he could from his treatment and there is no further programming that has been shown to decrease an individual risk of re-offense within the treatment community." He then added, under oath, that Ron "needed to go through all of the steps of the program again, not for Ron's edification, but "in order for the team to ultimately support Ron's request for a provisional discharge." When asked how long this might take, the good doctor said, "It could take, "years."

We had all taken an oath to tell the truth. My observation of the hospital psychiatrist's position was that the truth for him was staying aligned with the institution, no matter what, no matter how hollow a position that might involve or how inane his responses were to questions by the court.

Even if the recommended groups were useless and there was no defined benefit in repeating them, still he needed more of the same.

Between these periods of testimony there is a waiting period for the Court opinions to be shared. These are the times of additional personal trials and tribulations as one thinks about the course of the questioning and the responses offered. There have been times when I have swelled in pride and joy reliving the hearing or moments of my trial testimony that were really good, to the point, and informative. I can admit to even gloating over what I thought were right-on, dead-center responses offered to complex queries. Then there are the times when I put myself through a "second trial" of my own making; feeling critical of my responses and regretting not offering a different and better answer. I wondered if the hospital psychiatrist had similarly reflected on his responses.

Ultimately, following such proceedings the state and defense create reports, called "Arguments" that summarize their respective opinions. The State's closing argument began with an introduction and procedural history of Ron beginning in 1986, his acquittal of 1st and 2nd Degree Murder, his revoked discharge in 2001 reportedly related to a reduction in his medication dosage and his reportedly beginning to "exhibit symptoms of his mental illness including the hoarding of papers and other items in his room at Arrowhead House, his leaving the state to obtain a trailer and his return to WRTC. Noted was Ron's initial petition to the SRB for a full discharge, which had been denied in November 2006 related to his "refusing to participate in treatment and instead, focusing on the existence of a mental illness (sic); (this was the actual wording). The following bullets were enumerated:

1. "Ron-maintains he does not need psychiatric medication and therefore is unlikely to take them if discharged;"
2. "Ron should work toward a provisional discharge and toward demonstrating psychiatric stability and appropriate behavior without medication;"
3. "Ron continues to need supervision in a treatment setting;" and
4. "Ron should not be fully discharged from his commitment as he is not capable of making an acceptable adjustment to open society without supervision and continues to be dangerous to the public unless subject to supervision."

The Special Review Board had denied the first and subsequent petition presented to them; an alternative petition for provisional discharge which was also denied."

The State's legal issue was "whether clear and convincing evidence establishes that the Appellant, Ron continues to be in (sic) in need of civil commitment." Listed "Facts" included: "Ron declining to be interviewed at his most recent SRB evaluation and it being completed without his participation: that Appellant had no juvenile or adult criminal history except for the shooting of his girlfriend resulting in his commitment; his giving varying accounts of the shooting but not acknowledging responsibility for the shooting; his not believing he has a mental illness and does not need medication to treat a mental illness; and has declined to participate in treatment groups in recent years"

Also listed were Ron's "increased symptoms in 2006 in the Transitions Unit when he was taken off medications," including becoming agitated, (allegedly) threatening staff, and being disorganized in his behaviors and thought processes, (no specific examples were noted), then agreeing to resume medications under threat of transfer to a more secure area but again refusing them a week later. Later in March 2007 he was transferred to Unit 800, the most secure unit of the Minnesota Security Hospital and while there "allegedly" complained of being poisoned by the food and fumes and believed he had been secretly medicated; his psychiatrist declared a behavioral emergency and had Appellant placed on emergency medications."

These were contrived reasons: he had only threatened to sue staff, never to physically assault them; he did not resist resuming his medication, and he had no history of complaining of being poisoned ever in his history; he was placed on emergency medications absent the medical record verifying this in detail. No information was offered of this inconsistency; no information was noted that he asked for his attorney to be informed of what was occurring, no reason was given as to why he could be transferred out of the unit in five weeks, which was record breaking for this unit! And then he was not transferred to a treatment unit, but a unit preparing patients (supposedly) for discharge.

The State pointed out, "Appellants' treatment team consistently did not support Ron's request for a full or provisional discharge. They said he had demonstrated "no progress in understanding his mental illness, does not recognize his need for treatment or ongoing need for psychiatric medication and stepped backward in treatment."

Also cited was the treatment team "not believing Ron's plan to live independently with a friend even if coupled with the typical provisions of a provisional discharge plan that would allow him successful adjustment to the community.

They called attention to particular doubt that Ron would be compliant with taking psychiatric medication, or participating in therapy or case management, but offered no evidence to support this doubt. They noted he needed on-going treatment and supervision in his current treatment setting. Repeated was the petition for discharge not being supported by Douglas County Attorney's Office or Douglas County Social Services Department.

This first written provisional discharge plan was denied.

This denial was explained with the statement, "There is no support in the record for a full discharge except for the testimony of Dr. Linderman, who believes Appellant is not receiving useful treatment at the Minnesota Security Hospital and that the treatment offered to him would be a waste of his time."

A 2007 Risk Appraisal by a MSH psychiatrist was used to repeat much of the same information along with noting that "at one time Appellant expressed a change of mind, stating that he no longer wanted to leave the hospital for fear of his life (supposedly noted in a May 25, 2007 report) along with noting his meeting 5 out of 20 risk factors from the HCR-20 ("HCR-20" stands for Historical/ Clinical/ Risk score involving 20 quick checklist items for risk) that served as the basis of the physicians' opinion against discharge. This was pure fabrication, as Ron had no expressed or written desire to stay at the hospital. (Of the 20 risk factors with Historical factors representative of the strongest predictors of risk Ron had one Historical item noted as "major mental illness;" the paragraph defining this item noted that "the substantial majority of individuals with severe mental disorder do not behave violently, research generally indicates that mental illness increases the odds of violent behavior" with Ron's history absent violent behavior since his 1986 admission.

Next offered was "clear and convincing evidence" in the direction of non-support for release due to a lack of protection to the public which, while previously discussed now included new and novel items. These included, "no evidence that Appellant's conservator (Ron's daughter) as agreeing to the proposed arrangement, Appellant never seeking input from his Douglas County caseworker apparently because of his paranoia towards Douglas County, and the proposed plan lacking commonsense restrictions related to prohibition of the possession or use of firearms, alcoholic beverages and unprescribed mind altering drugs."

Factors offered in support of Ron's discharge were the following: "Ron not exhibiting psychosis from 1986 through 2006 and his return to St. Peter from Willmar due to the WRTC closing; Ron's not requiring a Jarvis Order to comply with his neuroleptic medication, as well as his ability to manage with a tapered dose of Risperdal while remaining under supervision. Also listed was his engaging in business dealings involving a large corporation interested in some of his real estate holdings that caused him increased stress, with staff noting his becoming obsessed with the transactions and acting demeaning toward staff without a display of noted/actual physical aggression. Ron was also identified as being sent to Unit 800 in March of 2007, later resuming his original dose of Risperdal and being transferred out of this unit.

The second Court Ordered Independent Forensic Examiner conducted her risk assessment on Ron noting he rated "Low" on the measure of psychopathy. She also noted that his score on a Violence Risk Appraisal Guide predicted an 8% chance of recidivism in the next 7 years and a 10% probability in 10 years, described as a Low-Moderate risk from a clinical perspective. She also noted that "Ron has never been involved in a physically aggressive incident during his commitment, representing a low risk of violence in the community, with his records noting the distinction that his dangerousness to others was seen as having been managed since October 10, 2006. It was further noted that the current provisional discharge plan "has the necessary elements to help him adjust to the community and could ensure public protection related to a focus on continued medication compliance and stability within the community."

Ron's MSH psychiatrist testified "Many of Ron's risk factors were historical in nature and cannot be changed or managed to reduce risk from an actuarial perspective; that his symptoms were managed, and he continued to take medications as prescribed. That Ron was not seen as impulsive and not found to be a present risk of physical aggression. However, the provisional discharge plan lacked specificity but insured medication compliance which would support Ron's success in the community. He stated that Ron had basically learned everything he could learn from his treatment and there was no additional programming shown to decrease his risk of re-offense within the community."

The last item noted by the MSH psychiatrist during testimony was, "Ron needed to transition back through the steps to be supported in a provisional discharge to ensure he would remain medication compliant as the primary justification for a continued in-patient placement." The estimated time for this to be accomplished was answered as **"Years!"**

Likewise, the MSH Social Worker reported, "Ron could not be provisionally discharged without going through the process of reduction in security beginning again in the Transitions Unit from which he was transferred to unit 800 and this process may take several years;" "that Ron could not be supported into transitions by his treatment team unless he attends programs he has previously completed and which will have low to no impact on reducing risk other than to assist him in gaining insight into his illness;" that Ron's current placement does not provide assistance in developing and support a provisional discharge plan and hoops to get out, noting that Ron basically had to jump through these hoops to get out, noting these hoops had at least, in Ron's case, little probability of reducing his risk beyond its present low level."

The Court came to multiple different conclusions: finding that the Independent Psychological Examiner who did the updated independent risk assessment, and Ron's Independent Forensic Expert, (me) to be consistently similar, and more importantly, persuasive.

The Court did NOT find the testimony of the hospital psychiatrist persuasive and cited the list of information he was unable to provide as examples.

The Court noted Ron had provided the outline of an acceptable provisional discharge plan but would require assistance in locating a residence and finding necessary services. They noted his plan included supervision and agreed he was seen as capable of making an acceptable adjustment to open society with supportive services.

The Court noted the Minnesota Security Hospital had failed to prove that Ron had a continuing need for treatment in his current treatment setting.

Ron's motion for a Provisional Discharge from his civil commitment was therefore granted; the Special Review Board's decision denying Ron's petition for provisional discharge was reversed, and the Court ordered the treatment team to work with Ron to ensure that the necessary supportive services were in place upon his discharge to the community.

One of the judge's concurring opinion attached to the final order summed up the significant issues in Ron's case as his having been "simply required to attend and complete programs with the proper attitude" because he was in a unit where these programs were expected to be completed. When he refused, he was identified as having a "negative attitude." It was also noted that his treatment team failed to support either a full or provisional discharge because they did not like it, and because he was in a unit were patients were not even eligible for discharge planning services. This judge noted that Ron was essentially in a Catch 22 situation.

The multiple mental health service delivery levels involved with Ron's case were blind to Ron's situation, and unfortunately to their own situation of being blind! Patient rights were being violated; the statutory criteria for release had been replaced by completion of a list of programs that had nothing to do with reducing risk. Not realizing that, they saw the only option after 20 years...as more of the same. The entire situation was seen as a shocking demonstration of the bottom line for a certain type of psychiatric care, patient rights, common sense, treatment excellence, professional acumen and human compassion.

It may have been that the hospital psychiatrist was never given a copy of the court findings, or that he may have never read the findings of the Appellate Court or known his information was described as "unpersuasive." He may never have seen the printed Order that Ron was to be released rather than repeating treatment groups that the doctor himself described as, "basically useless."

The best part about losing so many times before this great win was that the total victory now was so very, very, sweet. I was so pleased to have had a part in this process. We joined effort for someone who really needed us; we persevered in the face of abject disrespect for our cause by treatment professionals blind to reason/patient rights; we survived ineffective SRB hearings with technical problems and one hour time limits to present decades of information and lay the groundwork for a patient's rights; we endured SBR members tardiness.

Being consumed by Ron's situation was not difficult. Certainly, it was not entirely an experience of smooth sailing. And at the time of our wonderful gains, we knew there were challenges ahead. We just underestimated how many there would be, the varying levels of difficulty and how long they would last.

I couldn't have driven enough miles or hours to get tired of repeating this information over and over in my head. I loved every minute of the hearing. Finally, there was a verbalized set of opinions consistent with Ron's records, his personal statements and his behaviors over years and years of time. I would have been only happier, if the judges had lined up Ron's treatment providers and basically shamed them for capricious management of his case, empty treatment results statements unable to be supported from his record, and explanations related to the reason this patient kept repeating itself over and over. It was a fantasy, egotistically derived for what they needed to happen for them not him. Would never happen. I did wonder what it was like for this team to leave the court hearing with a different order to follow. What questions did they ask of each other? Did they feel ashamed professionally for missing the point of treatment for Ron? Did they learn anything?

And Ron, well, Ron was in disbelief. He was relieved, and pleased, and hopeful and tired, very weary of his long fight towards freedom.

The End is not The End

Surprises related to Ron's case never seemed to end. While the Court issued an Order for Ron's release from confinement at St. Peter in 30 days, I noted with mixed annoyance and exhaustion that his main file interpreted the order much differently. One of the psychiatrists in the unit wrote in his medical file that Ron would be "unable to get an appointment with a community psychiatrist for at least six months," as though the court order would have to be changed to accommodate an appointment with the doctor. She truly misunderstood what was happening. I guess she assumed Ron's freedom depended solely on the approval/acceptance of a new psychiatrist taking Ron's case.

But our newest and immediate challenge was bigger, unexpected and ugly to say the least. While over a dozen assisted living/group home possibilities were available for Ron, many of which he had visited personally, reportedly, Mr. Black, and Ron's conservator teamed up and dutifully called each one, informing them of Ron's history and the fact that their accepting Ron as a new resident might carry risk. Their message repeated Ron's "violent history," suggesting he may not be the kind of resident their facility would like to explain to the community. Who knew if his good behavior the past greater than two decades was a sure thing? How would people in the neighborhood like to know a killer was living next door to their family member or children?

Each and every one of the possible dozen placements yielded to the scare tactics and declined to accept Ron. One by one, each and every facility that had met and liked Ron would send the letter stating, "your criminal background is inconsistent with our community," or words to that effect.

When Ryan Magnus called me to share what was happening, I was surprised to say the least. I lived in the southern part of the state, far away basically from the central lake region in Douglas County, and I suggested he call an assisted living facility I knew about in my community, and tell them I would personally vouch for Ron, hands down. This assisted living facility was called Reflections.

Reflections also got the calls from Mr. Black and conservator. Ultimately, to their credit, Reflections handled this situation by saying they would *only* take Ron *if they did not have interact with the likes of Mr. Black and Ron's conservator.* I had more respect for this facility and their staff than ever. I loved their "pluck." We were not alone. Ron was not alone.

What I found out later, after Ron had passed away, was that he was not aware of the facilities he had previously visited and liked, that later declined to accept him, nor was he made aware of the reason Mr. Magnus was driving him to Austin, Minnesota where Reflections was located. Ron Jr. was also not aware of how his father ended up at Reflections until I shared this story with him in 2018. Ron Jr. said he thought his father being placed so far away from home was on purpose, by the hospital, to make his life separate from his family. For many years Ron Jr. had carried this resentment for a situation never asked about. When we were talking on one occasion and he commented "How in the world did the hospital decide on Reflections way down in the southern part of the state? It took me hours to drive to see him." When I told him the story he became very quiet. Apparently, he had carried a grudge related to this placement, that I did not know about. When he talked about what happened he could hardly believe the additional struggle his father had to endure basically related to Mr. Black and the conservator.

Despite applications for emergency funding was being sought during the time Ron lived at Reflections, it was actually Ron Jr. who footed the bill.

No funding was forthcoming from emergency sources by the time we needed to get Ron placed, and little to no money was forthcoming from Ron's conservator or Mr. Black who apparently were upset that, yet a new facility had been found, especially one that called their bluff and told them to back off. Ron was headed to Austin, Minnesota, home of the world famous SPAM museum.

Ryan called to let me know when he and Ron would be arriving in Austin, and my husband John and I met them for lunch at Piggy Blues, a local rib joint. When they arrived, there was Ron wearing his navy blue business suit, white shirt and navy tie, looking like he just won the lottery.

The magic was unbroken until we sat down to order. The waitress started with Ron and when she asked him what he wanted, for a few seconds he sat speechless, stunned almost. I guess this question caught him off guard because there were few to no waitresses at the state hospital dining areas and his having choice es and options related to food and eating, left him, well, speechless.

After lunch Ron was driven to Reflections, a large, Victorian style home on a corner lot, with beautiful oak woodwork, wainscoting in each room and sliding pocket doors common to the day, that closed or opened up a room depending on the need. It had been a rather elegant home of the past, converted into an assisted living residence. A covered open porch at the top of the entrance of stairs greeted guests; this would be where Ron would sit talking to his buddies on his very own cell phone that they gave him. The inside floorplan included an oak paneled living room, dining room, kitchen, and open staircase on the first floor with bedrooms and baths on the second floor.

The dining room had a round table and long windows that spilled sunshine into the homey room. The kitchen also had a large round table for breakfast and coffee with high windows that looked onto the back yard. Reflections housed eight residents. It was within walking distance to downtown and nearby cafés for coffee or lunch or burger places. Ron could walk around a quiet neighborhood where it was safe to ride a bike, and rides to the medical appointments were provided. The house became a holiday showplace at Christmas time. The residents were mostly elderly, and Ron talked easily with them all. He helped one gentleman who was his roommate who had periods of confusion. One day when I visited Ron told me a new resident had once lived in Alexandria and they could share memories about the city; Ron was excited that the person knew of his former grain dryer business and people from the area. In fact, only disadvantages were the bedrooms were small and he was a distance from Ron Jr.

During his time at Reflections, Ron attended family funerals and saw people he had not seen in years. He also regularly visited with the pastor at St. Olaf Lutheran Church in downtown Austin, seeking reassurance that he was forgiven for Margaret's death. I could imagine his walking into the large, prominently steepled, brick church, and in his sincere and folksy way starting a conversation to verify his salvation. His doubts would cause him to return again and again, to be sure.

Every nightmare possible, even those occurring in the daytime were hopefully over. However, Ron had many serious and unmet health needs, either overlooked or ignored by the state system or perhaps his estate paying for them. His teeth for instance, were worn down to his gums from years of grinding them during his sleep. As a result, it was just plain painful for him to eat certain foods related to their being too cold, too hot or too difficult to chew. Moreover, he needed new hearing aids. He had regular living expenses at Reflections and he needed spending money. His hard work for years prior to his hospitalization, huge estate and property holdings were expected to be there for him.

Alas, routine costs of care, let alone dental repair and hearing aid replacement were out of the question. Either a miserly insufficient amount of money would arrive late, or never at all. This was an ongoing battle without relief, related to Ron having a Conservator who was supposed to be assisting him by paying for the basic services he needed. Ron had complained about Mr. Black to the Lawyers Professional Responsibility Board (in 2007, no less) only to be informed by this board that Mr. Black was currently the attorney to the conservator, not Ron's attorney at all and Ron was basically on his own, without anyone, let alone a lawyer to help him. Whatever wealth he amassed for safe keeping was more than likely on less than solid footing. The attorney who at one time called me at the hospital in St. Peter demanding an explanation as to the reason I had access to "his client," was reportedly not now, and had not been for years, Ron's attorney at all.

If hearing aids were $4500.00, a check for half the amount might arrive after several weeks of requests and reminders. This situation became so problematic that monthly room and board payments required the intervention of Ron's county case manager and his social worker. The result of this situation, over time for it to sink in, was that Ron's needs, supposedly being taken advantage of, were now understood as true, and not part of a

317

convoluted delusional process. These things got paid when he was at the state hospital because Mr. Black and conservator wanted him to stay at the hospital. Now that he was out in the community, both people whose jobs were to support and protect Ron's rights, these folks were otherwise preoccupied. And the money, was never sent with any regularity.

Ron's first Thanksgiving in freedom was spent at Ron Jr's, who drove the several hours south to Austin to pick Ron up in the morning for the several hour drive back north, to his home. It was the first family Thanksgiving after entirely too long. The aromas of the turkey and stuffing must have been more wonderful than ever; the cranberry sauce more ruby red than Ron had remembered. The desserts had to have tasted particularly soft and sweet, easy to eat.

On Thanksgiving Day, Ron saw a woman and two children walk up the steps to the door of the house. Ron Jr. was busy with the turkey. Ron Sr. opened the front door, welcomed the woman and girls and stepped aside to let the mom and kids in. Then he introduced himself. At the same time, Ron Jr. came into the entry, and observing what was going on, asked if Ron recognized the young family. It was Ron's youngest daughter, and her two girls, his grandchildren. Ron had not seen his daughter for a least a decade if not more, and he had never met his grandchildren. They all hugged and cried until he was heaving to get his breath. All four of them embracing each other and their combined tears washed over their faces with a mixture of grief and joy. It was the best Thanksgiving Ron ever had.

During the time Ron lived at Reflections, he could not get his own lawyer despite more than one petition to restore his capacity, which is a process necessary following the awarding of a conservatorship. If he had been granted what is termed a "restoration of capacity," he would have been seen as able to manage his own affairs, with help. I and other psychologists had examined him related to this request, and we all made repeated recommendations for this to be granted by Douglas County Court. Each and every petition went unapproved by Douglas County. Of course, this restoration, if it happened would include his having the assistance of an attorney to aid him with his legal rights on so many levels.

Ron living at Reflections was a means to an end. He needed to establish a history of successfully living in the community, away from the hospital so as to eventually move to a different assisted living facility near Ron Jr.'s home. By the time he moved from Reflections after seven months, he had accrued over $12,000 of unpaid expenses. The funds that did arrive for his living expenses were always late, less than what was needed, or never arrived at all.

I would later be chagrined to discover that as of December of 2017 Reflections still had yet to be paid for their housing and care of Ron! From 2009 onward, after Ron had been released, Mr. Black and the conservator reportedly continued to pay themselves monthly fees out of the estate, for managing the estate. Most painful was my memory of Ron telling me he sent his Social Security checks for $1329.00 for years to be put into savings. Meanwhile, liens had mounted over years of time for unpaid services.

His time at Reflections did facilitate Ron's once critical Douglas County social worker's change of heart and mind. When he was at the state hospital, this woman was critical of Ron for years of time for just about everything except breathing, (as reviewed in his medical records). She considered him lying about what happened to Margaret, being arrogant and unruly to staff at the hospital and then complaining about needing more help from the county for his rights being violated. She had been critical of Ron not participating in his state hospital programming, so she mostly limited her face to face contact with Ron to observing him on Interactive TV during periodic meetings in which she could "view" him at a conference.

There was one instance when she actually visited him in the ward where he lived, only to report a criticism of his having what he called an "Indian quarter," consisting of a .22 bullet glued to three pennies, the kind of thing one might pick up at Wall Drug. Her professional assessment as entered within his records noted that "for a man who committed murder, this was evidence that he had no remorse."

She had been his social worker for years and now she had to follow him at Reflections. However, it was during his time at Reflections that she got to experience first-hand, the harsh reality that Ron was not being supported financially, without a continuous fight.

Ron entered Reflections in the fall of 2009. By the end of October, the weather turned cold and he had no winter coat! Efforts to find money for such a purchase consisted of the usual numerous requests without response. Finally, he got a winter coat for $10 at a thrift store. When I next saw him, he went on and on to me, about the great quality of this coat, and what a fabulous deal he had gotten. My husband gave him some warm pullover sweaters that he no longer wore and which we guessed would fit Ron. We couldn't believe it when he told us thanks for the sweaters, along with the story that the laundry lady at Reflections put them in the washer and then the dryer, causing them to shrink to a child's size.

The same Douglas County social worker I recently mentioned became part of Ron's release treatment team, so to speak. When he moved closer to his son, the same pattern continued. Every day, Ron struggled to meet his meager financial needs. All those years of setting aside his Social Security checks was for naught. Someone had his money, but it wasn't Ron.

Ron moved from Reflections in the late spring, early summer of 2010 to a single floor Assisted Living Facility near Ron Jr. that was more spacious, including Ron being able to sleep in a queen-sized bed. Ron Jr. got new tires for a used Cadillac, fired it up and accompanied Ron as he learned to drive again. The regular ritual of finding treasures at rummage sales resumed in a limited style, with Ron voicing concern that his provisional discharge could be revoked if he upset someone. All in all, though, life was getting better.

After two months at his new assisted living home, following years of confinement and state hospital challenges, Ron went to bed one night, fell asleep, drifted off, and died. He failed to show up for breakfast that next morning and the staff found him still in bed, dead. He had been out of the hospital for 10 months. He reportedly spent the evening before his death watching TV and turned in early. By this time, I had literally just moved to Florida and we were waiting for the moving van to show up with our furniture. Ryan Magnus called me the morning Ron had been found and I was shocked and devastated. Ron's death was just so unfair for him.

The day was solemn and hollow. I couldn't believe Ron's life was over when he was just getting started. Less than a year at freedom, less than a year to meet and learn about granddaughters, less than a year to drive to Ron Jr.'s home for dinner. Less than a year to come and go at will. The day was dark. It was, Unbelievable. I would have given anything to be at Ron's funeral. Our move to Florida had occurred only days before Ron's death; we were weary from packing, the long drive, and camping out in our house waiting for the moving van. Ryan Magnus sent a plant with our names on the card, but that was not even close to being at the funeral in person. I so regretted the timing.

Ron's funeral would be on his birthday, a fact he most certainly would have noted with some humorous reference. It took place on a pleasant Minnesota summer afternoon in Morris, Minnesota and included some family members and friends. His granddaughter spoke about her love for a grandfather she knew only a brief period of time. Ron Jr spoke of his father's struggles and what their newly forged bond meant to him. Mourners and family blended in tribute to Ron in a manner that would have made him proud. There were people from his former life, his life when he was struggling at the hospital, and life during his new-found freedom. The Ristrow brothers were amongst his pall bearers, carrying their friend to his final resting place.

On the front of his funeral program was a silhouetted design of a man fishing, with the caption "Peaceful Memories." Inside was a colored photo of Ron (actually the same photo of his face from the group photo taken of Ron, Ryan Magnus and I in front of Piggy Blues). The music was listed as, "You Gave Me a Mountain," "Help Me" by Elvis Presley, "Believe," by Brooks and Dunn, and "Lucky Old Sun" by Jerry Lewis.

Treasure Trove

In 2014 my computer was hacked, and my e-mail was compromised. After not hearing from Ron Jr. for a very long time, out of the blue, I received an email from him joking about some silly ads he had been receiving supposedly from me and we started re-connecting. I had not told him yet that I was starting to write a story about his father with the many documents I had related to the case.

I had no title yet for what I was writing, and barely a plan in mind for how to begin, let alone organize the information. I toyed with including the notion of "'willful ignorance," related to what happened to Ron involving a host of health care professionals, over time succumbing to a pattern of actions they most likely questioned if not considered was less than right or ideal.

When I shared my book plan with Ron Jr., he became excited and reported he had a garage full of boxes of his father's papers. I offered to pay for the cost of sending them and soon thereafter received nine banker boxes, ranging in weight from 35 to 50 pounds. The cost of these boxes was more than worth it. shipping and it was worth it.! My garage was transformed into a series of long tables that facilitated sorting and organizing these documents.

Receiving this shipment of assorted treasure boxes was overwhelming. Except that these boxes were the days and years of the lifetime of someone I had grown to know on a professional level first, who now had passed on, unavailable for further conversation. I was unprepared for the vast amount of information I would review in these boxes, or the memories of events and facts Ron had talked about with me. It was a humbling experience for me. Sorting through his records was undeniably fascinating along with feeling like an invasion of Ron's privacy. The worst part was that I could not call him with questions or to verify information about what I was finding with Ron himself.

The contents of these boxes greatly exceeded the areas of Ron's life we talked about as patient and psychologist. The other areas, such as his business dealings, family issues, personal relationships, hobbies and interests, and his mountain of letters to and from others were new territory for me. I learned more about grain dryers than I ever wanted. I learned about what drove him related to his goals, his plans for the future, his eventual dashed hopes and his apparent despair as he accepted being outnumbered and out-gamed.

When I interviewed Ron in 2006, he had been hospitalized for 23 years and exhibited no symptoms of an active mental illness. Some of his archived writings were from a very different time of his life when he was in deep and unending anguish, when his life had literally been turned upside down and he was struggling to find his footing on unfamiliar terrain.

I sat for hours reviewing documents depicting a time when he was severely depressed; his thinking disorganized and angry, blaming those he could and in anguish over situations over which he had little to no control. There were documents that added to the information he shared with an me about his family, grain dryers, his loves, his goals, successes, experiences of emotional ruin, followed by information that only raised more questions.

Most of the time, when one talked with Ron, his quirky humor was appropriately evident during the conversation. But some of these boxes had no humor. They were the trappings of a man alone; confused, alienated, abandoned, lost. I had underestimated the extent of his expansive curiosity on the landscape of so many areas. To say he was a voracious reader was an understatement.

Each evening, after having spent hours sorting through one box at a time, getting lost in reading the contents, organizing the paperwork and finally having to stop to rest I was struck by the wealth of information that represented a lifetime that was now spread out on folding tables in a double-wide garage a long way from their home.

Ultimately, the challenge was, how to organize and condense years of detailed information into a story of a man's life and existence, How I would have liked to be able to call Ron Sr. and ask more questions about his dryers, and his nemesis, Farm Fans and the details for his competitors wanting to eliminate his being the competition. I would have asked who he thought benefitted the most from his being out of the picture, so to speak, and if that was the case, I would have asked what he would have done differently, had there been a chance? I would have asked what he learned that was most important to him.

I pondered how my own life would look if all my experiences, relationships, mistakes, successes, loves that were lost and those that were never ending, were somehow categorized into file folders, shoe boxes, assorted envelopes and plastic bags. When I went through the sheet music Ron had kept, I wondered what treasured music I might keep because I still hummed the tune or thought about the words within the music. I wondered about the number of boxes that might represent my entire life.

I reviewed photos of Ron holding his children as babies, now adults, and seeing photos of Ron in his younger years. I became lost for hours reading about the details of court-related interviews, court reports done by other professionals, police reports, crime scene reports about details of which I had never seen before. Having grown up in a smaller rural community myself, I enjoyed vicariously learning new details about where Ron lived, and places, like Jim and Judy's where folks went for a beer and to hang out and talk.

I started out trying to organize box contents into categories of legal information, business records, hospital and mental health records, personal interests, and miscellaneous. There were literally bales of copied mental health information, diagnostic forms, medication research, newspaper articles related to mental illness, behaviors within mental illness and medication issues. For example, there was the Jeff Reardon article related to his illegal behavior when under the influence of medications, which Ron felt applied to him.

There were copies of copies related to letters Ron wrote to people with whom he was asking for assistance or lambasting them and criticizing their involvement in business efforts against him. There were letters to politicians from whom he was enlisting help. There were hundreds of pages that were copies from his MSH medical file and lists of people he had written to as well as letters he had received from some of these people warning him to cease or desist in contacting them by mail or phone. Some of these mail restrictions and lists of people were people that Ron was specifically warned not to write! One list was placed in his medical chart: "Do Not Write to: Washington Federal Savings and Loan, the Douglas County Attorney, Douglas County Hospital, the Douglas County Coroner, lawyers from the Foegred and Benson law firm, various personal employed at Farm Fans, Inc."

There were boxes of grain dryer product mailings, ads, inventory sheets, and dozens of pages of legal pad size notebooks covered with lists of names, figures related to his grain dryer inventory and figures of available dryers, and projected inventories and earning potential. These lists included entries of legal charges he felt were related to each individual and court case numbers that he apparently felt applied to these persons. These boxes were a glimpse into his world of researching nearly everything medical and legal that applied to him, his case, and his situation.

There was information that at the time of the shooting in 1986, that Ron reportedly requested Margaret Brown's children receive $400,000.00; no directions were included as to how this was to occur, and I wondered if it happened. In later review I noted that possibly Ron's insurance policy had awarded money to the Brown children. I wondered if these children had remained in the lake area and how their lives had turned out.

Also included in this motherlode were newspaper articles related to the 1986 shooting, the jury trial, the trial outcome and follow up articles in the *Echo*, the local newspaper in Alexandria. There were transcripts of the grand jury, interviews by examiners, court proceedings and their outcomes, various treatment programs in the MSH hospital, the Arrowhead House records, records from Miller Dwan in Duluth, the fiasco in his getting the U-Haul and the paperwork associated and involving Mr. Black.

Some of his early writings included long and rambling tirades noting "incapacitation from wrongful medications I had been prescribed and forced to take for mental illness disorders I never had, other than what the adverse side effects and inter-drug reactions caused that restrained me from preventing the illegal closing of my Farm Fans/Farm Systems lawsuit, and for personal injury to myself and the wrongful death of my intended wife while I was under the influence of wrongful medications I should never have been forced to take, by those who prescribed the meditations and those who failed to recognize the fact I was suffering from adverse drug reactions, not mental illness."

He would further lament how his caregivers had failed him, along with mentioning a plan, "to pursue my legal medical and other legal entitlements related to malpractice," noting that "every physician is required to insure him or herself for one-million dollars for malpractice coverage and every licensed nurse must individually insure him or herself as well, therefore we can recover a considerable amount considering how many misdiagnosed my condition."

Ron would later write about the anguish he continued to experience, noting, "it is now going to be ten years since then, and no one has lifted a finger to correct the wrong doings of others who have committed the worst crimes and yet are respected by others." He would note, "The shooting was not an intentional act nor was I mentally ill at the time," and then disassociate from what occurred and report, "if Margaret had not awakened unexpectedly the shooting would never have occurred, but Margaret apparently saw me in the dark holding the revolver and became frightened, grabbed my arm, I panicked, not knowing what it was, or who it was, in the state of mind I was in at the time."

He relived Farm Fans "terminating Transmatic as their largest distributor without prior notification, surrounding Transmatic with factory owned branch locations and competing with factory direct pricing which was a part of the conspiracy as this was done prior to the termination and after; knowing we had done nothing wrong to deserve being put out of business, we began searching for answers and found that enviousness was the first reason, and that over $300,000.00 worth of returned goods had not been paid for by Farm Fans at the time of the termination."

Within various differing documents he would repeat certain phrases along the lines of, "my illness was caused by the medications they had told me to take by force and coercion which I became the accused of premeditated and intentional "Murder," and then labeled "Mentally Ill and Dangerous," followed by the words, "Misrepresentation," "Misdiagnosis." Major legal topics in addition to psychiatric issues varied somewhat but mostly focused on areas related to "fraud, conspiracy, anti-trust, criminal negligence, breach of fiduciary duty, misrepresentation, negligence/contributory negligence/imputed negligence, penalties for deceit or collusion, conflicts of interest, duress."

There were stacks of treatment records over years that included highlighted treatment notes, some of them underlined, including his comments noting his threatening to sue staff or turn them into their boards related to what he saw as poor treatment. There were pages of Behavior Management issues noting Ron's infractions within his living unit including his having "admitted to selling a stamp to patient #44114; his admitting to "purchasing three movies from his peer but would not tell staff how much he paid for them;" his giving patient 44224 toothpaste, his trading stamps and a belt in front of staff;" Mr. Steen gave a peer envelopes and stated to the peer he was not charging the peer anything; he was remined it was against the rules to borrow/give/share any item with peers."

There were personal greeting cards one including a hint of a budding romantic interest with another patient and their shared dreams for the future. This discovery was to me an example of Ron's resilience against all odds. To be in such a long confinement and still have hope of future happiness was amazing. There were invitations to his 50-year high school reunion which he had hoped to be released in time to attend, and there was a note from the person who organized the reunion telling him that he had been missed and wishing him well.

There were copies of health fad information and inspirational/religious documents. There were dozens of tape recordings, legal pads covered with information related to his RICO suit and agendas with various attorneys. There were copies of reports written about him, and research he had conducted on his own, about his symptoms, side effects to medications, and how to deal with stress and depression.

One notably impressive feature was Ron's handwritten pages of his ornate writing style that looked like something Alexander Hamilton himself had scribed. He had lists of lists with names of attorneys, bankers, business persons, their phone numbers, case law topics he thought applied to each and every individual on the list and copies of letters he had received from people he met who supported him and some who did not want him to keep contacting them. There were long rambling letters to people he held responsible for his losing his business, his fortune, and his future.

There were pages of grain dryer "Profit Loss Charts" some stretching 15 years time spans, and "Updated Damage List(s)", also with un recovered losses including "personal injury hearing loss from fan noise...personal injury causing stress from expansion demands/termination," with numerical estimations in the millions of dollars.

Newspaper clippings spoke of corrupt officials, family members who swindled their relatives, people charged with murder, people found not guilty due to insanity. There were copies of Minnesota statutes, articles on the hazards of certain medications, side effects, conservatorship, a copy of the Federal Rules of Procedures, civil and criminal procedures and copies of letters from MSH to his friends who wrote to the hospital regarding what they interpreted as "inadequate care" given to Ron.

There was a copy of "The Jailhouse Lawyer," numerous documents from the Citizens Commission on Human Rights International which Ron had joined and to which he made regular contributions. There were copies of his MMPI that he claimed had been manipulated to make him look mentally ill and there were packets of information in a story form that he had created to tell his own story.

Some of the letters I found in Ron's boxes were concerning and included unabashed deceit. One letter from Mr. Black to Ron, dated

February 17, 2004, noted Mr. Black reporting to Ron's conservator after he had recently called her and engaged in a "long conversation," that he was aware of her being in a "tug of war" between lawyers and that "she should not have to be in that position...I do not want that you are placed in that situation and I do not believe it is in the interest of your father that such is the case." He then reminded her "she had the right to resolve matters as she saw fit and did not have to confide in anyone," followed by a list of suggestions that might be of benefit, such as, "Do not let your father hire a lawyer, do not give him money to do so, maintain control of the hiring of a lawyer, if such a lawyer does call you make it clear right off the bat you are not hiring a lawyer unless he can tell you what he intends to do, I am available to talk with you." I was more less than shocked about Mr. Black sinking to this lower level yet of despicable behavior.

Also, sadly, was a 2007 letter from the Lawyers Professional Responsibility Board to Ron, following Ron's complaint to the Board about Mr. Black, only to be told that Mr. Black was *not his attorney, but instead his conservator's attorney!* Had this Board missed noting that Mr. Black had changed clients, from Ron to that of his conservator? Ron would not have written to this Board had he been informed Mr. Black was no longer his attorney, and clearly the year (2007) was one year after Mr. Black had

337

informed me Ron was his client and what was I doing talking to him without permission?

Related to the huge number of documents in Ron's boxes, I had truly underestimated his verbosity, his unquenchable thirst for knowledge, information and trivia and his obsessive compulsive advantage interwoven therein. He was the King of pack rats and lead researcher of things of interest to him. At one point I considered the possibility that this constant thirst for information and collecting information may have been the way he coped with being at the state hospital and its' milieu therapy or the boredom and under stimulation of groups discussing "Blueprint for Change."

Amongst Ron's papers was his possession of the landmark mental health Supreme Court case law I have previously noted. He had a copy of "O'Connor vs. Donaldson." How he found this case is amazing. The hope it offered for him related to some of Ron and Kenneth's similarities must have consumed his thoughts on more than one occasion. I would have like to have listened to what Ron thought of this case.

Other documents in Ron's private papers included copies of Master Schedules for various wards in which he had housed and a variety of inspirational booklets, one entitled, "You are Forgiven." There were newspaper articles about attorneys convicted of taking their clients' assets, about officials charged with crimes and about dependent adult children taking their parents' property and assets.

There was a full-page story and obituary in the February 18, 1985 Business Twin Cities section about his famous Minneapolis attorney, John A. Cochrane whose history included winning huge million dollar antitrust litigation cases (except for Ron's). Noted cases included settlements netting "$202 million for makers of folding cartons; $23 million, ocean shippers; $53 million sugar and others. This man was described as a "burly St. Paul barrister" who reportedly had "rear class...for "talking loudly and blowing his nose in a red farmer handkerchief with others thinking he was a pushover until they learned differently." He was noted as one of "the Twin Cities wealthiest attorneys."

There was a copy of the "Patient's Bill of Rights," common to state institutions when Ron was first admitted to the state hospital system in 1986. Within this document were statements related to the defined "rights" of patients, such as a patient having the right to "polite and respectful care," with neither "polite and respectful" defined as though this would be a given.

Another paragraph spoke of patients' right to "help plan your treatment," again without definition or examples, including the fact that Ron's treatment, upon return to the confines of St. Peter had not varied in two decades.

"You have the right to privacy and to respectful treatment." No definition of privacy or respectful treatment. The psychiatrist who sent Ron to Unit 800, a ward designated for the most dangerous patients, who have demonstrated recent assault, dangerousness and discontrol, and from which no one is soon released, got away with it, and it was anything but respectful.

Also noted were patient rights related to friends:" You have the right to be able to choose your friends and talk or write wo whomever you wish in privacy. You have the right to have your own belongings as space allows to choose not to perform services unless they are part of your treatment, to be free from isolation except in an emergency." Notably, Ron's access to his friends was altered, then eliminated as a result of his declining to participate in group programming; for again not participating in this treatment program he was sent to a second placement in a separate building where none of his former hospital patient friends could visit. Additionally, one of Ron's best friends who visited him weekly was banned from the hospital grounds when he carried one of Ron's boxes of his personal legal information from his old room to his new room. The "Rights" continue, but you get the drift. You can try to discuss your rights, but do not think they won't be trumped by some other reasoning.

Ron's letters were legion in number, lengthy, painfully presented to the sender in question. In May of 2002 he penned a long letter lamenting the sale of some of his land to Dayton-Hudson for the pending Target store in Alex. He wrote about people to whom he had entrusted his assets continuing to disappoint him by failing to live up to the "fiduciary obligations" he had assigned them. His message remained that his diagnoses had been "falsified," his forced medications had added to his emotional and physical pain, his legal rights had been denied and eventually the statute of limitations expired related to his business ventures causing him "uncomprehend able pain." He could find no place of peace or solace; there was no haven where he could rest from what he described as "intolerable suffering."

There was a letter from one of Ron's high school classmates telling him, "The Class of 1958's 50th reunion is now history. It was a huge success with approximately 60 classmates and 40 spouses in attendance. You were sorely missed. Hopefully you will be able to attend the next one." She included a copy of the reunion booklet, earmarking his Elvis-look alike photo.

How Change Doesn't Happen

When state hospitals were originally established, they offered a long needed haven for families with mentally ill family members, and for mentally ill patients themselves. Ron was not the first person to spend over two decades in a state institution, and he most likely will not be the last. His continued confinement was not related to his being at a state institution in Minnesota, as research contains a long list of patients from an assortment of states who shared this fate.

When I contacted the hospital to clarify, how Ron's unit was organized, I was told his unit was not a medical model, but instead, a "rehabilitative model," preparing him for return to the community. At the time that sounded hopeful, but later on conflicted with testimony during his SCAP panel hearings when his treating psychiatrist and treatment team professionals testified he needed to remain confined where he was, in order to repeat programming that could take "years" to complete, despite his previous institution having assisted him in visiting numerous community housing opportunities for what was thought as him impending discharge! His path was hopeful, until he returned to the mother ship.

What happened? Where were the intervening powers, steps, staff, program personnel to advocate for the original plan, especially since his history of confinement was void of any act of behavioral decompensation, let alone violence?

Unfortunately, Ron's case was only one example of a system that mistreats thousands of patients every year, abusing their rights and keeping them in confinement well beyond anything rational.

I learned through reviewing an August 2017 research article, "Forensic Patients in State Psychiatric Hospitals: 1999-2016" by the National Association of State mental Health Program Directors, that overall national trend lines showed a 76% increase in the number of forensic patients in state hospitals from 1999 to 2014, a trend noted as inconsistent across all states. Subsequent populations of state hospitals between 2002 and 2014 indicated only one state's percent change in that there was a reduction is its forensic composition: the other 24 states experienced increases. All graphs suggested that for those with data available, state hospitals have seen increases in forensic patients receiving inpatient services from 1999 to 2014. This study noted that the more beds are occupied by these patients, the lower the state hospital turnover rate, meaning there are fewer openings to admit new patients. Also noted were "long periods of stay, low turnover rates, and overall increase in the number of referrals from the courts have added to increasing state waitlists."

One might expect that there would be a corresponding professional group, usually that of social workers/case managers, who are aware of each patient's designation as well as length of hospitalization at various periods of time. I never saw in Ron's records any attention called to the fact he entered state confinement in 1986 and he was still there in 2006, when I originally interviewed him. It would appear that a release planning component was not part of his medical file, not that of anyone else's record for that matter.

Within the August 2017 reference there was the term "forensicfication," used to refer to the proportional increase of state hospital's forensic populations. It made me feel somewhat better to know that there are professionals aware of this occurring. However, there was no mention of the suspected factors driving it on a larger scale, whether this was occurring on a national level, nor were there noted solutions. I noted some states like Colorado, Washington, Utah and Texas, noted a sharper rise in these populations of patients, along with the fact, that it is the courts, rather than the mental health system that controls the admission and discharge of forensic patients.

This study did not comment or focus on the length of confinement, perhaps because the mentality is that treatment takes as long as it needs to be successful. Ron's treatment had been moving laterally, at best, rather than towards an end goal and his treatment team in total had no qualms recommending he repeat programming that could take years of time, insisting he participate in programs labeled "useless" within the court record.

Most frightening is the fact that had his case for release not been pursued and heard by the SCAP court, he could still be buried in the system. The support by the SCAP judges was for his release; they articulated perfectly the problems within the system, and shared their frustrations with the lack of individuality in treatment, programming and release that had been ongoing and, as such had less and less to offer.

How is it that over decades of time we can identify a common problem, like patients not being released from decades of confinement, but not the solution? Is this situation the result of faulty staff management, a void in human rights, patient census issues, inability to assess divergent information, ineffective system management, staff politics, challenged resources, system management issues? I pondered the answer to this question during hours of driving, even tossing around the possibilities from personality clashes between Ron and staff associated with his case. My suspicion was that for all the good the state system intended for Ron, there was no evidence within his record related to his planned release at his former institution being picked up and continued to completion.

Research has determined that the greatest risk factors for release of mental patients includes their *diagnostic history,* (with schizophrenia, delusional disorders, schizoaffective disorder, bipolar disorder and antisocial personality disorder being highest on the list for relapse of symptoms and subsequent violence), *compliance with taking prescribed medication,* (Ron was prescribed and taking Risperidone, a newer generation neuroleptic successful in moderating his prior symptoms), and the existence of cooperative *attitudes towards treatment compliance (medication),* this last factor assured by his conditional release designation.

When I interviewed Ron, he acknowledged remnant doubts related to his diagnosis while also reporting his intention to continue taking Risperidone which helped his symptoms of anxiety. He had no history of

346

aggression in over two decades of confinement. He had no past history of substance abuse, and no history of antisocial personality disorder behavior; he had an anchoring history of business success and lifelong friends.

Cases involving long periods of confinement from a range of states have become landmark Supreme Court mental health law findings. Precedent-setting cases were heard and resolved, in many cases re-shaping implications involving civil commitment, criminal competency, the death penalty, insanity, the right to refuse treatment and the right to have an evaluation. One such case was the 1975 Supreme Court case of O'Connor v. Donaldson, of which Ron Steen had a copy in his massive cache of personal information.

Kenneth Donaldson had been civilly committed as mentally ill to Florida State Hospital in January of 1957. This commitment was initiated by Donaldson's father, who said Kenneth was suffering from delusions. Donaldson's diagnosis was paranoid schizophrenia and he was civilly committed for "care, maintenance and treatment." No evidence was found as to whether Kenneth Donaldson was incompetent to manage his personal affairs as he had been doing so adequately for 14 years prior to his commitment. Kenneth was kept in custody, against his will, for nearly 15 years until Dr. J.B. O'Connor finally retired from being the director of the hospital. During the subsequent trial, Dr. O'Connor, was questioned about the case and reported a belief that Donaldson would have been able to make a successful adjustment outside the institution but could not recall the basis for his conclusion or the reason Donaldson had not been released.

During the trial Dr. O'Connor argued that the court needed to assume that Mr. Donaldson was receiving treatment to justify his confinement because treatment was an issue left to the discretion of the psychiatric profession. However, hospital records noted Mr. Donaldson consistently refused treatment in the form of medication because of his beliefs as a Christian Scientist and because he claimed he was not mentally ill and therefore did not need any treatment.

Donaldson's records did not identify him as having posed a danger to others during his 15 years of "hospitalization" or at any point in his life. Dr. O'Connor conceded at the time of the hearing of the case that he had no personal or second-hand knowledge that Donaldson had ever committed a dangerous act, been suicidal or seen as likely to inflict injury upon himself or others. Donaldson had repeatedly petitioned state and federal courts for release on a number of occasions, with none of the claims resolved on their merit and no evidence that a review was ever held.

The record showed that because Dr. O'Connor believed that Donaldson could only be released to his parents, who were now too old and infirm to take responsibility for their son, the rejected offers of supported release for Donaldson. Despite the fact that at the time of this trial, Donaldson was now 55 years of age.

Noteworthy was the fact that Kenneth's care was described as, "milieu therapy," the same term used for Ron Steen's treatment in Minnesota from 1986 to 2009. This therapy in 1957 was noted as a "euphemism for confinement in the milieu of a mental hospital

"Milieu" is defined as, "a person's social environment, backdrop, setting content" "milieu therapy is defined as "a form of psychotherapy that involves the use of therapeutic communities. Patients join a group of around 30, for between 9 and 18 months. During their stay, patients are encouraged to take responsibility for themselves and others within the unit based upon a hierarchy of collective consequences."

The definition of milieu is confusing at best, as it basically says nothing; nor is the term "a hierarchy of collective consequences" defined.

The therapies that do get results are cognitive/behavioral and rational/emotive in nature. These therapies teach people to be aware of their thoughts and behaviors, how to intervene in such and change their internal responses to situations, actions and reactions to situations.

The Supreme Court ultimately opined that Dr. O'Connor, *as an agent of the state, did knowingly confine Mr. Donaldson thereby violating Mr. Donaldson's constitutional right to freedom.* After being held against his will for nearly 15 years and only being released when Dr. O'Connor retired as head of the hospital, Kenneth Donaldson took a responsible position in hotel administration. At issue was Kenneth Donaldson's having been confined against his will and his constitutional right to liberty in the absence of his being determined as dangerous. It is clear why Ron Steen's attention was drawn to this case and why he copied it to keep in his personal papers.

As noted, dangerousness is a concept widely associated with the term mental illness, and is, perhaps, the single strongest factor adding to its stigma. In 1972 a Wisconsin case, (Lessard v, Schmidt), a judge changed the basis of commitment from a civil commitment of involuntary hospitalization to a criminal procedure based on "dangerousness." Other states followed suit and reportedly by the end of the 1970's nearly e very state changed the criteria for hospitalization for those seen as dangerous to themselves or others. Add criminal acts related to "dangerousness," amongst the need(s) for or lack of psychotropic medication rights related to symptoms of mental illness, and here are the makings of what can become a very complicated storm involving illness, personal rights, public safety and decision making.

Another noteworthy Supreme Court case is that of Jackson v. Indiana in which criminal defendants found incompetent to stand trial were noted as *not permitted to be held indefinitely*: there must be some possibility of becoming competent in a reasonable amount of time. Ron was initially seen as incompetent to stand trial but later seen as competent with advancing freedoms.

Being held indefinitely in the state system had not been discussed between Ron and his caregivers. But this inevitability was obviously a reality. So how does treatment move from admission to transfers to return to indefinite confinement? How is it that some patients never get released? How is it that patients are held for years and years until they are eventually unable to manage on their own?

In the summer of 2018 I received from some friends who live in Nova Scotia, an article from *The Canadian Press* noting the story of a woman in Halifax. The headline was, "Patients stuck at Halifax forensic hospital for years," along with the stories of patients, some who of had been waiting for 4-5 years, one waiting over 6 years, for release. Noted issues included these patients being under "significant restrictions" (undefined) as preventing them from moving forward. The article noted some human rights groups *observed* this problem had been going on since 1995.

There were the common issues of lack of community service facilities where patients could be placed, the ongoing challenge of resources, and the stigma associated with former patients who were seen in the past as both mentally ill and having engaged in a violent criminal act. Observations noted patients in state hospitals seen as capable of living in the community who were nevertheless, prevented from moving on for whatever reason, deteriorating with depression and hopelessness.

A Politics & Government report from Western State Hospital in Jefferson County in the state of Washington noted in a report dated May 17, 2018 that "People ready for discharge can't get out," 40% of the hospital's approximately 580 civil patients were on the discharge list with the median time spent on the list being 104 days; in reality, some people have waited years, or even decades to be released after the hospital deemed them ready for discharge, according to hospital officials. Problems included lack of facilities to accept patients, a patient rejecting a facility due to its location far away from family, and the stigma associated with people who have received mental health treatment at a large institution. Patients having a criminal history also challenged their acceptance by a new facility.

When Washington state began offering construction money to those who wanted to build facilities, some states began to run their own step-down facilities. Financial incentives were also shared, such as a state hospital bed in Washington being $790 a day, and community placement just $95 per day. Ron's daily cost at St. Peter was $550.

Between 1955 and 1994, roughly 487,000 mentally ill patient s were discharged from state hospitals, lowering the number to only 72,000 patients. By 2010 there were 43,000 psychiatric beds available, equating to 14 beds per 100.000 people. "According to the Treatment Advocacy's Center's Report, "*Deinstitutionalization: A Failed History,*" this was the same ratio as in 1850.

While the focus of mental health policy over the past fifty years has been to close state hospitals, there are currently more than 200 state hospitals that remain open, serving a "declining but challenging" population. The state of mental health in America (MHA, Mental Health America) notes that one in five adults, over 40 million Americans, more that the population of New York and Florida combined, have a mental health condition. The rates of youth depression in 2011 was 8.5, increasing to 11.1 in 2014; even with severe depression 80% are left with no or insufficient treatment. The same search noted most Americans lack access to care and 56% of American adults with a mental illness did not receive treatment; reportedly, even in Vermont, the state with the best access to services noted 43% of adults with a mental illness did not receive treatment. In states with the lowest workforce, there is 1 mental health professional per 1000 individuals. Arkansas, Mississippi and Alabama have the least access to care and the highest rates of imprisonment. There are presently over 57,000 people with mental health conditions in prison and jail, enough to fill Madison Square Garden three times.

One in five adults have a mental health condition; youth mental health is worsening with severe depression increasing from 5.9% in 2012 to 8.2% in 2015; even with severe depression, 63% of youth are left with no or insufficient treatment, and that was before the rash of school shootings.

354

Additionally, there is a serious mental health workforce shortage with 6 times the individuals to 1 mental health professional including psychiatrists, psychologists, social workers, counselors and psychiatric nurses combined, as noted in the 2016 State of Mental Health in America.

Personally, I find it difficult to be believe that we are in a better place in 2018 related to mental health treatment for the general population or the mentally ill under court commitment. The fact that treatment settings continue to rely on "milieu" anything, a treatment from the 1950's that remains as hopelessly vague now as it was in the past, and that institutions and providers are satisfied with this level of indirection tells me that the only thing that has changed, is that time has passed.

The Weakest Link of the Chain

When I was in high school band the talented conductor, Mr. Thornton, would at times, frantically tap his wooden baton on his podium, halt our music, and sharply point out a problem existed with a particular section, sometimes the brass, sometimes the woodwinds. He would repeat his metaphor of the "weakest link in the chain." What he explained was that a long chain is only as strong as its weakest link; and if that link breaks, the chain itself fails.

The weakest link in the chain of mental health services is that related to withholding timely release of a civilly committed patient who has failed to demonstrate clear evidence of risk of harm to others. Mental health professionals understand that certain people are dangerous and require confinement for their safety and that of others. At the same time, there are people we only hear about after years and years of confinement, like Ron, who perhaps represent the tip of the iceberg of people whose loss of freedom is taken from them by others without justifiable causes. Prison sentences end; in mental illness there is no end of commitment without confirmation via assessment, which, too often, is taken in front of review boards who do not demonstrate an understanding of mental health law.

Being held indefinitely in the state system had not been discussed between Ron and his caregivers. But this inevitability was obviously a reality. So how does treatment move from admission to transfers to return to indefinite confinement? It might have to do with staff oversight of ethical courses of treatment or ignoring ethical checklists of treatment for patients who have been hospitalized for certain amounts of time with no evidence of discontrol. Ron's treatment team saw him after more than 20 years as not demonstrating control. The Court and some of us outside examiners saw his situation differently. Ethical review might have bought these groups closer together related to how his case was perceived and what safeguards were needed before his release.

It would be naïve to consider, that if and when the State Hospital Legal Department received the Findings of Fact ordering Ron's release, a careful review of his case resulted. Something truly egregious happened to Ron Steen in the name of "treatment." In an ideal world his psychiatrists, physicians and treatment team members would hear some information related to the findings of the judges and review them in detail so that this situation would not happen again.

For example, the staff member who made the decision to send Ron to the highest security unit in the hospital complex when he "failed to demonstrate evidence of aggression" should have resulted in the staff receiving some sort of correction, if not sanction. It is an interesting fact that physicians at state facilities have, in most cases, immunity from civil liability.

An article entitled "Physician Peer Review Immunity: Time to Euthanize a Fatally Flawed Policy" by Charles R. Koepke, M.D. in the Journal of Law and Health at Cleveland State University (2009) caught my interest. While this immunity can protect caregivers from frivolous claims of malpractice, could it also work against patient care? While it is true that such physicians have to accept all the patients assigned to them without being able to decline patients for who there is little hope of improvement, to have immunity seems like an invitation for problems related to care, or more specifically to the occurrence of good care.

I thought about the descriptions within Ron's case before the three SCAP Judges,' including statements of "meaningless rules of little to no

358

value," within treatment units. I thought about the Judges statements related to "unit heads needing to address, change and replace such rules with those concepts based on research that noted therapeutic change."

How could physicians, and other treatment providers be responsible to meet, identify, and correct, what the Judges cited as "endlessly changing and unclear and meaningless rules needing to be completed as a sign of progress" if treatment providers have "immunity? What about discussion related to what was noted by the SCAP Judges as Ron "not being the only patient," subjected to such practices? What about improved observations of unit programs and establishment of ethics committees to oversee treatment statistics noting improvement in patient behaviors and wider options of programming, so patterns of the past would not be repeated?

The need for individually scripted treatment plans should be verified as having occurred and treatment providers should be better trained to see individual differences in patients. There could be monthly seminars in mental health case law so employees within the state system could be better informed as to how patients enter the state hospital and what the criteria is for their release.

Were any recommendations forthcoming related to the development and workability of the "Special Review Boards," such as the quality of information, or lack thereof, coming out of such groups? Based on the effort exerted by the hospital professionals to dig their heels into denying Ron's release, in combination with open denial of their understanding of the legal parameters for release, would not training programs for staff prompt enlightened discussions to improve the experience of patients and professionals alike?

Certainly, Ron's case, both over time and at various junctures, involved ethical considerations related to applying the statutes that guided his confinement and aimed at his release. I thought back to Ryan Magnus first introducing me to Ron's situation by telling me a social worker at one of Ron's last placement had approached Ryan to tell him that Ron Steen was "stuck" in the system and needed legal help. After we got involved with Ron's case, in particular when we were facing Special Review Boards and the cumbersome process of our efforts moving at a snail's pace over years, the notion of being "stuck," took on new meaning.

Considering Ron had rotating treatment teams of a dozen or more professionals every three months over for years of time, how was it that not one professional questioned whether the team was on track for meeting Ron's civil rights for release based on the definitions of and within the release criteria? Where was the copy of the legal criteria for release in his medical file?

I considered the possibility that this was a case of willful ignorance, a term used to refer to situations whereby people ignore any input that appears to contradict their inner model of reality. Some references refer to willful ignorance as "tactical stupidity." Evidence suggesting willful ignorance is noted in the absence of established facts, like, perhaps the absence of the legal criteria for release from civil commitment in patient charts.

In Ron's case, and that of other state hospital patients, comments within the records did not include reference to the legal criteria at the heart of the current issue at hand. What was noted instead, was whether or not he went to his social groups that were used as gate keepers for his release, despite the lack of research that these groups reduced risk let alone aided in the healing of mental illness. Since patients in state institutions are involuntarily admitted under specific legal statutes, staff need to be trained to understand the specific statutory requirements involved related to their admission and their subsequent release, and document accordingly in patient records. In

361

Ron's situation it was clear staff did *not know* the statutory criteria related to his release, which contributed to violations of his rights.

Ron shed the designated "dangerousness" qualifier because of the length of time he went without his acting out physically towards others. It was not his declining to attend certain groups that changed his behavior. He had not declined his medications, nor had he exhibited uncontrollable symptoms of his mental disorder. He had followed all safety rules, and he had not engaged in acts of physical aggression. The things he did on a daily basis were not listed in any organized manner to support his remaining in the state hospital.

It would seem that in a large psychiatric center such as the state hospital, where budding professionals in law, psychiatry, psychology, social work, nursing and direct care services are drawn into jobs involving both medical and legal issues, would be a worthy location to discuss patient programming needs as supported by research as useful for problem solving. And for individuals who preferred and do better with more solitary activities, a different set of programming needs could be developed for therapeutic purposes. But neither would be the sole gatekeeper for release.

In 2013 the state hospital where the movie *One Flew Over the Cuckoo's Nest* had been filmed, was closed. In honor of the movie a section of the psychiatric hospital had been turned into a museum. Tours reportedly included information about the psychiatric hospital treatment of the day, noting "At the time hospital staff did their best."

The state hospital system has ombudsmen readily available whom patients can contact if they feel their rights have been neglected. Ron called a variety of such individuals to inquire about his seeing new doctors, yet all his efforts never effected any change.

The fact that change for Ron required a court order to be corrected suggests, if not speaks to the entrenched organizational schemata that resists correction/change unless discovered, pointed out and replaced with meaningful action.

The grains of truth and deceit in Ron's story may feel different for each person reading about his case. Lessons learned and new paths towards progress are possible with treatment supported by research, and accomplishing that which is claimed. If the facts do not support this happening more attention is required, not just ignoring the situation.

Epilogue

Ron Steen's successful business career lasted from 1959 to 1980. During this time, he thrived, honing his skills at marketing and selling grain dryers and driving thousands of miles in the tri-state area making deals and flourishing in his field. Amidst all his success, he missed the rising storm of a mental illness he inherited, he just did not see it coming. This illness changed the course of his life and his perception of things, and it also impacted his behavior, which caused him to spend decades in a state hospital for the death of his lover and friend, Margaret Brown. He would not walk freely again outside a state institution until 2009.

Those of us who were privileged to know him personally will never forget him, or the lessons we learned.

According to available records, the cumulative cost of Ron's state hospital care fell into the range of $2 million dollars; his personal responsibility, supposedly paid by his estate was approximately $500,000.00.

The final tragedy related to Ron's case, was the fact that from the time of Ron's death in 2010 until 2018 and counting, his estate, supposedly under the care of Mr. Black, and also Ron's early conservator, failed to pay Ron's list of bills from years past while reportedly continuing to earn their commissions prior to and since Ron' death in 2010. And because Ron died intestate, he had no will.

Ultimately, Mr. Black and Ron's conservator were relieved of their positions by Douglas County District Court in October of 2017, following the airing of issues earlier in July of the same year. While the court had ordered the estate to be settled in the usual two year time period, Ron's estate had remained unsettled for eight years! Both Mr. Black and the conservator were ordered to provide complete and accurate accounts for time spent working for the Estate and justifying their compensation as required by Minnesota law. Plans were made for the sale of remaining assets.

Mr. Black had unabashedly assessed himself a handsome amount from the Estate and Corporation for his time and skillset, along with noting "additional anticipated" payments would be owed him; the Conservator was also compensated and noted additional fees pending. Remaining family members reportedly objected to the claimed amounts still owed to these people and respectfully requested no additional assets be paid until a full accounting could be completed.

The lessons learned in this story vary, depending on the audience. Likely some people in the lake region never knew about Ron Steen Sr. or his Transmatic Big-R Save $ More Grain Dryer Capital Corporation or the story about his rise to success and later problems. Calling attention to Ron's long prevented release from the state hospital might suggest the existence of other patients also endlessly confined without cause.

The 1977 Lincoln Mark V that Ron loved and kept enshrined, caught the eyes of many who were privileged enough to know about it, or see it in person. Few were allowed to gaze on this prize, and only Ron had actually driven it. I can imagine the stories that were told when Ron and a few chosen friends were shown the car and stood around sharing Elvis stories and discussing which of his music was their favorite, talking about Elvis serving in the Army even during his stardom, his lifestyle, and the reasons the Lincoln was one of the Elvis' favorites. One of the persons reportedly interested in the Lincoln at least at one time, was also Mr. Black.

After Ron's passing and the onset of fall in 2010, just around the time the weather was getting chilly and crisp, the garage was opened to get the car out and sell it, along with some of Ron's other remaining property. The winding road out to the property was a pleasant drive, with miles enough to notice and enjoy the lake view and share some old stories of the heydays of Lake Miltona. Then it took a few minutes to park, and find the correct key to open the padlock on the large garage door, before moving the large doors aside to get inside.

When access to the garage had been accomplished, and everyone's eyes had adjusted to the dim light and were moving along the remaining objects left in the building, visitors realized the huge staging area where the car had once stood had been swept as clean as a dancehall. The place where the magnificent car had stood, was empty. The Lincoln was gone. Like a blast of icy cold water on a hot day, the anticipation of the treasured vehicle had been dashed. No one knew anything, and no one was found who knew more!

Because on some level, I think perhaps that empty garage might have brought a smile to Ron's face.

I also think it will be a very long time before I stop thinking of Ron Steen when I see a vintage automobile that has been meticulously maintained and is still enjoyed. I can imagine Ron driving the Lincoln, in all its glory, the windows down, his arm resting on the driver's side window ledge, smiling and nodding or waving to folks he was passing on the road of life.

Ultimately, the words of George Orwell best sum up the realities of Ron Steen's case: "We are all capable of believing things which we know to be untrue, and then, when we are finally proved wrong, impudently twisting the facts so as to show that we were right. Intellectually, it is possible to carry on this process for an indefinite time; the only check on it is that sooner or later a false belief bumps up against solid reality, usually on a battlefield." George Orwell, 1946

"Truth is like the sun. You can shut it out for a time but it ain't goin' away."

Elvis Presley

* * * * * *

Photographs

Margaret Brown's Home

Echo Press

1986

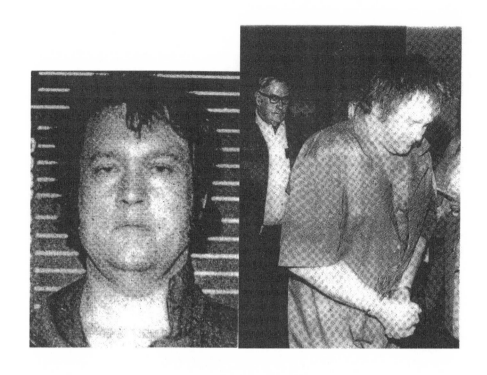

Booking and arrest photographs

Echo Press

1986

Ronald Steen

Lake Region Echo

June 18, 1986

RECEIVED

MAY 7 1987

LAWYERS PROF. RESP. BOARD

Appeal   April 23, 1987

I Ron Steen, Hereby Present My Appeal To the

Office of Lawyers Professional Responsibility

I Hereby Request A Complete Review of My Previous File I Sent to this Office Be Directed By Whomever I Had Spoken to Regarding the Explanations I Had Prepared In Expection of A Comprehensive Followup of the Seriousness of What My Ex-Attorneys Have Done to Me And My Business.

As of this Morning I Received the Determinations of Phillip J. Nelson Stating that He or Whomever Had Found No Cause of Discipline Based Upon My Explanations of What Is Not Only Violations of Ethical Codes But Criminal Acts and Crimes of Felonious Magnification.

I Was Sent A Copy of "Complaint And Investigations Procedure" Along With One Complaint Form which I Used to Identify Four Minnesota Licensed Lawyers As All Four Are Guilty In the Mismanagement of the Same File of Intent, But Fraudulently Handling of What Has Resulted In the Destruction of My Life And My Business And Many Assets I Do Not Want to Lose.

Correct Me If I'm Wrong! It States "What Will or Will Not Be Investigated. Complaints that Lawyers Have Acted "Unprofessionally" Are Investigated.

Example of Ronald Steen's 'copperplate' handwriting

372

Competitor Advertising

The Canary

September 28, 1978

The Canary

November 2, 1978

THEY'RE ALL COMING
OVER TO DRYMOR

First the service people came over to DryMor because of less problems. Then the salesmen came over because they didn't have to lie about the price, capacity, service, delivery, full savings, etc. Plus they don't have to go to court to get their commission!

Now, because of the high cost of fuel, a company that services, the ability to dry sunflowers safely, facts, and truth in pricing - the owners are coming over!

Pictured below are some of the latest trade-ins on DryMors. It's amazing that some of them are the same year as (the repainted) so called 'New' ones on other lots!

FARM FANS AB-18B

230V IQ   **$11,500**

243 hours (actual time). Should dry 100 bu. per hour (corn), including load and unload, dry and cool.
(We don't recommend for Sunflowers.)

- 450 GRAIN CHIEF
  $4500
- 275 MORIDGE
  $3750
- 375 BEHLEN
  $2500
- 8-13-10 KANSON
  $6600

FARM FANS AB-8

230V IQ   **$4500**

1381 Hours (ready to go). Should dry 50 bu. per hour (corn) including load and unload time, dry and cool.
(We don't recommend for Sunflowers)

4 USED

FARM FANS AB-8B

IQ 230V   **$4500**

1266 Hours (Looks like New) Should dry 50 bu. per hour (corn) including load and unload time, dry and cool.
(We don't recommend for Sunflowers)

FARM FA?
AB-18B
IQ 230V
$10, 00
452 ours
(Same as ne?
Should dry
100 bu. per
hour (corn) i?
cluding loa?
and unload
dry and coo?
(We don't
recommend ?
Sunflowers?

So, if you're thinking about a new conventional "Barrel" type dryer give us a call. We're taking in daily like-new ones at a fraction of the cost of new -

The Canary

May 24, 1979

Ronald Steen

The Echo Press

1996

Ryan Magnus, Ron Steen & Dr. Rose Linderman

2009

Made in the USA
Columbia, SC
22 December 2018